CELEBRITY/CULT[...]

- Why are we so fascinated by people who make no material impact on our lives and are, in many respects, just like ourselves – ordinary?
- Why do we care about people who have no conspicuous talent?
- Has there ever been a time in history when so much time, energy, and money has been devoted to following the exploits of people we have never met, are never likely to, and who don't know we exist?
- What are the likely effects of this collective obsession with celebrities on politics, race, and the media?

In answering these and many more questions, Ellis Cashmore takes his readers on a quest that involves visiting the Hollywood film industry of the early twentieth century, the film set of *Cleopatra* in the 1960s, the dressing room of Madonna in the 1980s, the burial of Diana in the 1990s, and the *Big Brother* house of the early 2000s. Author of *Beckham* and *Tyson*, Cashmore collects research, theory, and case studies en route as he explores the intriguing issue of celebrity culture: its origins, its meaning, and its global influence. Covering such varied perspectives as fame addiction, the "celebrification" of politics, and celebrity fatigue, Cashmore analyzes the relationship celebrity has with commodification and the consumer society, and investigates the new media and the quest for self-perfection.

This absorbing new book skilfully explains why we have become so captivated by the lives and loves of the celebrity and, in so doing, presents the clearest, most comprehensive, wide-ranging, and accessible account of celebrity culture to date.

Ellis Cashmore is Professor of Culture, Media and Sport at Staffordshire University, England. His recent books include *Beckham* (Polity, 2004), *Tyson* (Polity, 2004), *Sports Culture: An A-Z Guide* (Routledge, 2000) and *Making Sense of Sports* (Routledge, 2005).

CELEBRITY/CULTURE

ELLIS CASHMORE

First published 2006
by Routledge
2 Park Square, Milton Park, Abingdon, Oxon OX14 4RN

Simultaneously published in the USA and Canada
by Routledge
270 Madison Avenue, New York, NY 10016

Routledge is an imprint of the Taylor & Francis Group, an informa business

Typeset in Stone Serif by Keystroke,
28 High Street, Tettenhall, Wolverhampton
Printed and bound in Great Britain by
TJ International, Padstow, Cornwall

British Library Cataloguing in Publication Data
A catalogue record for this book is available from the British Library

Library of Congress Cataloging in Publication Data
Cashmore, Ernest.
   Celebrity/culture/Ellis Cashmore.
     p. cm.
   Includes bibliographical references and index.
   1. Mass media and culture. 2. Celebrities. I. Title.
   P94.6.C376 2006
   302.23–dc22   2006004386

ISBN 10: 0–415–37310–7 (hbk)
ISBN 10: 0–415–37311–5 (pbk)
ISBN 13: 978–0–415–37310–4 (hbk)
ISBN 13: 978–0–415–37311–1 (pbk)

CONTENTS

CULTIVATING/TASTES

: voyeurs and players

"My drug hell"-type headlines are now commonplace in the tabloids. You'd be forgiven for assuming we've always had a ghoulish fascination with the lives of other people, especially the parts of their lives we: (a) are thankful we never have to experience; or (b) would love to be part of. But we've been incited. In the 1960s, we wouldn't instantly and greedily gobble up stories about the so-called private lives of the rich and famous. Now many of us probably spend more time following the lives of celebrities than we do familiarizing ourselves with "legitimate" news. It may be harmless, but surely it wasn't spontaneous. We didn't suddenly become ravenous for insider information on celebrities' sex lives, or label-by-label breakdowns of what clothes they wear, or what bar they were drinking at last night. Our appetites have been whetted, our tastes cultivated. How, when, why, by whom, and with what consequences?

You could argue that most interesting things about celebrity culture are the least important – the celebrities. Less interesting but much more important is *our* preoccupation with famous persons whose lives never intersect with our own and whose fortunes make no material difference to us. Also interesting is the reason for the extravagant value we attach to the lives of public figures whose actual accomplishments may be limited, but whose visibility is extensive. Then there is the global industrial apparatus geared to producing talent-free entertainers, or even "ordinary people" who crave fleeting renown. Or, consumer society and the relentless drive to convert everything and everyone into commodities that can be sold like items on a supermarket shelf. These all seem worthy of our attention.

You can't understand anything without context: the circumstances surrounding something, the conditions under which it comes into being and the situations that precede and follow it. Celebrity culture is no exception. It didn't pop out of a vacuum: there were conditions, triggering episodes and deep causes. The conditions include the proliferation of media in the 1980s and the loss in confidence in established forms of leadership and authority that happened around the same time. I'll deal with these in chapters to come. By triggers, I mean specific events and the people involved in them: like the scandalous picture of Elizabeth Taylor and Richard Burton, the emergence and death of Diana and, most importantly, Madonna. Again, all these will be covered. The cause of celebrity culture insinuates us in a larger story, that of consumer society and, in a sense, this story runs throughout the book, though I'll expand a little before we go on. (I also lay these and other key features out in a timeline toward the end of the book, pages 270–9.)

The cast of characters that make up today's generation of celebrities couldn't be more saleable if they had barcodes. You don't need to be a cynic to realize that the instant someone scales the heights of public visibility and makes it into the headlines or onto television, they start selling. If they're not directly selling dvds, movies, cds, concert tours or books, they're indirectly selling cosmetics, cars, household appliances and every other imaginable piece of merchandise.

Some might argue: that's what they're for – to sell. A straightforwardly one-dimensional assessment, perhaps, but one with some merit. After all, entertainers and sports stars have, for years, sold tickets to cinemas or sports events on their name value. They've also operated sidelines in endorsements, allowing their names and images to be linked with products they might never have used in exchange for hard cash. Contemporary celebrity culture brought with it a significant change.

Other writers whose work I review in later chapters argue that today's celebrity culture is an extension of a collective preoccupation with the famous. It has long-standing historical antecedents. I think differently: there is something distinct about today's celebrity culture. Instead of just being devices for marketing films, music or the consumer products they endorse, the celebrities have become products themselves. They are now commodities in the sense that they've become articles of trade that can be bought and sold in a marketplace. Obviously, you can't buy *them*, but you can buy their representations, their sounds and the products with which they're associated. Consumers pay for that presence.

You'd have to be a conspiracy theorist to leave it there, though. The image of a cabal of capitalist supremos huddled around a table plotting the next phase of consumer society and contriving the idea of changing famous people from moving advertisements to actual commodities is a delectable one. But it doesn't really play. We need a more detailed investigation into the changes that led us – the consumers, the fans, the audience – to embrace the celebs and, significantly, spend money in the process.

This is less straightforward, though not a project that will plunge us into hopeless confusion. We just need to backtrack to the days when digital meant fingers and toes, and rap was something you got across the knuckles for misbehaving. Celebrity culture became a feature of social life, especially in the developed world, during the late 1980s/early 1990s, and extended into the twenty-first century, assisted by a global media which promoted, lauded, sometimes abominated, and occasionally annihilated figures, principally from entertainment and sports.

We became progressively preoccupied with famous persons whom we endowed with great meaning though without really reflecting on why. Their public visibility, or profile, seemed to be more crucial than what they said or did. Only rarely did we ask: "Why do I want to know about this person?" or "Why did this person become famous in the first place?" The phrase "famous for being famous" was once a tautological joke. It eventually became a reasonable explanation of why someone or other was fêted.

By the end of the 1990s, the bar had been lowered: in previous decades famous figures, or "personalities" as they were often called, had to work harder to achieve fame or notoriety. The Rolling Stones had to trash countless hotel rooms and get busted for drugs. The Sex Pistols had to remain determinedly obnoxious even on their days off. Even Elizabeth Taylor, who reigned empress-like in the 1960s, intrigued her global audience with extra-marital improprieties. And they had to produce music and films too. (More on Taylor in the next chapter.)

Now, their essays in sleaze and scandal seem unacceptably devoid of depravity. We demand something different of today's celebrities. What's more, we don't want to wait for it to be discovered: celebs must surrender themselves to life in a kind of virtual Panopticon – the ideal prison where the cells are arranged around a central watchtower in which concealed authority figures can inspect without being inspected. We, the fans, are in the watchtower and the celebs are open to our inspection. The moment they withdraw or become reticent, we lose interest and start peering at others. Just as we vote wannabe celebs out of the Big Brother house, we can send celebs to oblivion. And we know it.

Skilled in the art of celeb-making and celeb-breaking, we consumers have more power collectively than at any time in history. Contrary to how we're often depicted, we're not hapless chumps who just luxuriate in whatever is dropped on us. We're educated in the arts of celeb-production by the very channels that present them. Put another way, we don't just look at the pictures: we've become able readers. In fact, we do most of the work. This is Joshua Gamson's argument and one I find completely persuasive. His 1994 study *Claims to Fame: Celebrity in contemporary America* portrays fans as knowing and savvy participants in the celebrity production process: "The position audiences embrace includes the roles of simultaneous voyeurs of and performers in commercial culture" (1994: 137. Year of publication followed, where appropriate, by page numbers will be given in brackets throughout the text, with a full bibliography at the end of the book).

All the celebs did was make themselves available. Madonna might have been the first celebrity to render her manufacture completely transparent, but everyone who followed was almost forced to do likewise. Even if celebs were bashful about revealing to their fans evidence of the elaborate and monstrously expensive publicity and marketing that went into videos, cds, stage acts, movies and, indeed, themselves, fans were aware enough to figure it out for themselves. The pleasure in being in celebrity culture is that the consumer observes, secure in the knowledge that he or she is actually not just an observer, but a player too.

Consumers know that the accomplishments of many of the people they follow are insubstantial and that their effects on society are inconsequential. They know that so-and-so became famous because she slept (and told) with someone who was vaguely a "somebody." And that a former reality show's contestant earns several million a year in spite of a self-acknowledged absence of intellect, taste, knowledge, skill or anything worthy of merit. We know these things: we just choose not to dwell on them for long or see them as reasons to stop following them. It's more enjoyable to participate in the joys of celebrity culture.

And, crucially, we are prepared to keep dealing: we pay and the celebrities supply us with . . . what exactly? They don't exactly sell their labor, or expertise so much as their presence. In other words, they just appear. It could be argued that some celebrities do have valuable skills to peddle. But are we fascinated by, say, Tom Cruise because of his dramatic performances, or because of his weird affiliation with Scientology, his stern repudiation of the suggestion that he is gay, and his serial marriages? The celebrity's talent has no necessary relationship to his or her celebrity status. Contestants on a reality television show have no conspicuous talent, yet they often get status, if only for a short period. Once they're in the celebrity labor market, they can start dispensing the same resource that makes Hollywood actors and global rock stars celebrities: not talent, but presence. They just appear in tv shows, gossip magazines, internet sites, advertisements – everywhere they can. As long as consumers maintain an interest in them, they remain celebrities. And there are consequences, many of which will occupy us in chapters to come.

Like it or loathe it, celebrity culture is with us: it surrounds us and even invades us. It shapes our thought and conduct, style, and manner. It affects and is affected by not just hardcore fans but by entire populations whose lives have been changed by the shift from manufacturing to service societies and the corresponding shift from plain consumer to aspirational consumer – a change we'll focus on shortly.

: new game, new rules

"The mass media with their cult of celebrity and their attempt to surround it with glamour and excitement have made Americans a nation of fans and moviegoers," wrote Christopher Lasch in 1980. Reflecting on what he called *The Culture of Narcissism*, Lasch added: "The media give substance to and thus intensify narcissistic dreams of fame and glory, encourage the common man to identify himself with the stars and to hate the 'herd' and make it more and more difficult for him to accept the banality of everyday existence" (1980: 21).

Since then, we've been further encouraged to identify with the stars. But, far from making it more difficult for us to accept the "banality of everyday existence," celebrity culture seems to have had the opposite effect: it enables us to accommodate it. True, we might secretly harbor and perhaps quite explicitly express dissatisfaction with our lives, but the invisible attachment to the glitzy world of the celebs functions as a lifeline. We survive by dreaming those "narcissistic dreams" Lasch thought to be so damaging. Maybe they are. That's an issue we will need to consider toward the end of the book rather than the start. For now, let's take Lasch's point about the media (we tend not to use "mass" nowadays).

A peculiarity of celebrity culture is the shift of emphasis from achievement-based fame to media-driven renown. This is captured in the contrived verb *to celebrify*, which, while never formally defined, might be interpreted to mean "to exalt; praise widely; make famous; invest common or inferior person or thing with great importance." In his *Illusions of Immortality: A psychology of fame and celebrity*, psychologist David Giles submits that: "The ultimate modern celebrity is the member of the public who becomes famous solely through media involvement" (2000: 25).

While the "ultimate" celebrity's rise might be attributable "solely" to the media, celebrities typically perform some deed, however modest, to attract initial attention. That deed might involve an appearance on a television quiz show, a criminal action, or an inept showing at a major sports event: in other words, conduct that would hardly be regarded as commendable and deserving of recognition in earlier eras, perhaps as recently as the 1980s.

During the late 1980s and early 1990s, however, our concept of merit changed. Figures who traditionally earned distinction and drew praise for their efforts vied with characters whose achievements were often uncertain. Literally worthless individuals, it seemed, began cropping up. What's more, they commanded interest for nothing in particular. In fact, they were not completely worthless, worth being an equivalent value of merit conferred on someone or something by a population. Whether the neophyte celebs actually deserved reverence is not a question I'm going to answer in this book. But I'll give the reasons why so many others believed they deserved it. All sorts of characters who, in another age, might be viewed as unworthy of attention ascended from obscurity to public visibility and, in some cases, global fame without seeming to do anything at all.

What they *did* do was appear; their images were relayed to millions via television and internet sites; newspapers recorded their exploits; magazines recounted their thoughts. "Media involvement," to repeat Giles's term, was the key: celebrities engaged the media. And we were delighted: at least, the response to the new generation of celebs suggested this. The world was being persuaded that people with no talent, no obvious gifts, nor any characteristic deserving of distinction were worthy of our serious attention just because they were in the media. It worked.

There are reasons why the media changed its focus and with such dramatic effect. The first is in the iconoclastic tendencies of photographers that became known collectively as the paparazzi (and I deal with their rise in Chapter 2). Fatigued, perhaps bored and certainly inured to the anodyne output of the Hollywood film industry, fans eagerly devoured the work of journalists who ignored the unwritten rules about the boundaries between private and public life. The entertainment industry had previously controlled the release of information on stars' private lives. The paparazzi discovered that fans had an appetite for another version: the one in which famous faces were caught in embarrassing moments, doing things they weren't supposed to, and looking like they shouldn't.

So, by the time of the extraterrestrial changes in broadcasting, consumers had become quite habituated to peering into the hitherto well-protected private lives of movie and music stars. Few could have predicted how the time-space compression introduced by media technology would have affected their ability not just to peer but to examine and scrutinize in forensic detail. The globalization of the media introduced the capacity to transmit large volumes of information around the world, not just quickly, but instantly. By information, I mean news, entertainment and, perhaps most crucially, advertising.

Satellites, or transponders, were the instruments of the media's global expansion. By wrapping the world in an invisible network of communications, satellite broadcasters were able to bounce information off satellites and send it literally anywhere. Satellite television companies recognized no national boundaries. This effectively meant that virtually everyone on earth was part of one huge market. It also meant that the size and power of corporations grew, leading to increasing control over economic and institutional resources and, much more importantly, an enhanced capacity to shape popular attitudes, beliefs, and values (more on this in Chapter 3).

Rupert Murdoch, perhaps more than any other media figure, exploited the opportunities offered by the satellite technology pioneered in the 1960s, and the deregulation and privatization of the television industry in the 1980s and early 1990s. In February 1989, Murdoch's European satellite started beaming programs via satellite through his Sky network. A decade later, his various channels reached 66 percent of the world's population.

The problem with having so many channels was content: what do you fill them with? MTV supplied a clue. To keep so much of the world riveted to the screen, television networks needed a formula. Televised programming detached itself from fixed content and began firing off in the direction of entertainment, for which we should read *amusement* – something that occupies us agreeably, diverting our minds from matters that might prompt introspection, analysis, or reflection. This is not to suggest that drama can't provoke contemplation, nor that critical examination can't be entertaining too, nor even that the narratives of soaps or cartoons are not open to critical reading. And it certainly doesn't underestimate the viewers' speedy acquisition of skills for screening and skimming information. But, for the most part, entertainment doesn't prompt us to modify ourselves in any substantive way.

Light entertainment, to use a more indicative term, became a staple of a formula that demanded only a modest level of attention from viewers. Music + movies + sport. Asked to respond to this in 1990s, an informed person might have said: people will soon get sick of it; they will feel as if they're suffocating under a superabundance of froth. This didn't prove to be the case. Of course, the communications revolution didn't end with television, and the proliferation of multimedia brought a further layer of information conduits, notably the internet.

These changes in the media's orientation had an impact on the relationships between performers and the newly emergent media. Even before it was called showbusiness, the entertainment industry furnished individual artists who drew acclaim and were used as selling points. From nineteenth-century minstrel shows, through ragtime, the British music halls, silent film, radio and, of course, theater, popular entertainment forms invariably provided a showcase for figures who distinguished themselves from their contemporaries. The Hollywood star system, beginning in the 1940s, was able to exploit this as no other industry ever had, operating a smooth-functioning, factory-like production line in which "stars" were treated much as commodities. Their use value was in generating box office sales, as we'll see in Chapter 4.

While the concept of producing stars rather than waiting for them to emerge stayed largely intact until the mid-1980s, the newly prolific media both offered different opportunities and demanded a different kind of engagement with artists. Madonna, more than any other entertainer, realized this. After the success of her fourth album *Like a Prayer* in 1989 Madonna appears to have seen the future: the days when people got to be famous and stayed that way through just making movies, hit records or writing bestsellers were approaching an end. The most important feature of the coming age was visibility: doing was less important than just being in the public gaze. With so many channels of communication being filled up with all manner of entertainment, there was bound to be an overflow of entertainers, most of whom would make little impression on the public consciousness.

The ones who did were those who would not just make themselves visible, but transparent – there was no contradiction.

Madonna not only epitomized this, but helped it materialize. She seems to have struck a bargain with the media. It was something like: "I will tell you more, show you more about me than any other rock or movie star in history; I will disclose my personal secrets, share my fears, joys, sorrows, what makes me happy or sad, angry or gratified; I will be more candid and unrestricted in my interviews than any other entertainer. In other words, I'll be completely see-through. In return, I want coverage like no other: I want to be omnipresent, ubiquitous, and pervasive – I want to be everywhere, all the time." It was a captivating *quid pro quo*. As the 1980s turned to the 1990s, Madonna was, as she wanted to be, everywhere.

Madonna's dressing room on the Blonde Ambition tour of 1991 must have been like an echo chamber for celebrity culture: massed media workers would cram in to probe for information and would probably not leave disappointed. Fourteen years after the Blonde Ambition tour, which was diarized in the movie *Truth or Dare*, or *In Bed with Madonna* as it was called in Britain, Gwen Stefani griped about the media, but shrugged: "I understand how the game works" (quoted by Duerden 2005: 12). The rules of that game were drafted in the late 1980s and Madonna played no small part in their formulation. You almost wonder whether Madonna set out to reinvigorate the popular culture by continually breaking rules and getting rewarded for her misbehavior. Probably not. But, encouraged by her early successes, she seems to have used them as guides. I won't reveal my argument yet. I'll just chain together the words: disclosure ➜ scandal ➜ ubiquity.

: a world of glitz, glamour, and luxury awaits*

* bring a credit card

"In contemporary marketing, the naturalization of consumer desires has been codified into a set of timeless emotional needs," writes Juliet Schor in her *Born to Buy: The commercialized child and the new consumer culture* (2004: 44). Consumer culture was originally built on the avarice, envy, and possessiveness that flourished in the postwar years. But it became ordinary, common, and everyday so that we eventually came to understand ourselves as the kind of creatures that had spending in our DNA. Consuming was, to use Schor's word, naturalized.

Some writers have pointed out the ways in which celebrities, perhaps inadvertently, promote aspirational consumption by becoming mobile advertisements. In this sense, celebrity culture is at one with with commodification – the process whereby everything, including public figures, can be converted into an article of trade to be exchanged in the marketplace. As early as the 1930s, the advertising industry had sensed that people didn't buy products just because they needed them: the needs had to be coaxed. Desire worked much better. If someone desired something, the second they procured it, the desire was gone. So, the trick was to keep pumping up new desires: as soon as consumers upgraded the fridge, they needed to start thinking about a new car. As soon as they got the car, they started thinking about a new house. "The accelerator of consumer demand," as Zygmunt Bauman calls it, is pressed hard down as new offers keep appearing on the road ahead.

In his article "Consuming life," Bauman argues that one of the big feats of the consumer culture has been in liberating the pleasure principle from the perimeter fence beyond which pleasure-seekers once could venture only at their peril. "Consumer society has achieved a previously unimaginable feat: it reconciled the reality and pleasure principles by putting, so to speak, the thief in charge of the treasure box," Bauman concludes (2001: 16).

In other words: in the past consumers wanted to own goods, but knew they couldn't afford everything they wanted. So they resigned themselves to it. Not now. They look at celebrities and want to be more like them, have the kind of clothes they wear, drive the cars, eat in the same restaurants and so on. They realize that much of this is out of their reach. But this is doesn't stop them wishing they could get at the celebrities' treasure box. So they'll opt for the nearest thing and keep wishing and hoping. This might have seemed irrational as recently as the 1980s. Now, it's normal: we would all like to be a bit more like celebrities.

This is reflected in the way we shop. Shopping is now considered glamorous, not utilitarian. The consumer is encouraged to declare his and her worth by spending money on items that will help him or her look like, play like, or in some other way, be like someone else. That someone else is the celebrity, or more likely, celebrities with whom they feel or want to feel an attachment. In this sense, the consumer's enterprise is as much to express a sense of bonding or even identity with the celebrity as acquiring new possessions.

It's tempting to see the whole purpose of celebrities in this light. When people ask, "What are celebrities for?" an answer might be "to keep us spending." After all, they seem to match products with basic human needs. Even the phrase "must-have" is evocative of a primal drive. We see or read about a celebrity and begin to wonder whether we could have what he or she has. And we delight in discovering that we can get pretty close.

We have to examine celebrity culture and consumer society as a tennis fan watches a match: constantly switching focus from one to the other. One can't exist without the other any more than a tennis player can play against herself. This is most visibly demonstrated in endorsements. Celebrities are paid to say nice things about products which they may or may not use and encourage consumers to buy them. Advertisers have always used famous people as spokespersons or "faces of" whatever piece of merchandise or brand they are trying to sell. But next time you watch television, or skim through a magazine, try to notice how many ads feature "names." Consumers might once have been quite susceptible to the hidden persuasion of advertising. But, today, as I've pointed out, we're in on the act. We know what's going on and discriminate accordingly when it comes to shopping.

The same processes that produced today's celebrities have changed us into savvy consumers "whose attitudes, aspirations and purchasing patterns are unlike any before them," as David Lewis and Darren Bridger put it (2001: 3). We don't buy to possess the same kind of products as celebrities so much as to be more like them.

I elaborate on this in later chapters, especially Chapter 9, and it is a key theme of the book. The gigantic changes that resulted in a refocused media and a newly acquired taste in irrelevance have also turned us into deliberating and judgmental consumers who have taxed advertisers and manufacturers to respond ingeniously. If consumers know more about products and brands and use that knowledge when they make purchases and if many of the products on sale are, for all intents and purposes, identical, advertisers have to figure out ways of selling them something more than the actual product. Celebrities have provided a solution.

Two themes, then: changes in the media and changes in consumer society. You don't need to be a scholar to fathom out that both of these are in some way connected to each other and to the rise of celebrities: the job of this book is to lay bare the connections. The consumer society written of in the late 1950s by J. K. Galbraith in *The Affluent Society* and Vance Packard in *The Status Seekers* has reinvented itself. The narrow ideal of the good life with all its material requirements is still there. Now, access to it is less restricted. In fact, it's universally available. The exhilarating prospect of buying into celebrity culture has both dulled and stimulated the senses of a generation. A world of glitz, glamour, and excitement awaits anyone with enough money. Celebrities perform as ever-present titillations, relentlessly teasing us to make ourselves more like them. Buying commodities is usually our only recourse.

All the time, we're shrewd enough to know this, but too charmed by it all to resist. The ethos of excess and the emphasis on impulse promotes new demands that are assuaged by the consumption of new commodities. This gives celebrity culture an almost addictive property, consumers craving the products celebrities dangle in front of them.

So much so that we're actually encouraged to be dissatisfied and crave the things we haven't got, but which pose a solution to some problem we either have or will have once we've familiarized ourselves with enough ads. An ordinary day brings us into contact with such topics as cosmetic surgery, phones, self-help, diets, headache cures and any number of other items which both indicate a problem and a solution. We might expect all this to have eaten away at the capacity for analysis. As I'll argue in the pages to come, this is not the case.

My account of celebrity culture necessarily questions some of its myths. There is less room for spontaneity, randomness, and sheer luck than the reader might think. All the same, there are people and events that either accelerated change, or transferred wider changes into the realm of the personal. So, while I stress the effects of the media and the development of consumer society, I make space for Madonna, whose appearance worked like a synthesizer, bringing several elements together and producing something new. Or Beyoncé, who has to be understood not only as a glorious diva but as propaganda for a race-free society. And the all-purpose moving advertisement David Beckham, whose opulent, novelty-filled life is propaganda of a different sort.

Events too shaped the contours of celebrity culture, or, as I put it earlier, worked like triggers. I open the next chapter with one such trigger and its proximate effects: the public outrage generated not so much by Elizabeth Taylor's indiscretion with Richard Burton, but by the photograph that captured a moment of it. Technology played a part in this: it wouldn't have been possible without the telephoto lens now used by paparazzi. Satellite television was another technological innovation that precipitated changes far beyond its original scope. Any argument that strives for comprehensiveness needs to take account of these kinds of particulars as well as the generalities of cultural change.

Celebrity culture is a phenomenon that is simultaneously well known and little known. Many are fascinated by celebrities without actually understanding why they are fascinated. They know they are part of the process, yet not sure which part, nor how the process works. Everyone is aware of celebrity culture while remaining ignorant of when, where, and why it came into being. Maintaining this paradox is arguably the greatest triumph of celebrity culture.

MAKING/NEW RULES

: liquefying stardom

A million. It was unheard of. She might have topped the *Motion Picture Herald*'s "top ten box office" draws. But no female actor, or actress as it was in the 1950s, could seriously demand one million dollars for a single movie.

In September 1960, Elizabeth Taylor arrived in London to begin work on *Cleopatra*. Twentieth-Century-Fox agreed to her unprecedented and perhaps preposterous fee. Then again, this was the world's foremost screen goddess, a sparkling extravagance that mesmerized the world, not just with her acting, but with her turbulent private life. Famous enough to adorn the cover of *Time* magazine in 1949 when aged only 17, Taylor transformed from child star to superstar, commanding the attention of the planet.

In the course of her rise, Taylor had made a habit of getting involved in relationships that, while not scandalous, were out of the ordinary. She had been either involved with, or married to men who had turned out to be abusive, alcoholic, or philandering. She'd also been attracted to the gay actor Montgomery Clift and married to Michael Wilding, who was 19 years her senior.

When she started shooting *Cleopatra*, she was married to Eddie Fisher, who happened to have been her ex-husband Mike Todd's best man at her wedding with Todd. Fisher himself had left his wife Debbie for Taylor. Ensconced at London's Dorchester hotel, Taylor's entourage, which included three children, several dogs and cats and a large staff, lived up to expectations, having food specially brought in from around the world and embarking on shopping trips of heroic proportions. The movie script was in such dire need of rewriting that no actual filming got done before Taylor became dangerously ill and flew back to California to recuperate.

By summer 1961, the film was already beginning to look doomed. Members of its original cast dropped out and its director Rouben Mamoulian was replaced by Joseph L. Mankiewicz. When shooting resumed in September, the location was switched from London to Rome. All the time, the production costs were mounting. *Cleopatra* would eventually become the most expensive film to date at $20 million.

Among the several personnel changes was the substitution of Richard Burton for Stephen Boyd in the role of Marc Antony. Burton landed the part after appearing as King Arthur in the Broadway production of *Camelot*. Having established himself in theater rather than film, Burton had distinguished himself playing many of the major Shakespearean roles. He had also received an Oscar nomination in 1952 for his part in the screen adaptation of Daphne du Maurier's *My Cousin Rachel*, in which he played opposite Olivia de Havilland.

While he was a respected actor, in terms of global fame, Burton wasn't in the same league as Taylor. And yet, together, with the enthusiastic assistance of a newly rapacious media, they were to figure prominently and collectively in one of the most dramatic changes in popular culture of the twentieth century.

Prior to *Cleopatra*, neither Taylor or Burton had been tormented by the invasive photojournalists who had been memorably parodied in Federico Fellini's 1960 *La Dolce Vita*, a quite prophetic film in which one of the characters named "Paparazzo" is a photographer who resorts to often manic means to secure his shots. Like other great fictional characters, such as Lothario,

Romeo, and Pangloss, Paparazzo contributed his name to the popular vocabulary. In Italy, photographers were zealous chroniclers of the lives of those deemed worthy of public interest. Anita Ekberg, who had been in the Fellini film herself, had famously taken a bow and arrow to an especially inquisitive photographer and had unwittingly contributed to what was to become a genre – that of the paparazzi.

The 1950s and early 1960s defined a kind of golden age of glamour. Hollywood stars, in particular, were parts of a pantheon: like deities, they seemed to exist at a level above that of other mortals. They lived lives of such opulence, such splendor, such sublime beauty that they seemed unapproachable. And, in a genuine sense, they were. They secured themselves away and drip-fed their fans with occasional personal appearances and carefully controlled silvery images. Even stepping off a plane was a procedure so meticulously rehearsed that ensuing photographs looked like portraits. This was an age when cameras were affixed with flash attachments and the pop of a bulb was an announcement that a star had arrived. Every picture evoked a wonderworld, one that was at once remote, yet touchable, distant yet close.

Some photographers, however, were experimenting with a new piece of technology: the zoom lens. One of them was Marcello Geppetti. Maybe he suspected that there was something going on between Taylor and Burton, or maybe he was just reconnoitering the exclusive sector of Rome's Mediterranean coast where the privileged moored their elegant crafts. Whatever his motives, Geppetti must have felt his pulse race as an image of Taylor and Burton came into his sight. Not just any old image either. Taylor lay on the deck of the yacht serene in the comfortable knowledge that she was away from prying eyes. Burton was craned across her body in an embrace that was unmistakably that of lovers. Geppetti snapped as his subjects kissed.

As an illustration of theories about the unpredictability of distant events, the closing of the lens shutter is not comparable with the flutter of a butterfly's wings somewhere over tropical Africa. But its unintended influence on subsequent events could hardly have been predicted. And, if there was a chaos theory of cultural change, this might qualify as evidence.

Geppetti's shot depicted Taylor and Burton, two married adults, a mother and a father, in the capital of a Catholic country, indeed in the spiritual center of the Catholic world. Remember: this was 1962. The image signified an adulterous relationship. The product of Geppetti's initiative encircled the world, newspapers and magazines featuring the picture alongside stories of an affair that started secretly but was now the most famous liaison in the world. Even the Vatican was moved to condemn the relationship. The US State Department was urged to revoke Burton's entry visa on the grounds that he was "detrimental to the morals of the youth of our nation."

Taylor's status as one of the world's most accredited beauties and, of course, the foremost female movie star ensured that the story would travel. Burton, a handsome thespian, though with no track record of amorous affairs, made a great foil. But it was the fact that they were both married with children that elevated this above the level of an ordinary scandal. The outrage it prompted also signaled a new age was beginning.

Once it was possible for Hollywood stars to divide themselves, presenting a public persona to their adoring audience while reserving a space for their private selves. The parts of their lives they preferred not to reveal were warily kept from the fans. The industry was geared up for this kind of dualism: after all, it thrived on images. The stories of the screen were complemented by the stories of the lives of those who inhabited the screen. Even compellingly newsworthy figures, like Taylor, were able to keep their distance: there might have been curiosity about her private life, but her audience knew only as much as she or her advisers thought appropriate. There was a respectful relationship between the media and objects of their attention. All that was about to be mixed up.

It wasn't just the Taylor–Burton image that changed the relationship. But there was a sense in which it signaled the change. As the dog days of summer succumb to the freshening fall, so the stars' days of peace and quiet gave way to an open season. They were now fair game.

Not even Taylor, perhaps especially not Taylor, could prevent the intrusively ingenious Italian media spoiling her privacy, a privacy that had never before been seriously infringed. In Rome, the media weren't nearly as respectful, nor as obedient as they were in the USA. And, armed with a telephoto lens, they had the hardware to challenge most attempts to cordon off the private lives of stars.

A new era was beginning. Actually, it had been taking shape in continental Europe for some years before 1962. *La Dolce Vita* was a riotous yet not entirely false rendition of the Italian media. Its central character secures his exclusives by gatecrashing parties thrown by and sometimes seducing the rich and famous, who then become scandalized by his stories. He gets caught up with a news item that could easily have jumped off this week's front page of the *National Enquirer*: CHILD SPOTS THE VIRGIN MARY.

Anita Ekberg, who was in the film, was involved in a life-follows-art altercation with disturbing cameramen (they were all male) outside her villa in Rome. Along with Brigitte Bardot, whom Geppetti caught lying sans bikini top in St Tropez, Gina Lollobrigida, and Sophia Loren, Ekberg was among an elite of women whom European photographers pursued.

Whether by accident or on purpose, photographers discovered that these and lesser stars were more interesting when provoked to anger than when allowed to present themselves in peace. As Tazio Secchiaroli, a contemporary of Geppetti and a probable model for the "Paparazzo" character in Fellini's film, reflected: "We found that, with small events created on purpose, we could earn 200,000 lira, while before we got 3,000" (quoted in Richards 1997: E.01).

Nowadays, off-guard shots of celebrities are more common than poses: we're used to seeing them shielding themselves, caught by surprise, fleeing or gesticulating irritably as if stung by having their privacy invaded. In the 1960s, the stars were used to being photographed in the way they, not the photographer, desired. They wanted to be seen as majestic, dignified, graceful, pleasing to the eye. The kind of way *Vogue* would portray them on its front cover. Photographers who specialized in catching them bleary-eyed during a night on the tiles, their mascara smudged, their bra straps showing, were unwelcome.

If photographers could earn almost 70 times as much for these kinds of shots as they could for straightforward poses, then there must have been a market for them. Audiences might initially have been shocked to glimpse their favored stars in unusual circumstances with their dignity compromised. But they clearly got used to it and, eventually, came to expect it. Stylized shots must have seemed bland by comparison.

The Taylor–Burton shot was one of the triggers of celebrity culture: it sort of liberated not just photojournalists but the rest of the media, releasing them in new directions; but it also set off a chain reaction among the stars and, perhaps most importantly, the fans. They were the ones whose attention and money were needed, not just by the film industry that helped both develop and make use of the stars, but the entire media surrounding that industry. After all, they all lived in a symbiotic world, in which the existence of each party benefited the others. Even the fans, whose cash kept the wheels of the industry turning, profited; they wouldn't watch, read about, and follow the exploits of the famous if they didn't get something from it. Their tastes were changing.

The fans were not like passive alien abductees whisked away and reprogrammed by the marauding media, then sent back with new appetites for humiliating pictures and salacious gossip. Yet there was a sense in which tastes changed to accommodate the variation in images. Compared to the output of the new generation of photojournalists, the designed shots seemed antiseptic, tame, bland, colorless, even disingenuous and, worst of all, downright dull. After glimpsing the stars in the raw, so to speak, audiences would never be satisfied with lush, dreamy portraits that had been such staples of show business.

The images and words that accompanied them might have piqued a routine curiosity in the stars. But never much more. The major Hollywood studios employed in-house photographers who, as Amy Henderson puts it in her essay "Media and the rise of celebrity culture," "created a style of portraiture that crystallized stardom" (1992: 5). The representations offered by the paparazzi had the opposite effect: the stars deliquesced like ice crystals on a radiator.

Scarcely credible as it was, onlookers watched the hitherto untouchable stars dissolve into characters who bore a remarkable resemblance to themselves. Did this make them any less fascinating? No: if anything, interest in them grew. Fans may previously have been served up answers to questions they never really cared about. Now, they were asking different questions, the answers to which had to be sought outside the official studio sources.

: just as wretched as you

In 1968, Generoso Pope moved the editorial headquarters of one his magazines from New York to Lantana, Florida. There, beneath the cerulean skies, among the oleanders and palmettos, amid the cicadas and flamingos, the magazine grew just like hibiscus. Its circulation went from one million to three million.

Pope had bought the *National Enquirer* 14 years before and changed what used to be a horseracing guide into a weekly catalog of incredible and gruesome stories with headlines like I CUT OUT HER HEART AND STOMPED ON IT and I ATE MY BABY! The only news items consisted of stories about the excesses of

Hollywood stars. Judy Garland, in particular, was a bountiful source of news: her drunken binges, overdoses, and serial marriages were stock items. When she died in 1969, the *National Enquirer* might have faced a crisis. But it adapted quite efficiently, specializing in stories about the Hollywood set's miscreant behavior.

In the 1960s, stars were much more circumspect about their lives; so the stories had to be pursued with vigilance. The Taylor–Burton story was like a hardy annual, popping up at regular intervals over several years. Its power to move magazines off newsstands was undeniable, though the *National Enquirer* hit the equivalent of pay dirt when Sonny Bono and Cher LaPierre emerged as television show hosts, as well as the recording artists they had been in the 1960s. When the too-good-to-be-true couple started heading for their 1974 breakup, the magazine featured them consistently, taking a keen interest in either one's indiscretions. Warning shots about the end of private lives had been fired in the 1960s, as we've already documented. Sonny and Cher's marital collapse happened in full view of the world. The *National Enquirer* was selling five million copies per week by the mid-1970s.

Cher was developing into a kind of prototype contemporary celebrity. When she appeared with apple cheeks and bluejeans in 1965, she looked like she might have walked straight in from a trailer park. Then it was like Mountain Dew turning to Cristal champagne. But, unlike today's celebs, she was stung by tales of her extravagances. Billy Ingram, in his "A short history of the *National Enquirer*," recounts how, in 1976, Cher reacted gruffly to a report in the British newspaper the *Observer*, which, on her account, described her: "This woman lives in a two million-dollar house, spends 500 bucks a week on manicures, drives one of her three Ferraris, when she's not using her Rolls-Royce or Mercedes, has 600 pairs of shoes, and 1,000 beaded dresses, and she's not happy" (nd: p. 6). Nowadays, celebrities might be embarrassed by such frugality.

Cher became a regular with not only the *National Enquirer* but with the other comparable publications that were launched in the mid-1970s. These included the Rupert Murdoch-owned *National Star*, *People* and *Us Weekly*, all appearing in 1974 and all specializing in the same mix of gossip and muckraking. Cher's relationships or alleged relationships were legion. Journalists covering her exploits had a simple remit, according to Ingram: "Just throw in a few other bizarre details, true or not, it didn't matter – because it's perfectly legal to print just about anything you like about a celebrity" (nd: p. 7).

It wasn't quite "perfectly legal" but the comment summarizes the thrust of tabloids as competition intensified in the late 1970s. Pictures of celebrities became the currency of choice and the pushy approach pioneered by Italian paparazzi came to the fore. When Elvis Presley died in 1977, the *National Enquirer* featured a picture of him lying embalmed in his coffin and was rewarded with sales of seven million. Celebrity deaths proved to be dependable boosts to circulation, as strong sales following the deaths of Bing Crosby and John Lennon indicated.

The shrieking headlines that told of sightings of Elvis in the most unlikely places years after his death were what made *National Enquirer* internationally famous. It didn't just capture the spirit of the 1970s and 1980s: it caged it and taught it to do tricks. But as those times changed, the *National Enquirer* wasn't so quick to adjust as some of its rivals, and the sightings, the accounts of alien abductions, and the gory reports seemed dated alongside the celebrity muckraking of its rivals like the *Globe* and the *Star*, both cheap newsprint tabloids that sold off the stands near the supermarket checkouts. *People*'s recipe was the most congruent with the times. Its "focus was entirely on the active personalities of our time" (Neimark 1995: 86).

In the 1990s, Bill Clinton's affair with Monica Lewinsky (of which more in Chapter 11) and Jesse Jackson's "love child" were the kind of stories that sold magazines more effectively than "Loch Ness monster ate my husband," though the Grand

Guignol of the O. J. Simpson trial in 1994 was the most important signpost event (as we will see in Chapter 8). Attention switched from the ordinary to the celebrated sectors of society and the emphasis changed from the extraordinary to the ordinary. The success of magazines such as *People* and, in Britain, *Heat* and *Hello!* indicated that people preferred to read about everyday events in the lives of fantastic people rather than fantastic events in the lives of everyday people. There's also evidence that this preference was reflected in traditional news media. "From 1977–1997, the amount of 'soft news' (celebrity, scandal, gossip, and other human interest stories) in the American news media increased from 15 percent to 43 percent," according to Kathy Koch (1998: 5).

The fortunes of the *National Enquirer* fluctuated as the traditional newspapers softened and tabloid rivals adapted more flexibly. The *Star*, for example, in 2004 reinvented itself as a glossy mag, which, as the *Economist* of July 8, 2004 reported, "treats celebrities as people to envy (better clothes, better dates, better sex and, inevitably, better body parts) but also, if captured from a slightly different angle, as people who are just as wretched as you."

By the time of the *Star*'s new beginning, our preoccupation with celebrities – in the sense we use the term today – was in full evidence. In particular, interest in the foibles and fallibilities of celebrities seemed to issue a personal demand to magazines such as the *National Enquirer*: "Show us how cosmetic surgery can go grotesquely wrong. How age corrodes the most sublime beauties. How marriages made in heaven can descend to Stygian depths."

It was as if an entire culture had been redefined in personal terms, as seen through the eyes of celebrities. As Jill Neimark wrote in her "The culture of celebrity": "Our national passions, cultural watersheds, sexual mores, gender and racial battles, and political climate are viewed through the ever-shifting kaleidoscope of stories about people" (1995: 84).

In its own bizarre way, the *National Enquirer* has been a cultural heart-rate monitor, providing a visible display of changes without revealing their sources. The magazine, which remains the mother of all tabloids, did more than record changes: it contributed to them, providing the basic elements of rumor and fanciful stories that fermented into soft news. One of the challenges in this book is to apportion causal priority to the chicken of the media or the egg of public taste. Which came first? Did the softening of the news media with its focus on personalities and their trivial pursuits change us? Or did we demand insights into the glitzy world of entertainers, confessions of their personal failings, and prurient details of their private lives?

: a victim for all seasons

"Like the making of sausage or violin strings, the minting of celebrity is not a pretty business," observes Lewis H. Lapham. Both the chow that makes such a tasty breakfast and the twine that produces the mellifluous sound are prepared from the intestines of pigs, sheep, or horses.

Writing for *Harper's* in the months following the death of Diana, Princess of Wales, Lapham detected a Faustian bargain between the media that confer "temporary divinity" on individuals and all but guarantee "the gifts of wealth and applause" but in return for "remnants of his or her humanity" that are made available to "the ritual of the public feast" (1997: 13).

Diana always gave the appearance of "having been granted every wish in Aladdin's cave – youth, beauty, pretty dresses, a prince for a husband, and Elton John for a pet." Her fans, who came from all quarters, cherished her for her neediness, which was, on Lapham's account, "as desperate and as formless as their own" (1997: 13).

Interest in the royal family had been largely reverential. Onlookers were exactly that: detached observers, watching as subjects rather than participants. Only Queen Elizabeth's sister Princess Margaret induced a more involved curiosity, her trysting occupying the paparazzi, though without sending them into the kind of frenzy as Diana did. As celebrities go, Diana was *ne plus ultra*: the highest form of such a being. No woman or man has ever commanded such reverence, respect, and collective love from such a wide constituency, in her case, the world. Even the most sober account of her life and death seems like a fairytale that got out of hand. It has the staples of love and death, as well as liberation, deliverance, and tragedy. Like other great fairytales, its motif was transformation. As ugly ducklings turn to swans and sleeping beauties awaken, Diana was changed from ingénue kindergarten teacher in a London school to the nearest the twentieth century had to a Goddess.

Unlike other fairystories, Diana's transformation was no magical affair. It was, as Lapham suggests, a more prosaic business, akin to that of the sausage-maker or the manufacturer of violin strings. In other words, a production in which raw materials are refined into items of taste and grace.

Not that Diana herself was without her own immanent elegance. Born in 1961 at Park House, the home that her parents rented on Queen Elizabeth II's Sandringham estate, she was the third child of Edward John Spencer, Viscount Althorp, heir to the 7th Earl Spencer, and his first wife Frances Ruth Burke Roche, daughter of the 4th Baron of Fermoy. So, her aristocratic credentials were sound. She became Lady Diana Spencer in 1975, when her father became an earl. Returning to England after attending finishing school in Switzerland, Diana grew close to Prince Charles. They announced their engagement in February 1981 and married later in that year. The wedding ceremony was televised globally. Their first child, William, was born in 1982 and their second, Henry, or Harry as he was to become known, in 1984.

Over the next eight years, interest in Diana spiraled upward. Already the most admired and, perhaps, accepted member of the royal family, she contrived to remain imperious while developing a common touch. Time and again, people would testify that "she touched me" even though they might never have met her, or even seen her in the flesh. There was a tangible quality not so much in her presence but in even her sheer image. And this was made possible by exhaustive media coverage that occasionally, in fact once too often, became dangerously invasive.

The image was a cross between Cinderella and Rapunzel: a beautiful, yet lonely princess imprisoned in a loveless marriage with a prince, whose suspected infidelity with an older and less attractive women was the talk of the court. Trapped and with no apparent escape route, she seemed defenseless against a powerful and uncaring royal family. Diana made an enchanting victim, a vision of sacrificial womanhood. She kept her mask of motherly serenity, smiling beatifically to her millions of followers. Her popularity seemed to grow in inverse proportion to that of her husband. She threw herself into charitable work and aligned herself with great causes, visiting people living with AIDs and children in hospitals.

The separation was one of those worst-kept secrets. When it was finally announced in 1992, both Diana and Charles continued to carry out their royal duties. They jointly participated in raising the two children. Diana continued with her charitable endeavors, attracting battalions of photojournalists wherever she went. If there was a high point during this period, it came in January 1997, when, as an International Red Cross VIP volunteer, she visited Angola to talk to landmine survivors. Pictures of Diana in helmet and flak jacket were among the most dramatic images of the late twentieth century. In the August, she traveled to Bosnia, again to visit survivors of landmine explosions. From there she went to see her companion, Dodi Al-Fayed in France.

Late in the evening of August 30, 1997, Diana and Al-Fayed, their driver and bodyguard left the Ritz hotel in Place Vendome, Paris and drove along the north bank of the Seine. Ever-vigilant, the media were soon alerted and pursued the Mercedes in which the party was traveling. Remember: by 1997, Diana's every movement was closely monitored. Interest in every aspect of her life was genuinely global. Not only was she fêted the world over, she was inspected too. The appetite for news – any kind of news, however insignificant – was devoured. "Diana," remarked Lapham, "was a celebrity of the most vulnerable and therefore the most nourishing type, a victim for all seasons."

At twenty-five minutes past midnight, nine vehicles carrying the media and a single motorcycle followed Diana and Al-Fayed into an underpass below the Place de l'Alma. As the Mercedes sped away from the pursuing pack, it clipped a wall and veered to the left, colliding with a supporting pillar before spinning to a halt. There followed a few moments while the chasing photographers paused to consider their options. Inside the wrecked Mercedes were four motionless bodies, including that of the world's most famous, most esteemed, most adored, most treasured, and most celebrated woman. Photos of the wreckage would be hard currency. But to delay helping her and her fellow travelers might jeopardize their chances of survival. The paparazzi took their shots.

Diana was still alive when she was freed and rushed by ambulance to a nearby hospital. Attempts to save her life were futile and, at 4.00 a.m., doctors pronounced her dead. Of the Mercedes passengers, only Trevor Rees-Jones, Al-Fayed's bodyguard, survived. None of the others were wearing seat belts. It was later revealed that the chauffeur, Henri Paul, had been drinking earlier in the evening. The media people were cleared.

There followed the most extraordinary expression of public grief ever. This is unarguable: the scale, scope, and intensity of the response to her death distinguished it from any comparable manifestation of sorrow. The deaths of John F. Kennedy in 1963, Elvis Presley in 1977, and John Lennon in 1980 had been occasions for conspicuous mourning, though they were of a different order and, perhaps, from a different age.

The response to Diana's death defined an emblematic moment, one of transferred emotion. In the days leading to her funeral on September 6, over a million people flocked to pay their last respects, many leaving bouquets at her London home at

Kensington Palace. Her funeral attracted three million mourners who cast flowers along the entire length of the journey. A global television audience of two and a half billion watched the day's events.

Diana's friend Elton John sang and later released a rewritten version of his "Candle in the wind," in allusion to Diana's Aeolian frailties. While John's venture was not born out of commercial greed, there were plenty of exploitable byproducts to follow. A foretaste of the celebrity value of Diana came when the first issue of *Time* magazine following her death sold 750,000 more copies than usual. Sales of a commemorative issue exceeded 1.2 million. *National Enquirer*, in a somewhat hypocritical gesture, refused to published pictures of Diana's death scene, despite having headlined a story the week before DI GOES SEX MAD.

Then came the merchandise. A planned comic book featuring Diana raised from the dead and invested with superpowers and entitled (following the Bond movie) *Di Another Day*, was ditched by Marvel Comics amid protest. But less offensive products, such as statuettes, decorative plates, and "Cindy"-like dolls began to appear on the shelves within months of the tragedy.

The near-inevitable conspiracy theories surrounding the death were equal to those of the moon landing, the JFK assassination, or 9/11. More rational attributions of blame centered on the chasing pack of paparazzi. Diana's brother, Earl Spencer, offered this view: "I always believed the press would kill her in the end," quoted by Jacqueline Sharkey in her 1997 article "The Diana aftermath." He said: "Every proprietor and editor of every publication that has paid for intrusive and exploitative photographs of her, encouraging greedy and ruthless individuals to risk everything in pursuit of Diana's image, has blood on his hands" (1997: 18).

If they hadn't been so manic about getting their photographs, they wouldn't have pursued her car so heedlessly. Sharkey reflects on how "the public and some members of the press denounced the photographers – and journalists in general –

as 'barracuda,' 'jackals,' piranha' and 'vultures' feeding off celebrities" (1997: 18).

So went the argument. Few wanted to extend that same argument further. If they had, they would have concluded that the paparazzi were motivated by money offered by media corporations that could sell publications in their millions to consumers whose thirst for pictures and stories of Diana seemed unquenchable. In the event, the photographers were cleared of any wrongdoing by a French court in 1999. The fact remains: all parties, from the paparazzi to the fans, were connected as if by invisible thread.

And then something interesting happened. As Donna Cox puts it in her "*Diana: Her true story*: post-modern transgressions in identity": "We became voyeurs to our own displays of 'suffering', playing 'Diana' to ourselves through blinking television monitors" (1999: 330).

The audience not only watched the Diana fairytale reach its denouement, but saw themselves as bit-part players in that same fairytale. This narrative transformation was both revealing and concealing. The media's part in the death of Diana might have been laid bare, but consumers' complicity, though recognized, was left unexamined, at least not in a deep or critical sense. While audiences might have agreed with Earl Spencer and condemned the media, they rewarded them with high sales and record viewing figures.

Perhaps transformation overstates the change. Anyone who was aware of Diana – and it's difficult to imagine anyone who wasn't – was forced to inspect the way in which news values had been subverted by entertainment values. After all, Diana's greatest triumph was not so much in ushering in world peace, or saving the planet, but in offering so much pleasure to so many people.

Yet the inspection was momentary. It didn't bring to an end the gathering interest in figures who, like Diana, offered pleasure while presenting absolutely nothing that would materially alter people's lives or the lives of any other living thing. The interest in recognizable people was probably interrupted by Diana's death. Then, after a spell of earnest introspection and critical evaluation of the media, the interest resumed.

During the 35 years that separated the Taylor–Burton scandal and the death of Diana, the word "paparazzi" was inducted into the popular vocabulary, as was "tabloid" and "celebs." "Reality tv" would arrive soon after. Diana had become the paragon of celebrity. Taylor may have been the most famous, perhaps most revered, woman of the 1960s, but, by the time of Diana's emergence in the 1980s, the simmering pot of interest in the rich and famous had been brought to the boil. In 1992, when her separation from Charles became official, the pot boiled over. Diana was news: not just what she was doing or saying or even wearing. People seemed to gasp in wonder at the very mention of her name.

In the 1960s, the most adventurous clairvoyant would have been hard pressed to predict the tumult of interest in Diana. Something had happened. Not to Diana, but to *us*. We, the living human beings who attributed to her so much celestial power, were the ones who changed. And, after her death, we would go on changing.

Following the death of Diana and Al-Fayed, *Time* magazine writer Margaret Carlson observed: "By the time of the couple's dinner at Paris' Ritz Hotel, the rules of engagement sometimes observed between the photo hounds and the princess had gone completely by the board, as the street value of a grainy shot of Diana with al Fayed reached six figures" (1997: 46).

"Rules of engagement": it's an interesting choice of phrase, carrying connotations of the principles that bind the actions of parties involved in some sort of conflict or competition. That wasn't the case here, though the circumstances of Diana's death certainly had the elements of opposition. Carlson's point is that "the run-ins between celebrities and those who take pictures of them are growing increasingly ugly."

The likes of Geppetti and Secchiaroli weren't exactly welcomed by the stars of the 1960s, but they became parties to an initially uneasy accommodation, which later became symbiotic, benefiting both. A renowned exception was photojournalist Ron Galella's near-obsessional pursuit of Jacqueline Kennedy Onassis. Incensed by the ceaseless attention, Onassis secured a court order that prevented Galella encroaching on what she considered her private space. In this case, the rules of engagement were enshrined in law – and the well-documented run-ins were truly ugly.

The media weren't going to let their subjects appear as if they'd come straight from a makeover. Nor were they going to run anemic copy like: "Her favorite recreation is motoring and she is never so happy as when spinning along a country road, the fresh air blowing in her face" (this is actually plucked from the fan magazine *Film Weekly* by Matthew Sweet in his book *Shepperton Babylon*).

Elsewhere, a self-perpetuating mechanism was being developed. The *National Enquirer* and other tabloids with their relentless focus on the exploits of famous personalities were, as Neimark put it, reducing the scope of world events to individuals (1995: 84). We, in turn, became habituated to a softening of news in which entertainment – and I use this in its widest sense: anything that amuses or occupies us agreeably – became an increasingly large staple in our intellectual diets. Our interest in politics took on a personal focus, as we were drawn to politicians as much if not more than their politics – we will examine this in Chapter 11.

We started to understand the world through people rather than events, processes, or actions. Interest that, in the 1960s and perhaps 1970s, would have been seen as unwholesome or downright salacious became much more commonplace. The scandal precipitated by Taylor's affair may not have started this, but it was the single most important episode in the transition to a culture in which almost everything we knew arrived via the media and everything we did was designed to take us closer to a life of endless novelty, pleasure, and commodities.

GIVING/IT ALL

: public property

Fame is . . . it's such a strange thing, isn't it? You never quite get used to being public property, really. Take our conversation now. You have just walked into this room and started telling me shit about myself and that's, like, weird, it's crazy, because we are strangers.

Gwen Stefani (quoted by Nick Duerden, 2005)

In 1981, the year of Diana's marriage, the mention of dvd, pc, CNN, vcr, BSkyB or cd would have probably elicited puzzlement. They're now parts of our everyday vocabulary and we could justifiably say that they've come to signify technological progress. But there's a price to pay for everything, especially progress. It might offer the prospect of genuine liberation, including a release from many of the irksome restrictions of life; it might actually produce life-altering benefits. On the other side of the balance sheet? Consider burning fossil fuels: it produced the energy that fired the industrial revolution, but left us with a global warming that endangers the planet. The internal combustion engine revolutionized the way we travel, the scope of our travel, and affected just about everything in the twentieth century. Inventors of that piece of technology couldn't have conceived of the number of deaths that would result either directly from travel or indirectly from pollution. And what of the cellphone, or mobile?

Few of us would gladly dispense with this small but enormously convenient instrument, despite the accumulating evidence that it may be emitting brain-damaging radiation.

There were two periods in the twentieth century when social change and technological change converged dramatically, and both have a bearing on our understanding of celebrity culture. The first followed the end of World War I. For all its destruction, the war had widened the horizons of allied forces, particularly the notoriously insular Americans, two million of whom had glimpsed European cities, their culture, their liberal sexual morality. Women, having played a vigorous role in the war, had challenged the illusion of the female as a delicate creature in need of men's protection. A vocal and effective suffragette movement was prising open new areas in politics and education. The sense of emancipation was enhanced by the the consumer goods that became available after the war: the radio, the affordable car, and the talking movie. These didn't just change they way we spent our leisure time: they changed our entire social experience.

People were brought together as never before: they could have the same feelings at the same time, despite being thousands of miles apart. The power of the media was stunningly revealed during the 1927 boxing match between Gene Tunney and Jack Dempsey when five radio listeners supposedly died from heart attacks. The car was equal in its impact: as ownership rose, so social and physical liberation came together. Places that were once remote became accessible (by 1930, 23 million Americans and 2.3 million British owned cars). New towns, new counties, even new states were within reach. Conceptions of physical space concertina'd, collapsing and compressing distances that once seemed unimaginably great. This complemented the sense of immediacy introduced by radio and, later, modified by the cinema and, more importantly, television.

Those who purloin the gifts of science and technology are often punished, though in less spectacular ways than the demigod Prometheus who stole fire from Olympus and taught humans to use it, but was later chained to a rock and preyed on by vultures. Television is like fire: it illuminates, ignites, and affects us in ways we rarely dwell on. Most of us could hardly bear thinking about life without television. As essentials of contemporary culture go, it has no challengers. Yet, it's been held responsible for, among other things, shortening our attention spans, precipitating violent behavior, and reducing local cultures to insignificance.

During the second half of the twentieth century, television transformed the way we thought and behaved. It affected the way we relaxed, the way we learned, the way we communicated. The complete cultural landscape was transfigured by television, to the point where we are hardly aware that we see the world as if through an invisible filter. So much of what we know about the world is gleaned from tv that we find it tough to think where else we find out about some event or other. The internet has, of course, emerged as an alternative.

It barely needs stating that celebrity culture wouldn't have been possible without television. Prior to its acceptance as a domestic appliance in the 1950s, we knew about prominent figures mainly by their names or artist's impressions, still photographs or newsreels shown at the movies. "Television, bringing famous faces and sounds into our homes, has created different kinds of celebrity," writes David Giles in his *Illusions of Immortality: A psychology of fame and celebrity* (2000: 32).

Television brought with it intimacy: we were able to see moving images and hear voices – in our own homes. It also brought replication: those images and sounds were not just one-offs: they could be repeated time and again, exposing us to the famous in a way that stirred us to new interest. We saw people that were previously remote and perhaps unknowable as ordinary humans with the same kinds of mannerisms, faults, and maybe foibles as the rest of us.

Giles argues that the proliferation of media, specifically television, in the late twentieth century expanded the opportunities for people to become famous. In material terms, there were more tv screens on which they could appear and become known. Viewers could not only see and hear a new array of people: they could almost reach out and touch them. In a way, they could almost swear they knew them. The more they felt they knew them, the more they became entranced.

Giles invokes a term from a 1956 article in the journal *Psychiatry* to capture the emerging relationship between tv figures and viewers: "parasocial interaction" (Horton and Wohl coined the term in 1956). The 1950s was the decade of growth for television: at the start, few households had a tv; by the end over 90 percent of households in the USA and 70 percent in the UK had at least one set. Viewers were forming unusual attachments. They were developing "friendships" with television characters, some fictional and others real (like announcers, or weather forecasters). They also "hated" some of them. Familiarity led to a sense of intimacy. Viewers actually thought they knew the figures they saw on their screens. They interacted with them parasocially. The relationships were and still are strictly one-way.

It's called parasocial because *para* means beyond, as in paranormal. The attachment might only have been as strong as a beam of light from a cathode ray tube. Yet it was experienced as real and meaningful. Consumers actually felt they knew people they had never met, probably never seen in the flesh, and who knew nothing of their existence. So there is no actual interaction (*inter* means between): it's one-way. This doesn't stop the consumer feeling like there's a genuine interaction. In this sense, parasocial is an interesting term that captures the way we think and feel about people we don't know and who don't know us but who sometimes unwittingly and unknowingly move us to act, occasionally in erratic and irrational ways.

: the vision of MTV

As Prometheus can confirm, anything can go awry when trying to snatch wisdom. In his case, human fallibility was exposed by the gods. In the case of tv, it was the impressionability of viewers. Television may have started with the best of intentions, with no brief to pander to audiences. In Britain, the BBC ostentatiously promised a theater of the airwaves. And, although it was funded by advertising revenue and had to remain audience-friendly, US television harbored similar aspirations in the 1950s.

Television used wire transmission: sending electrical signals over various types of wire, including coaxial cable. In 1962, the BBC sent the first communications satellite into orbit. Satellite systems allowed the exchange of television or telephone signals by means of microwaves, which are very short electromagnetic waves – the same things that heat your food. Telstar was the first of several similar satellites launched in the early 1960s. Signals were bounced off them while they orbited the earth so that telephone conversations and live television transmissions were made through space. In 1964, coverage of the summer Olympics in Tokyo were sent around the world via the Syncom 3 satellite. In 1969, the Apollo 11 satellite beamed images from the moon's surface into people's living rooms.

Technological developments over the next few years made it possible for some stations to use satellite delivery of all their programs. HBO, for example, began its service in 1976, transmitting from the Philippines the heavyweight title fight between Muhammad Ali and Joe Frazier known as the "Thrilla in Manila." HBO offered something different from the usual television menu: films, concerts, and sports events. Other channels to use satellite broadcasts included the Star movie channel, WTBS, Ted Turner's "superstation," as he called it, and the Christian Broadcasting Network, later to become the Family Channel, all breaking away from the traditional varied makeup of programming and opting for just one type of program.

The cable tv industry, which had started in 1948 as a primitive solution to the reception problems experienced by those in mountainous areas, quickly followed the early examples. Turner's CNN specialized in news, Nickelodeon in children's programs and ESPN in sports only. But most influential in the development of celebrity culture was Warner's MTV station.

Imagine two tv execs leaving a movie theater in 1977 after seeing *Saturday Night Fever*: impressed by the disco music that throbbed throughout the film, one suggests to the other that they start a channel on which they show nothing but the kind of material they've just witnessed. The other laughs: "Look, that was 119 minutes and it was held together by a plot. Why would anyone want to watch music clips nonstop without even a story to sustain their interest?"

Four years later, in 1981, MTV defied the cynics and began transmitting music videos, which were intended to promote record sales. In fact, the distinction between promotional material and entertainment was smudged if not erased by MTV which showed pure music clips, including concert footage at first. (Fanciful as the *SNF* scenario seems, it actually isn't too far from the truth: MTV was started by two CBS producers and an NBC radio programmer, who collectively dreamed up the idea.)

The program content came from record companies, which were eager to grab what was effectively free advertising. Pop videos were not then at the point where every commercial single was augmented by a video, but they were moving in that direction. MTV's income came from advertising revenue, which went up in proportion to their viewing figures, and its share of cable subscriptions. So there was a genuine symbiosis: all parties benefited from each other. While it seems a perfectly brilliant idea today, in the late 1970s, it must have seemed preposterous. Yet, here we are in the twenty-first century with MTV stations transmitting literally everywhere in the world and more imitators than iPod. MTV's global venture started in 1987 with MTV Europe and continued with such stations as MTV

Mandarin, MTV Japan, and MTV Africa. Record companies still crave the inclusion of their videos on MTV's playlists and advertisers love the demographics the station serves up: 18–25 with no dependants and disposable income.

Have you ever thought what's happening when you watch MTV? Are you being entertained, or held captive in front of a three-minute commercial? You could ask a similar question of sports: does enjoying the competition implicate you in witnessing advertisements for cars, razor blades, beer, and all the other kinds of products aimed at the sports fan market? Does it really matter? After all, television keeps us engrossed, absorbed, and amused. We usually have little inclination to analyze whether the hidden persuaders are surreptitiously bending our shopping preferences to their own requirements. Advertisers and tv companies figured this out long ago. MTV was, in its own way, a prototype. As its imitators proliferated, blurring the difference between entertainment and marketing became passé: making the two one and the same thing was the task. The band Dire Straits satirized the tightening relationship between pop music, television, and consumerism in their 1985 track "Money for nothing" in which they boast of getting to "play the guitar on the MTV" while acknowledging their unwritten responsibility: "We gotta install microwave ovens/custom kitchen deliveries/ we gotta move these refrigerators/we gotta move these color tvs."

: devouring Madonna

"We have far too much information about celebrities these days," according to Jill Neimark. Writing in *Psychology Today*, she lists some of the superfluities as "their love affairs, their private conversations on cellular phones, the color of their underwear, how many nose jobs they've had, how many intestinal polyps" (1995: 57).

Actually, this is about as wide of the mark as you can get. The whole point about celebrities is that there can never be too much information. There might not have been too much interest in Elizabeth Taylor's underwear, or, if there was, it would in the 1960s have been regarded as prurient. But there was certainly major interest in her love affairs, especially the association with Burton. Today, no detail of a celebrity's private life is privileged: to be a celebrity means to be willing to go public with the minutiae of what might, at another time in history, be known as a private life. No one recognized this as clearly as Madonna Louise Veronica Ciccone.

Around the time of the release of her album *Like a Prayer* in 1989 Madonna seems to have had one of those "Eureka!" moments. Or maybe it was more like a peek at a crystal ball (Baccarat crystal, of course). She seems to have arrived at the conclusion that a new age was upon us, one in which celebrities would rule the earth. "I have seen the future," she might have declared, "and it is one in which the fans will demand more and receive more; and those who are prepared to give them what they want – or even more – will prevail." Over the next five years, she did precisely this. "Madonna would later comment that this entire period of her life was designed to give the world every single morsel of what they [sic] seemed to be demanding in their invasion of her private life" (http://en.wikipedia.org/wiki/Madonna).

The world didn't so much "demand" details of or "invade" her private life: they were inescapably, unavoidably, obligatorily surrounded by a life which might have been "private" in one sense, but was opened up for full public inspection. Before her, stars had tried to section off parts of their lives. After, they either gave up trying, or gave up trying to be a star.

The organizing themes of Madonna's career, 1989–94, were classic celebrity: finely judged scandal, continuous media exposure, a cycle of dramatic makeovers, and sex. Its momentum was such that it carried her through over two decades as a leading showbusiness performer. She sold more records than any other female in history (250 million and counting) and amassed personal wealth of over $600 million. She earned paeans, prizes, and plaudits and drew censure, condemnation, and jeers.

Her first album *Madonna* was released in 1983 and sprung three successful singles, all of them heavily featured on MTV, then in its ascendancy. The music channel could legitimately be credited with making many artists – Duran Duran included – and stymieing the progress of others – numerous African American artists had their videos turned down by MTV and it took pressure from CBS to ensure a place for Michael Jackson's "Billie Jean" on the playlist in 1983. Madonna, however, was perfectly congruent with MTV's preferred profile: white, twentysomething, tons of junk jewelry, and a wardrobe that might have been put together from a flea market. Anyone could look like Madonna; millions actually did.

Then she assumed a new image: a bottle-blonde Marilyn Monroe manqué dripping with Harry Winston diamonds for her "Like a virgin" video, Madonna kept changing, keeping her fans guessing as to what she looked like. Two movies, an appearance in a Broadway play, a tempestuous marriage, the publication of nude photospreads (against her wishes: the shots were taken in the early 1980s), and multi-million record sales had turned Madonna into a major performer. She could have opted to stick with the formula: more albums, more chameleon-like changes of image, and occasional ventures into drama; in which case, she would have been remembered in the same way as her contemporaries, like Whitney Houston or Mariah Carey.

In the golden age of Hollywood, adultery, under-age sex, abortion, alcoholism, venereal disease, and suicide were rife. But journalists in the main refrained from gossiping about the hedonistic excesses of the stars. Controversy and scandal were unwelcome detours on the professional highway for movie and music stars. Often they were roads to oblivion. The media respected this and limited their criticisms to on-screen performances. In 1989, Madonna deviated with what might have been suicidal recklessness. For five years, she all but dared the media not to get involved.

1989. In the video for the title track of the *Like a Prayer* album, Madonna appeared with long raven hair, portraying a prostitute who witnesses a rape and murder. After a black man is falsely accused and jailed, Madonna goes to church, where a status of St Martin de Porres resembling the accused comes to life and kisses her passionately. The video which also featured burning crosses, was denounced by the Vatican (echoes of Taylor) for its "blasphemous" eroticism and misuse of Catholic symbolism. Pepsi-Cola pulled out of a $5 million endorsement deal with Madonna. The furor placed Madonna at the center of an international news story and helped turn the album into a global success: three more hit singles were taken from the album. (Pepsi was also embarrassed by endorsers Michael Jackson and Britney Spears, the latter photographed while drinking Coca-Cola.)

1990. MTV banned "Justify my love," a single with sexually explicitly lyrics ("You put this in me . . .") and an erotic video with gay and lesbian scenes to match. Being banned by the very medium that had been key to her initial success was a delicious paradox and the media devoured it. Over a million copies of the cd were moved. The visual style of the "Vogue" video bore gay influences.

1991. For the feature documentary *Truth or Dare*, or *In Bed with Madonna*, as it was entitled in Britain, Madonna allowed cameras access to areas of her private life. What audiences remembered was her bitchiness and self-regarding wit, but also her sensitive visit to her mother's grave and her softer, reflective side. Even talking bitchily behind the scenes of her "Blonde Ambition" tour, she came over as an ordinary mortal. It's difficult to imagine any other performer inviting cameras to examine them close-up in this way. But, as Joshua Rich reflects in *Entertainment Weekly*: "A warts-and-all movie confessional – rare from a diva of her stature – made total, perverse sense" (2002: 84). By coincidence or perhaps synchronicity, during the 1991 Persian Gulf war, millions of viewers turned to CNN to watch the war occurring in real time. The cable tv channel offered viewers a novel and unique way of viewing a real event "unplugged," so to speak.

1992. No book published in the same year received as much publicity. Inside the sheet metal covers of *Sex* Madonna could be seen in poses that suggested lesbianism, anal sex, and sadomasochism. The book sold in a vacuum-sealed cover at $50. Its publication coincided with the release of *Erotica*, an album that complemented the book thematically. The accompanying video featured Madonna dressed androgynously. This was a star at or approaching the peak of her popularity, fabulously rich, with several hugely successful albums and a presence in movies, baring herself and playing out sexual fantasies to anyone who cared to look. For what? Mischief? Outrage and media exposure were umbilically connected. Her intuitive brilliance in both brought rewards in the form of a seven-year $60 million deal with Time-Warner. Around this time, softish porn material from her background began to emerge, so her stylized bawdiness functioned as a distraction from this.

1993. Even in failure, Madonna created news. Playing opposite Willem Dafoe in the execrable *Body of Evidence* she was mercilessly maligned and lampooned. She weighed in as a dominatrix who introduces her defense attorney to the delights of having hot candle wax dripped onto his genitals. Masturbation, sodomy, and bondage fill the holes in the plot. Her much-discussed friendship with cross-dressing basketball player Dennis Rodman, then at the height of his celebrity rating, was one of those singer/athlete affairs that were to become popular in the years ahead (*cf*. Posh and Becks).

1994. The subject of the single "Secret" was that of a love affair between a straight man and a transsexual, though the infamous episode of Madonna's year was reserved for *The Late Show with David Letterman* on which she let loose with fifteen repetitions of the word "fuck," all bleeped. From one perspective, it was a coarse, undignified, unnecessarily offensive display from a woman who could lay claim to being the world's leading female singer. From another, it was another example of Madonna's capacity to turn the unlikeliest event into a showcase for herself. (The transcript of the interview is at http://www.allabout madonna.com/interview_1994_david_letterman.php.) In the same year, the trial of O. J. Simpson for the murders of his ex-wife and her friend generated unprecedented global media coverage.

Over the next decade, Madonna transformed from *grande amoureuse* to *grande dame*. Playing the eponymous *Evita* in the 1996 movie, she won a Golden Globe award. She converted to the Judaic sect known as the Kabbalah (changing her name to Esther in the process), teamed up with producer William Orbit in 1998 for one of her best-received albums *Ray of Light*, wrote children's books, had children, married, and moved to London. MTV banned her video "What it feels like for a girl" which featured a suicide, though it was tame compared to her earlier material. She was also subpoenaed to give evidence against stalker Robert Hoskins. (In the 1990s, stalkers were essential accessories for A-list affiliates, as we will see in Chapter 5.)

By 2000, Madonna was using vodocoderized vocals as she line-danced dressed in jeans and check cowboy shirt (not any old jeans and shirt, though: hers were by Dsquared) for "Nothing really matters" from *Music*. Nine million fans watched her concert "live" from London online. And, as if to remind the world that she could still make news whenever she wanted, she appeared, age 45, at the 2003 MTV Music Awards with two of her epigones, Britney Spears and Christina Aguilera. "In the most eye-popping encounter in MTV history," as Mara Reinstein, of *Us Weekly*, puts it, Madonna and Spears "sealed their brand new big-sister-little-sister bond with a sultry onstage kiss – tongue and all – that upstaged everything else" (2003: 52).

But the transition was complete and the MTV snog was a tiny reminder of Madonna's once-mighty potential to shock rather than a return to old values. If anything validated this, it was Madonna's appearance in a 2003 television commercial for Gap. This was a fashionista of the first order swapping her Gaultier conical bras and Versace gowns for sensible tee-shirts and khakis "The onetime mistress of reinvention once negotiated her celebrity like a game of chess – precisely by not catering to the masses," writes Danielle Sacks in her article "Who's that girl?" (2003: 32). "She sought out controversy. She sought to offend." But: "You can't be a pop icon and a spiritualistic writer and sing about the flaws of American consumerism and make out with same-sex pop stars half your age and be the face of one of the most generic brands in America all at once" (2003: 32).

This might read like a criticism, though it's no more than a complimentary observation: it doesn't diminish the overall impact she made on popular culture. Commemorating two decades of her influence, *Harper's Bazaar*, in September 2003 (issue 3502), held that "the ultimate pop-culture icon('s) . . . influence is endless" (p. 303). Even allowing for exaggeration, the point is that, Madonna changed "how the game works," as Stefani later put it: the principles that bind the actions of parties involved either cooperatively or competitively with the media. "I'm going to provoke, surprise, aggravate, and generally upset as many people as I can and I'm going to let you watch me do it," Madonna might have promised the media. "In the process, I will disclose more of myself than any pop or movie star in history. My body, my sexuality, my erotic fantasies: nothing is out of bounds."

The deal was simple: Madonna wanted and got more saturation media coverage than anyone, present and past. She was operating in an age of global media, when entertainment was becoming the hard currency of tv and when having a video vetoed by the likes of MTV made international news. Compellingly newsworthy in everything she did or said, Madonna was ubiquitous for at least the first half of the 1990s. Thereafter, her presence may have faded, but her influence remained. After her, no one could aspire to becoming a celebrity if they wanted anything resembling a private life. The boundary-blurring that had started in Rome in 1961 was completely obliterated during Madonna's rise, or, as some might have it, diabolically masterminded descent.

Writing for *Rolling Stone*, Britney Spears offers the view: "Madonna was the first female pop star to take control of every aspect of her career and to take responsibility for creating her image, no matter how much flak she might get" (2004: 124). It's a common observation, though one that misses the more important point that, in taking control of her own career, she needed the assistance of a media that had, by the end of the 1980s, become potent makers and breakers of careers. Hers could have finished prematurely in a comic shambles if her 1986 tale of a teen pregnancy "Papa don't preach" had been dismissed as a contrived attempt to inflame conservative moralists and prompt further outrage. Instead it was hailed by the media as a daring and inventive attempt to break away from the insubstantialities of pop music.

She did risk the flak, as Spears points out, but, as with all Madonna's gambles, it was a carefully calculated one. Emboldened by her success, she deepened her liaisons with the media until confident she had won them over. She provided great copy; they provided great coverage. The rules changed.

From the vantage point of the twenty-first century, Madonna is a middle-aged diva who reigned long and who made good music. Some might suspect that I exaggerate the extent of her influence. I'm not arguing that she singlehandedly introduced celebrity culture. But she, more than anyone else, effected a change in the style and manner with which stars engaged with the media. And, in this sense, she both epitomized and helped usher in an age in which the epithets "shocking," "disgusting," or "filthy" didn't presage the end of a career. On the contrary: when treated appropriately by the media, they occasioned the popping of champagne corks in celebration.

Almost every requirement of celebrity culture was met by the time of Madonna's fusillade of expletives on Letterman's show in 1994: a prying, ravenous media hungry for every "morsel"; a proliferation of global television networks with little else to fill their channels apart from entertainment; a breakdown in the traditional public vs. private domains; and a class of figures of world renown who had been changed as if by sorcery into what we now call icons – the word actually deriving from the Greek *eikon*, meaning a statue of a revered person, sometimes thought to be sacred itself. There is still something missing: us.

: people who play people who do great things

There was a time when we admired, respected, and followed the exploits of heroes. These included statesmen, scientists, explorers, and military figures, people – usually though not always men – who distinguished themselves by their accomplishments. Whether on the battlefield, in the laboratory or atop mountains, heroes were great achievers. They were known for their deeds rather than their "well-knownness," this being a term coined by Daniel Boorstin in his book *The Image: A guide to pseudo-events in America* (1992: 67).

We've changed. At least according to Len Sherman who writes: "We have forsaken our traditional heroes and replaced them with actors and athletes . . . where we once admired people who do great things, now we admire people who play people who do great things" (1992: 26).

Sherman means actors who play great historical characters, such as Alexander the Great, or athletes who talk about winning a football game as if they've conquered Everest, or pop stars who believe their status entitles them to make pronouncements on how to save the planet, solve third world debt, or bring peace on earth. For Sherman, celebrities have replaced heroes, but without having to inherit the responsibilities attendant on heroic status.

He means by this that heroes "embodied the best of their people's convictions and hopes. They consciously aspired to live in such a manner to as to serve as examples for the rest of society" (1992: 26).

By contrast, today's replacements make a point of operating "outside the morals and ethics and rules by which the rest of populace lives." We may go so far as to say that maintaining a celebrity status is contingent on breaking a few rules here and there, just to demonstrate that a disregard of norms that govern or guide the conduct of the rest of society. Madonna's contrived transgressions served notice that she could violate as many rules as she wanted with impunity.

While Sherman is specifically interested in the ways in which athletes were and are able to flout social conventions in a way that attracts publicity and so reinforces their status, his point is worth extending. Perhaps we have changed to the point where we've "forsaken" (itself an revealingly quaint word) or given up on traditional leaders and shifted our allegiance instead to people who don't actually do much, but appear everywhere. While Sherman doesn't refer to them, the Watergate affair and the anti-Vietnam war movement increased cynicism about not only government, but the media too.

When Sherman was writing in the early 1990s, there was less evidence about than there is today. His claim seems more solid now than then: we lack respect and hold in contempt many of our political leaders and regard men of the church as out of sync with contemporary values; we may be aware of the quests of mountaineers and pathbreaking scientists, but we're unlikely to be able to name them, let alone know much more about them.

Why? The spread of the market economy and the rise of democratic, individualistic values. That's the view of Charles Ponce de Leon. These have "steadily eroded all sources of authority," argues Ponce de Leon in his *Self-Exposure: Human-interest journalism and the emergence of celebrity in America, 1890–1940* (2002: 4). Our faith was being shaken by the start of the twentieth century; by the start of World War II, we thought about public figures in a less reverential way, questioning their wisdom and credentials for making pronouncements. These, we may note, are signs of progress: a healthy mistrust, a constructive skepticism, and a privileging of corroboration over faith are surely signs of a ripening modern democracy. But, as we'll see, they had the ironic effect of inclining us toward other non-traditional sources of authority.

We need to augment the arguments of Sherman and Ponce de Leon. In times of crisis, we have little alternative but to look to established leaders. We want and need them to make the decisions; our well-being depends on it. Political, military, and religious leaders are burdened with the expectations of many. Whether they make the right or wrong choices, people's lives are affected. This becomes particularly acute when security at home is under threat. At times like these, leaders seem to have intrinsic, impermeable value. We have no choice but to trust them. Names like Roosevelt, Churchill, MacArthur, and Montgomery ring out through history. Their status has a imperishable quality that time can't erode. Their reputations were founded on actions rather than . . . well, reputations.

Pioneers were also venerated, not because of what people believed about them, but because of what they pioneered, whether, like Albert Einstein, new scientific boundaries, or, like Edmund Hillary, natural limits. Religious and spiritual leaders were respected by virtue of their position, but were also obliged to dispense wisdom of practical utility in guiding their followers, especially in troubled times. They too earned their status, rather than having it dropped on them.

Only excessive and unjustified respect could produce a world at once so meek and so fickle that its heroes are configured in a loop of images. That, in effect, is the argument put forward by Boorstin, whose work is still resonant, over four decades after its original publication in 1961 (with the different subtitle of "or what happened to the American dream"). The image has become more important than the substance. Celebrities are "fabricated," according to Boorstin and what passed for their achievements were no more than artificial contrivances, what he called "pseudo-events." He saw American culture in the throes of change, entertainers replacing genuine heroes, their public "personalities" eclipsing what they stood for, did, or said. Boorstin might have been interested in the 1977 film *MacArthur: The rebel general* in which the archetypal American World War II hero was portrayed by Gregory Peck, himself venerated, though, in his case for "being one of those people who play people who do great things."

The fragile simulation of Peck would have been no match for the real thing in the 1940s in Southeast Asia, but, in the 1970s, with Vietnam appearing as an avoidable rather than inevitable conflict, the dark handsomeness of Peck would have won out.

You could plot a graph of the rise and fall of faith in established leaders, the horizontal axis ordered chronologically, the vertical measuring collective confidence. The spikes would appear in times of crisis, particularly when domestic security is under threat. In Britain, trust in political leaders has probably receded since the 1970s, after the IRA bombings grew less and less frequent. Following the Pearl Harbor attack, the USA's boundaries were not breached until September 11, 2001, by which time celebrity culture had taken root even in politics. So we can understand the waning reliance on the great statesmen and church leaders in terms of our not actually needing to trust, or have confidence, less still faith in them.

It's also possible to explain our gradual abandonment of inventors and explorers as the result of a combination of world-wearying adaptations. After electricity, the internal combustion engine, television, the cure for tuberculosis, and gene therapy, what's left to discover? And, with Everest and the lesser mountains conquered, the world circumnavigated several dozen times by boat, and the Amazon charted, adventurers now have to devise their own challenges rather than rely on nature. The end of the cold war and the emergence of panic induced by the specter of an all-pervasive, ever-present yet invisible enemy against which political figures seem ineffective served to undermine established authority even further.

There wasn't an automatic transfer of confidence, though consumers became less interested or concerned about leaders, less deferential about their opinions. They also became progressively engrossed with celebrities who, by the mid-1990s, were "worthy of our slavish devotion, attention and respect," as Mark Harris of *Entertainment Today* put it (quoted in Neimark 1995: 90).

But, if our lack of conviction in more traditional leaders is comprehensible, our sometimes preposterous, diverting interest in celebrities, or as Boorstin might say, their images, needs more explanation. Before moving to an explanation, let's keep in mind the constituents of celebrity culture, or at least those we've covered so far. Think in terms of a DNA double helix, except with three strands coiling inside each other like some Philippe Stark-inspired spiral staircase. One strand represents a predatory, persistent, and progressively omnipresent corps of photojournalists who showed none of the respect or mannered deference of their predecessors in their search for new prey. Emerging as a force in the late 1960s, the paparazzi dissolved the previous demarcation lines between the public and private spheres. Their presence signaled a kind of open season.

New rules of engagement weren't far off. If it hadn't been Madonna who rewrote them, it would have been some other starlet with savvy enough to cut a different type of deal with the media: "I show all and you tell all." Media coverage would never be the same. This is a second strand and it wove together perfectly with the newfound value attributed to entertainment in the late 1980s, a time when television channels were multiplying like tribbles (those prolifically reproductive creatures from the classic *Star Trek* episode).

The sudden multiplication is the third strand. "As the number of shows and Web sites increased, so did competition for audiences and ad dollars," writes Howard Altman of *CQ Researcher*. "In turn, that raised the demand for more cheap content, such as the latest celebrity gossip, to fill the burgeoning amounts of broadcast airtime" (2005: 2).

Entertainers found themselves on display like never before. More outlets, more time, and more viewers. Light entertainment was like hard currency on the international televisual exchange. You didn't have to be a Hollywood star to be an entertainer: tv was the medium of choice and it gave rise to a new class of celebrity. Members of this class, or more accurately, images of and gossip about them, accessed resources of power not from any hitherto untapped natural resources, but from us. Our change from hero-worshippers to idolaters of images was all that was needed to complete the transition to celebrity culture.

Too neat? Absolutely. There had to be a process as industrial as the kind of process that produces household products, except designed to manufacture celebrities. "Celebrity as the fleeting product of a vacuum cleaner/sausage maker," is how Joshua Gamson describes this process (1992: 1). We'll consider it in more detail in the next chapter.

FABRICATING/FAME

: calibrating the balance, 1880–1930

How many tightrope walkers can you name? No, I didn't think so. But, in the mid-nineteenth century, Jean-François Gravelet was one of the most famous people in the world. Performing as Blondin, the Frenchman owed his fame, not to mention fortune, to his feat of crossing Niagara Falls on a rope suspended 160 feet above the deadly cataracts. After his first crossing in 1859, he repeated the stunt with variations: blindfolded, in a sack, pushing a wheelbarrow, on stilts, carrying a man on his back, and while preparing an omelet.

Few people outside his inner circle of friends knew much of Blondin's love life, his personal preferences, nor probably even where he lived. Yet he was internationally famous and he lived in the glare of publicity wherever he performed. He toured the world, executing spectacular aerial tricks, his last performance being in Belfast in 1896. As his career came to an end, a new century, a new era, and a new culture started. Performing during the Victorian period, 1837–1901, meant that the likes of Blondin depended on live performances, or reports of their exploits.

Photography was used progressively through the second half of the nineteenth century, but the halftone print (in which light and shade is represented by dots) wasn't used until the 1880s. Once newspapers and magazines started to use halftones extensively, pictures were added to names and descriptions. It was possible to recognize the famous from their actual images rather than illustrators' impressions. (Daguerreotypes, the type of photographs named after their French inventor, while commonly available, were not suitable for reproduction.)

Newspapers and journals had been around since the early 1800s. In the absence of radio and television, fame was disseminated via the publications. The invention of the rotary press in the 1840s and the construction of newswire services both quickened the rate at which reports could be made available and broadened the scope of circulations. News was what happened yesterday, not the week before. Nor was news necessarily reportage of people and events that directly concerned the reader. Newspapers covered items of interest, that is, information that appealed to "novelty, interest and curiosity," as Neil Postman puts it in his *Amusing Ourselves to Death* (1985: 65).

Rising literacy rates, when combined with technological innovations and improvements in transportation, resulted in a 400 percent rise in the circulation of daily newspapers between 1870 and the end of the century. Some publications, such as *McClure's*, chronicled the feats of admirable and heroic figures, not just military leaders, but inventors and heads of business corporations. There was also another type of curiosity: entertainers intrigued people. In her "Media and the rise of celebrity culture," Amy Henderson quotes an American newspaper story written in the 1880s: "It is remarkable how much attention the stage and things pertaining to it are receiving nowadays from the magazines . . . it has become a topic of conversation among all classes, furnishing an endless gossip to the trivial, and intellectual interest to the serious" (1992: 2).

In the first half of the twentieth century, reporters together with their photographer colleagues developed ways of exciting and exploiting public curiosity in famous people, not just their deeds, but their personalities. During the first three decades of the twentieth century, the print media, aided from the 1920s by radio, elevated diverse figures to the realms of world fame. Like Blondin, some of the famous figures at the turn of the century were showmen, such as William F. Cody, or "Buffalo Bill," who toured the world with his Wild West Show, and Harry Houdini, the great escapologist. Both achieved even greater fame later in the century, when they became subjects of Hollywood films, the former several times over, the latter in George Marshall's 1953 *Houdini*. In fact, the lives of practically all the heroes of that time were later turned into biopics: *Dempsey* (1983), *Lindbergh* (1990), and *The Babe* (1991) included.

Arguably more interesting and revealing were the people who went to great lengths to avoid being famous, yet were not so much publicized as mythicized by the media in the 1930s: Howard Hughes and Greta Garbo were recluses but their lives were turned into public property almost independently of them. Both sought obscurity, at least ostensibly – in Garbo's case, her trademark plea "I want to be alone" became an effective marketing tool. The myths surrounding them grew immeasurably larger than the people themselves, suggesting a new role for print and wireless radio media in creating public interest rather than merely publishing and broadcasting in response to public interest. (Hughes, the eccentric movie producer, plane-maker and hotelier, was the focus of a 2004 movie, *The Aviator*).

One actor, perhaps more than any other, espied the emergent interest of the media in entertainers as individuals with person-alities, rather than as just the occupants of screen or stage roles. Taking advantage of the shift in journalistic priorities, Errol Flynn conducted his private life in a way that mirrored his on-screen persona and adventures. A modest actor with little training, the English-educated Tasmanian made his mark in Hollywood with swashbuckling performances in the title roles of *Captain Blood* (1935), *The Adventures of Robin Hood* (1938), and *Gentleman Jim* (Corbett, the prize-fighter) (1942). His off-screen affrays suggested a symmetry between the personal and the professional, though it was his amatory performances that launched gossip of mythic dimensions. "He seemed to wish to elevate the artistic self to the mythical status of his fictional creations," states his entry in the Biography Resource Center (2004). By the time he took on another title role in *The Adventures of Don Juan* in 1949, when aged 40, Flynn's reputation had grown to the point where there was an almost perfect congruence.

Stories of artists behaving badly had become almost a sub-field of journalism. Decorum was preserved by presenting these as having genuine "human interest," a euphemism for voyeuristic appeal. Flynn apart, few entertainers actually seemed set on scandalizing themselves. Most tried to accommodate the demand for information on them by releasing it in controlled bursts.

The mission to illuminate and expose the "real self" behind the screen or stage façade, meanwhile, galvanized journalists. In his *Self-Exposure: Human-interest journalism and the emergence of celebrity in America, 1890–1940*, Charles Ponce de Leon argues that one of the effects of the ever-more intrusive media's reportage of the private lives of the famous was in "promoting the notion that success, happiness and self-fulfillment had little to do with material goods or social status – a comforting thought for people to embrace in a society increasingly characterized by stark inequalities of wealth and power" (2002: 108).

With the Victorian era consigned to history, twentieth-century modernity brought with it different aspirations, goals, and ambitions as well as opportunities for achieving them amid the inequalities germane to industrial society and the market economy on which it was based. Entertainers were conspicuously achieving individuals and, in this sense, became models of success. And yet they still struggled to find true happiness. People of limited means could read and hear about their efforts and, in the process, identify with them. While there was voyeuristic pleasure, which they took from peering surreptitiously through peepholes or eavesdropping on putative private conversations, there was also comfort from the reassurance that the rich and famous had home lives just like everyone else.

In his 1990 book *Picture Personalities*, Richard deCordova offers the thought that audiences were fascinated by the secrets of the stars, especially salacious secrets. Virginia L. Blum adds: "Early on [in the twentieth century] we find audiences interested in undermining the very equivalence between real and 'reel' lives" (2003: 149).

The rules of engagement, as we called them earlier, were being rendered inoperative, with journalists eager to venture into hitherto occluded aspects of entertainers' lives and entertainers eager to allow them in, but only so far. If the private self complemented the public self, then there was harmony. Discord was another thing entirely. So it was important to grant the media access, but offer them only cosmetic fidelity. The most famous casualty of the failure to harmonize was Roscoe "Fatty" Arbuckle, a silent-screen comic, who became the first actor to earn a million dollars a year. At the height of his powers, his crushing personal unhappiness became known: an alcoholic and smackhead, he was framed for both rape and murder. His ruination served as a valuable caution that, in a part of the world known for its earthquakes, reputations were as precarious as matchstick models. (More about Arbuckle in Chapter 8.)

The response was effective. As Robert W. Snyder puts it in his "American journalism and the culture of celebrity": "Image managers learned how to calibrate the balance of public exposure [and] journalists were caught – knowingly and sometimes with their own connivance – in struggles for interview time with celebrities that compromised their own independence" (2003: 441).

Publicists, agents, managers, and the gamut of other personnel exploiting, working for or attending to the needs of the entertainers became self-taught guardians of images. Far from being interrogators, the journalists whose livelihood depended on access to those entertainers either accepted the stories that came out of the dream factory's publicity departments or conspired with them to produce anemic stories. It was a cozy alliance designed to protect the famous, most of them from the "flickers," as the silent films of the early twentieth century were called, or vaudeville, the variety music hall entertainment. It relieved the entertainers of pestering journalists, while satisfying those journalists by providing them with good "human interest" copy.

Perhaps the event that presaged the appearance of the media not only as conveyors but as creators of information was the faked car accident and supposed death in 1910 of "The Biograph Girl," as Florence Lawrence was called (after the Biograph Studio to which she was contracted). Previously, screen actors had performed anonymously. Carl Laemmle, the pioneer mogul and later founder of Universal Pictures, signed Lawrence from Biograph and contrived his ingenious if deceptive way of getting her name into lights. It worked and, in so doing, alerted the industry to the value of managing public images. In this sense, it inaugurated a new era in the film industry.

By the time "talkies" replaced the silent movies in the late 1920s, there was an embryonic public relations industry. The P. T. Barnum-style "no publicity is bad publicity" canon looked manifestly untrue: pr was predicated on producing news, not just any news, but news that enhanced or complemented a particular image. Press releases, press conferences, press accreditation: these were all parts of an apparatus assembled in the first decades of the century. They helped establish the industrial unit known as the film industry, the star system, or the Hollywood machine.

The machine cranked into action by the Lawrence hoax proved an efficient and reliable way of turning base ore into precious metal – box office gold. The studio chiefs might secretly have known that there was no such thing as god-given star quality, but they were not about to admit it: not while movie fans seemed enchanted by the notion. The big studios perpetrated and perpetuated the concept of a Hollywood cosmos that was populated by luminous celestial bodies who were remote and untouchable, quite unlike the rest of us.

The studios never actually perfected the machine. After all, for every Rudolph Valentino, Cary Grant, or Greta Garbo, there was a John Gilbert (a silent-screen star who vanished with the talkies), Jennifer Jones, whom David O. Selznick tried to turn into a star, or Anna Sten, Samuel Goldwyn's would-be successor to Garbo. But, for the most part, it was the machinery that produced stars and, in this sense, it was an early version of vertical integration (a term we'll consider more in Chapter 11). Actors were the studios' primary materials: they were contracted to appear in films that were produced, marketed, and distributed by those same studios. It was an "economic system," according to Douglas Gomery (2005).

: industrial action, 1930–60

In 1932, the Frank Borzage film of *A Farewell to Arms* brought its source book's author Ernest Hemingway international praise and recognition. According to Leonard Leff, this initiated a struggle between Hemingway, the authentic man and author with serious aesthetic ambitions, and "Hemingway," the macho persona lauded by the media for his non-literary pursuits. Leff's 1997 book *Hemingway and his Conspirators* is a study of "the making of American culture" and details how Hemingway's publishers, agents, and the film industry that turned his novels into block-busters – *For Whom the Bell Tolls*, 1943, and *To Have and Have Not*, 1945, were among the others – collectively created a public character with which the writer was never comfortable. Leff suggests that there was something fraudulent about the on-stage "Hemingway": he uses inverted commas to distinguish this media creation from the authentic artist.

The public representation was a construction of a developing apparatus of production. Hemingway, while anguished, colluded with the film industry, not only by making changes to style and content, but in perpetuating the image of a venturesome, testosterone-pumped man's man who was as happy in a bar or a bullring as sitting behind behind his typewriter. Leff's interpretation of the two Hemingways chimes with Daniel Boorstin's "guide to pseudo-events" which records the predominance of the image and, by implication, suggests that authentically "real" people lay behind the premeditated performances and designed personalities on offer to consumers (1992).

Whether that distinction holds true today is open to question and we'll interrogate it later. For now, it's important to realize that in the early 1930s there began a "period of industrialization," as Joshua Gamson calls it. It yielded "a developed profession of public image-management, and an elaborate and tightly controlled production system mass-producing celebrities for a widely consuming audience" (1992: 6). The title of Gamson's essay gives away his emphasis: "The assembly line of greatness: celebrity in twentieth-century America."

Heroic deeds were the traditional route to great renown, but the Hollywood assembly line was beginning to churn out figures of what we might call faux greatness: actors who played characters, fictional or real, who performed heroic deeds. Errol Flynn was one such actor, of course, though the archetypal faux hero was to arrive in 1939 with the release of John Ford's seminal western *Stagecoach* in which John Wayne played the Ringo Kid, an outlaw seeking revenge for the murder of his father and brother. Although he'd appeared in earlier films, *Stagecoach* launched Wayne on a career of – and this time, the cliché is apt – epic proportions. As James T. Campbell writes in his review "'Print the legend': John Wayne and postwar American culture," he became "not only one of the most recognized figures in the world but one of the most influential, the seeming quintessence of American manhood" (2000: 466).

How was this possible? After all, Wayne never saw real military action. Despite this, he was regarded as an all-purpose hero. "Reality and representation," as Campbell points out, were becoming "so interwoven as to be inextricable" (2000: 465). Wayne's screen exploits saw him as Davy Crockett at *The Alamo* (1960), on *The Sands of Iwo Jima* (1949) in World War II, or leading *The Green Berets* (1968) in Vietnam. It was hard to think of Wayne as separate from these roles.

In a similar way, it was difficult to imagine James Cagney the actor as distinct from the two-fisted tough guy who shot fast and talked even faster. Four Warner Bros gangster classics from *The Public Enemy* (1931) to *White Heat* (1949) created an imperishable image of Cagney as a scowling, pugnacious mobster whose natural environment was the mean streets of interwar America. Like Wayne and, before him, Flynn, Cagney became indistinguishable from the fictional characters he played. The melding was achieved, in large part, through careful selection of film roles, of course. But there was also precision in the way other kinds of images were presented. Gamson argues that the development of sound and film realism in the 1930s signaled the end of entertainers as "popularly 'elected' gods and goddesses" and the start of stars as ordinary mortals with whom audiences could feel "a sense of connection and intimacy."

"Crucial to this process was the ubiquitous narrative principle of the 'inside' journey into the 'real lives' of celebrities," writes Gamson (1992: 8). Fans were treated to larger and larger amounts of information about the stars' so-called private lives. So, it was imperative that all the information dispensed complemented rather than contradicted screen representations. Flynn's career would have been jeopardized if the "revelations" that he was bisexual published in 1980 by Charles Higham had been released during his heyday in the 1930s and 1940s. As interest in the "real lives" of entertainers grew, the film industry was forced to exercise greater control over material in popular publications, such as *American Magazine* and *Photoplay*.

Managing publicity became a smoothly functioning machine-like practice. The trick, according to Gamson, was to preserve the notion of natural talent, so that the stars appeared as ordinary people, in one sense, but ordinary people who were gifted with a little something extra: charisma, magic, *je ne sais quoi* – an indefinable quality that made them stars. The publicity machine's job was to highlight or amplify the natural qualities of their subjects. Unlike their predecessors, they weren't inclined to fabricate stories or stage stunts.

On Gamson's account, the success of the manufacturing process depended on its ability to obscure its own rationale. If it presented its subjects not as real people but as studio artifice – which is what they were – the entire narrative would have collapsed. It would have been like the conmen who made the Emperor's New Clothes letting the crowd in on their hoax before they let the naked monarch go strutting among his public. Not that cineastes were totally gullible. While most magazines enjoyed a snug relationship with the major studios' pr machines in the 1930s, some were staking out a critical distance from them in the 1940s. The idea that fame was manufactured rather than the result of some natural divination became popular and this caused the occasional contretemps. "But the skepticism heightened by increasingly visible publicity activities was contained more commonly by being acknowledged," Gamson remarks (1992: 12).

The same author elaborates this point in his book *Claims to Fame: Celebrity in contemporary America*, where he writes of the irony that became more pronounced from the 1940s, when studios "luxuriated" in stories of artificial production. Far from trying to conceal their aims, they prided themselves on their machinations. On Gamson's account this visibility was later to become a key feature of a celebrity-production process in which fans were "simultaneous voyeurs of and performers in commercial culture" (1994: 137).

While Gamson doesn't mention it, an event in 1950 effected an modification to the production process. James Stewart, who like other Hollywood actors was under studio contract, negotiated a different kind of contract for the Anthony Mann film *Winchester '73*. In taking a share of the profits as well as a flat studio rate, he paved the way for others to assert their independence from studios.

Obviously, without an audience, no one can be famous. Fans genuinely make certain people famous. The publicity machine's conceit was in telling audiences exactly that: "You are the ones who deserve the credit for making such-and-such famous. And the reason you've made them famous is because you recognize their abundant talent!"

This message was perfectly consistent with what Ponce de Leon, as we noted earlier, called "the spread of the market economy and the rise of democratic, individualistic values." Ponce de Leon argues that the growth of fame in the way we understand it today was accompanied by the development of a definition of achievement that fitted neatly with the consumer culture that was emerging in the first decades of the twentieth century.

Let me illustrate this with a classic study from the 1930s. Robert Merton concluded that our ultimate goal was material success, which we wanted to display and display conspicuously (1969). Good clothes, cars, electrical appliances: these were all commodities that were relatively recent arrivals in the market-place and ones that people wanted, perhaps craved. People valued their ability to consume and they were encouraged through various media, such as schools and particularly advertising, to maximize this ability – within certain boundaries. Merton's view was that the boundaries defined the legitimate means through which people could achieve their goals. There are right ways and wrong ways to achieve them. When people strove for material goods but lacked the means to get them, they often opted for the wrong ways. In other words, they stole the goods that the advertising hoardings and the radio commercials were telling them they should have. The "non-conforming" conduct, as Merton called it, was a response to this condition.

The study underscored the point that the market was turning us all into avid buyers of consumable products – consumers. Merton was writing at the cusp: at time when consumable goods were more available, but before we had fully arrived at the view that happiness, satisfaction, and fulfillment could actually be bought and sold. That became more visible in the 1950s and 1960s. In the 1930s and 1940s, the pursuit of modest success became possible through purchasing. Commodities gave people a means of defining success.

They also provided an important, if restricted, autonomy: people could choose what they wanted to buy. This may seem a minor privilege, but it hastened a sense of individualism. In exercising choice in the way they spent their hard-earned cash, people were offered the chance to see themselves as shapers of their own limited destinies.

The period saw the growth of status-consciousness as newly affluent workers began to entertain the possibility of social mobility, rising through a hierarchy in which the central criterion was not so much wealth or income as possessions, specifically the kind of possessions that brought kudos, cachet, prestige – status.

People began display their status through their transport, accommodation, and attire. So cars were no longer a means of traveling from A to B, but ambulant advertisements of relative success. Homes were powerful signifiers of standing, their location becoming more important than their number of rooms. While the term designer label didn't come into popular usage until 1977 – when Warren Hirsh, of Murjani, persuaded American socialite Gloria Vanderbilt to lend her name to denim jeans – the concept of advertising success through clothes is much older; in the 1940s, clothes began to acquire new potential. Looking successful became a precondition of actually being successful.

If earlier generations had understood their social position as relatively changeless, as if fixed by immutable forces, the postwar cohort understood it quite differently. Position, rank, or station were temporary. This was underlined in a series of studies. In many ways an exemplary product of its time, *The Affluent Worker* research of the early 1960s showed British industrial workers motivated by a desire for self-improvement, especially through the acquisition of material possessions (Goldthorpe *et al.* 1968). In the USA, there were several studies, many of them synthesized by the widely read scholar Vance Packard who, in 1959, published his argument that personal fulfillment and social recognition were twinned in the minds of newly aspirational Americans who were striving for consumer symbols of success. They were, as the title of Packard's book suggested, *The Status Seekers*.

: consumption as a way of life, from the 1960s

When Packard was compiling his data, television was still in its infancy; by the time his book was published, the tube had found its way into nine in ten American households; the ratio was similar in Britain. Consumers were ambushed by television. It was as if advertisers had been lying in wait, biding their time while waiting for the arrival of the medium that would trans-form the entire industry, not to mention the lifestyles of the population of the USA and, eventually, everywhere else. In Britain, commercial television didn't arrive until the mid-1950s when BBC lost its monopoly. But, in the USA, advertising drove television from the outset. Commercial "messages," as advertisements were called, punctuated every program, stealthily refining their approach so as to target precise demographic sectors.

Advertising quickened the change to consumer society. In a sense, we've always been consumers. From the mid-1950s, we became aspirational consumers, buying not just to subsist, but to make statements about our progress in the world. The commercials we saw on tv provided a kind of blueprint. They didn't just show merchandise, they revealed their hidden properties. For example, shampoo was ostensibly to clean hair, but it provided shine, silkiness, and radiance. Cars were to be experienced rather than driven. In the 1950s, advertising was relatively primitive. Today, every advertisement tries to sell something other than the actual product: a lifestyle, an image, or a solution to a problem with which it has no obvious association. As Christopher Lasch pointed out in his *The Culture of Narcissism*: "Advertising serves not so much to advertise products as to promote consumption as a way of life" (1980: 72).

Part of Lasch's thesis, which we'll examine in more detail later in the book, is that, once the economies of the US and, we might add, most of what we now call Old Europe had reached the point where technology was capable of satisfying basic material need, they started to rely on the creation of new consumer demands – "on convincing people to buy goods for which they are unaware of any need until the 'need' is forcibly brought to their attention by the mass media" (1980: 72).

What is luxury? Costly homes, clothes, furniture, food? Expensive vacations? Anything that we desire for comfort or enjoyment but that isn't indispensable? In other words, what we could actually do without. Microwaves, cellphones and personal computers for example? Cars, air conditioning, central heating, television? Most people would call these necessities rather than luxuries. It wasn't always so. During the second half of the twentieth century there was a redefinition of luxuries as essentials. Items that were once seen either fantastic toys or the exclusive property of the seriously rich were incorporated into a culture of consumption. From where we're now standing, there seems no end in sight for the incorporation: it just goes on and on. This is a global process too: commodities that would have once been seen as extravagances now circulate around the world as fluidly as the images and messages that advertise them.

Packard's other studies, on *The Hidden Persuaders* (1957) of the advertising industry and *The Waste Makers* (1960) who designed and built commodities so that they would become obsolescent in a few years, collectively portrayed a society in which traditional values, such as abstinence, prudence, and frugality were replaced by the ethic of well-being. The narcissistic impulse to pay close attention to one's own physical self was complemented by an endless supply of commodities that would, in some way, enhance, enrich, or just improve experience.

The advertising industry was central to the transition to a consumer culture. It governed the depiction of reality in which material goods became constituent parts of a good life "conceived as endless novelty, change and excitement, as the titillation of the senses by every available stimulant," according to Lasch in *The True and Only Heaven* (1991: 520).

Advertising became ubiquitous: not just on the hoardings, the television set, or the movies; but in every aspect of a media that, by the 1960s, had become the dominant source of information. The media of the consumer culture inverted the idea that success, happiness, and self-fulfillment had little to do with material goods or social status – which, as we should recall Ponce de Leon argued was promoted by the media in the early years of the century (2002: 108). It proved an intoxicating prospect: success, happiness, self-fulfillment – the good life – could be bought.

Through the 1960s and 1970s, the media, especially advertising and television, became increasingly interested in, or, if Lasch is to be believed, obsessed by youth, glamour, sex, money, violence, and celebrity. The media implicitly promoted the conception of a good life: the one lived by the affluent consumer with a cornucopia of material goods. Hollywood stars fitted the bill.

In a sense, movie stars were exemplars, though, by the 1960s, musicians, particularly rock musicians, were jostling for a place among the elite. Frank Sinatra had reaped the benefits of a career-transforming role in 1953's *From Here to Eternity* and became a prototype for many other singers, most notably Elvis Presley. In this period, success in the music industry was never enough: film was still the *sine qua non* – the ultimate qualification. The big band leader Glenn Miller didn't make the transition himself, though he was so ably portrayed by James Stewart in *The Glenn Miller Story* (1953) nine years after his death in 1944 that his reputation grew posthumously as a result.

The expansion of demand for consumer goods and the continual revision of criteria of luxury and necessity were products of a market economy and a culture in which the ethic of individualism prevailed. People were consumers, aspirational consumers at that. And they were sovereign decision-makers: they made the choices about what to buy. The ethic is stronger now than ever. Active citizenship mean having a say in your own destiny.

A change in the way we visualize ourselves was vital to what was later to become celebrity culture: as masters of our fortune and deciders of our own fate we had the means to distinguish ourselves from others. We saw ourselves not so much as parts of a design but as designers ourselves. Some writers on America, like Warren Susman, believe that this change in orientation is as recent as the 1930s, when the concept of divine providence began to weaken (1984). We were no longer creatures who enjoyed the protection of god: we were out there fending for ourselves. As such, we wanted to make the best we possibly could out of ourselves and, when successful, display this to others. Advertising provided us with ways of defining and exhibiting ourselves. The stars were its accomplices.

: Into commodities

"Beginning in the 1950s," writes Gamson, "celebrity began to be commonly represented not only as *useful to* selling and business, but as business itself, *created by selling*" (1992: 14). He means that, while Hollywood stars and other figures of renown had been used to declare their approval of commodities – endorsers, in other words – they began to be treated as commodities in their own right.

Both functions fitted hand-in-glove with the emergent consumer society. If you wanted someone to give a product credibility, who better than a well-known and possibly respected figure from the media? It would have been reassuring for consumers to see figures they knew, liked, and in whom they had confidence giving their support to a product – even if they suspected they'd been paid to do so. The unexpected bonus arrived when, as Gamson suggests, the figures themselves became products that could be bought and sold on the marketplace just like any other piece of merchandise.

The process through which any person or thing can be converted into a saleable object is known as commodification. The stars became raw material that needed refining, developing, and packaging before they could be turned into marketable wares to be displayed in films, theater, and, later, television. But, once they were commercially viable, they were like property.

This was and is a key process in celebrity culture: making people tradeable commodities, objects for consumption. Remember: the publicity machinery was already running. No one needed reminding of the importance of creating and maintaining an image, or a fabricated, popular representation that could be widely circulated and accepted by consumers. Commodification effectively doubled the ways through which those images could be manipulated and consumed.

The consumers were anything but passive. If Gamson is to be believed, they were empowered by the development, recognizing their roles in making and shaping careers, as well as ending them. Elisabeth Bronfen, in her essay "Celebrating catastrophe," points out "how the intensity of our gaze upon celebrity not only transforms the famous into commodities, but usually ends up destroying them" (2002: 181). Once our voyeurism reached a certain pitch, there was no other way to satisfy us other than ruining the very celebrity careers we had helped make. After consuming them, audiences consigned them to what Bronfen calls "the shadowy limbo of oblivion." We discarded them just like the commodities they were.

The trend continued, so that, by the mid-1990s, Jill Neimark was able to sum up: "Celebrities are borne aloft on images marketed, sold, and disseminated with a rapidity and cunning unimagined by the heroes of old, and then just as quickly cast aside" (1995: 56).

But, in the 1960s, the star-as-commodity idea was still in its infancy. It was a protracted infancy, according to Gamson, who reckons even early Hollywood "greats" such as Clark Gable and Myrna Loy in the 1930s were conscious that they were property owned by both the studios and, in a sense, the public (1994: 34–5). Yet this is not quite the same as being a commodity that can be produced, traded, and marketed. As Graeme Turner expresses it, in his text *Understanding Celebrity*: "In this context, the celebrity's primary function is commercial and promotional ... the celebrity is defined instrumentally, in terms of the role they play within the operation of the mass media, promotion and publicity industries" (2004: 9).

This is the "primary function" of contemporary celebrities, as far as Turner is concerned. It isn't their only one: in other words, they don't exist exclusively to assist in marketing operations. But, from the 1960s, marketing did become a bigger part of any star's remit. The very mention of their name could trigger an image powerful enough to change market behavior. Whether consumers bought a movie theater ticket, a long playing record (the forerunner of cds), a magazine, or any of the other countless items associated with the star, there was money transaction. And cumulatively, transactions drove consumer culture.

There is, as Michael Newbury puts it, "more to the well known than well-knownness" (2000: 272). "Fixing celebrity's origins requires the examination of something more than individual figures, though concentrating on such individuals may usefully make larger cultural processes concrete."

Over the past two chapters we have examined several individual figures, always staying mindful of the distinct circumstances in which they emerged and, crucially, in which they were consumed. Popularity, fame, or reputations are not constant qualities: they change over time and the only way to make sense of celebrity today is to, as Newbury recommends, "document a change in the cultural comprehension of renown" (2000: 273).

The way we understand fame and celebrity today is particular and unique. A celebrity emerging from a reality tv show in the twenty-first century is just not known in the same way as Buffalo Bill was at the turn of the twentieth century, or Errol Flynn in the 1930s, Elizabeth Taylor in the 1960s or even Madonna in the 1990s. They all, in a way, surrendered parts of their selves to an apparatus of promotion that became progressively elaborated through the twentieth century. And they could all lay fair claims to international fame. But the cultural contexts in which they came into view were as different from each other as they are different from today's context.

Celebrity, at least in the sense we recognize it, has origins in the late nineteenth century, when the circulation of newspapers featuring halftone photographs climbed and news was redefined as something that happened days rather than weeks before. Subsequent developments in the media, at first magazines and radio, then film opened new horizons, while setting new limits. The free flow of both news and entertainment entitled populations to share in new sources of information; yet it also initiated something of a dependency. We not only relied on the media for information: we trusted and had confidence in them. The consequences of this are all around us: from where else do we get our information, if not the papers, radio, tv, or the net? What would we do if we had to do without all these, if only for a day or so? For right or wrong, the media became the machinery of addiction.

The "period of industrialization" and the serial production of public images began in earnest in the 1930s as motion pictures ascended to their paramount position in popular culture. Fraudulent as many public images were – Rock Hudson, who was gay, was projected as a rakishly handsome lady's man, for example – they were emblems of a culture in transition. Consumerism and the market economy that encouraged individualism, freedom of choice, and unvarying demand for commodities effectively modernized populations into customers. They became aspirational shoppers in a marketplace where public figures could be bought and sold as readily as breakfast cereal or washing machines (themselves symbols of consumer society).

Looking at celebrity culture in this way is like removing the back of a watch to expose its mechanism. You can see the cogs, springs, and levers moving synchronously, but you won't be able to tell the time till you glance at the dial. As the twentieth century unwound, the visible drama, the narrative, and the personalities were all open for public inspection and consumption. The overwhelming success of the entertainment industry throughout the twentieth century was testimony both to the reach and influence of the media and its elasticity in responding to changing tastes. The united power of the print and electronic media was irresistible. But, while remaining respectful of the stars, particularly those products of Hollywood, the media were also adaptive and, as tastes meandered away from straight-and-narrow, the media too deviated.

When audiences gawped with relish at "candid" pictures of the famous that began appearing with rapidity in the 1960s, they may just as well have called time on the unwritten code that had protected the stars' private lives. If, as some suspected, "authentic" people operated separately from the fabricated personae that appeared on screens and in print, then they were under siege. The paparazzi of the early 1960s wanted the image behind the image. This is why the shot of Elizabeth Taylor's indiscretion with Richard Burton was such a harbinger: it foreshadowed a change between the media and the stars. It declared a kind of open season.

Publications that traded in amazing tales and gore exchanged gore for gossip and became unofficial organs of the rich and famous. The *National Enquirer* was the *primus inter pares*, introducing a new education in the indecencies of Hollywood life. Sales figures, as we noted, reflected a lively interest in the racy aspects of life at the top. Fidelity was not an issue.

If any single figure validated the power of the media in the 1980s and 1990s it was Diana. She was virtually hijacked by paparazzi every time she appeared in public. Even when she didn't, there were enough quisling confidants to guarantee supplies of insider accounts. Diana's near-divine status wasn't solely the creation of media manipulation. Diana "was a celebrity," as Lewis Lapham confirmed, "and celebrities are consumer products meant to be consumed" (1997: 11).

In a way, the entertainment industry had always treated its stars as consumer products, though it adjusted to meet the changing requirements in the 1980s. The multiplicity of television channels specializing in light entertainment opened up new opportunities, but it also set a new question for aspiring showbiz types: are you going to resist the brazen, usually disrespectful, often insidious, and always inquisitive media; or meet them half-way when they come snooping into your private affairs? Put another way: you are a consumer product; are you going to be like a Lamborghini Murciélago at around $330,000 with a waiting list of up to eighteen months, or a Hyundai coupé?

Madonna didn't singlehandedly start celebrity culture, as we know it. What she did was realize that Hyundais are accessible, affordable, and move out of showrooms in greater numbers than Lamborghinis. Abandoning any vestige of the old public vs. private domains, Madonna made her whole self available for commodification. She became the complete product. The dawning of her era saw the stars' music taking second place to what they looked like, whom they were dating, which diet they currently favored, and where they last did rehab.

After Madonna's seemingly inexorable rise, the rules of engagement changed so fundamentally that no entertainer could survive without extensive concessions to the media. Even then the prospect was not scary enough to deter the legions of wannabes who couldn't wait to bare all in their efforts to become famous, albeit momentarily.

There are several levels to celebrity culture. The consumer-oriented market economy lies beneath a change in popular consciousness, with freedom of choice and individual preference becoming primary values. An attendant technology-driven enlargement of the media had implications for the way we receive and consume, not only information but the products conveyed by that information. This, in turn, fueled consumer culture. In this way, consumers were both creators and creations. We – consumers – created celebrity culture with our voracious desire for new figures. We were also creations of an industrial process that fed us like rats in a maze, but which went wrong once we tasted the more scrumptious fare served up by voyeuristic journalism. It was at this point that celebrity culture, in the particular way we understand it today, began to take shape. Being a consumer no longer meant standing on the outside: it meant being an active player – a creator as well as consumer of celebrities.

WORSHIPPING/
FROM AFAR

: intimate feelings

Charlie Parker, John Coltrane, Miles Davis. These were leading lights among a firmament of jazz musicians appearing in the 1950s. They were the epitome of cool – then meaning a sense, style, attitude, and approach to music that signified an indifference to audiences and which stuck a defiant swivel-on-it finger toward mainstream society. "These musicians were less secular stars than quasi-religious figures and their fans often referred to them with godly reverence," wrote Nelson George in his *The Death of Rhythm and Blues* (1988: 25).

There's nothing unique, nor indeed unusual about bestowing divine status on mere mortals. History is full of characters who actually encouraged their followers to do so (the Caesars, Aztec leaders, Pharaohs) and, in the modern world, millennial cults are typically led by charismatic figures claiming messianic powers. Even musicians who have scorned such attributions, like Bob Marley or Bob Dylan, have been endowed with deistic eminence by fans. Marley had an oracular presence and his songs were infused with Rastafarian prophecy. Dylan perplexed one generation, while inspiring another with his sour condemnations of war and prejudice. Their influence makes their veneration comprehensible. But Kylie Minogue? Jennifer Aniston?

Integral to celebrity culture is the enthrallment in the lives of figures who have, for some reason, become well known. This much is obvious. So far, we've examined the changing social conditions under which celebrities came to occupy positions, not just of prominence but exaltation – and I use this word carefully, indicating the way in which celebs today are praised, dignified, and often ennobled by rapturous fans. Often, the objects of the fans' praise seem to have done nothing to justify such reverence. Such is the peculiarity of celebrity culture: ostensibly undeserving people are richly rewarded as much for being as doing. They offer themselves for acclaim rather than actually accomplishing something that might merit it. This may sound like a cynic's evaluation, but it's intended as a prompt. Why do fans worship celebrities who just don't appear to deserve it?

First, we should clarify what we mean by "fan." There are two versions of the sources for the word. One traces it to the adjective fanatic, from the Latin *fanaticus*, meaning "of a temple"; so the fan is someone who is excessively enthusiastic or filled with the kind of zeal usually associated with religious fervor. The term crept into baseball in the late 1880s, but as a replacement for the more pejorative "crank," according to Tom Sullivan, writing for the *Sporting Life* of November 23, 1887. The alternative is even older: the fancy was the collective name given to patrons of prize-fighting in the early nineteenth century. There are references in Pierce Egan's 1812 classic *Boxiana*. Whatever its etymology, "fan" lost its religious and patrician connotations and became a description of followers, devotees, or admirers of virtually anybody or anything in popular culture.

The origins are less important than the relationships today's fans have with celebrities. In a sense, we're all fans of varying degrees. Even those who are disenchanted by or even despise celebrity culture's meretricious excesses would be hard pressed to avoid watching and listening to celebs. Just reading a newspaper, watching tv or going to the movies implicates someone in celebrity culture and thus turns them into a fan of some order.

For reasons that will soon become clear, we'll call this group of hard-bitten yet celebrity-aware fans "agnostics," as distinct from what Lynne McCutcheon and her research colleagues call low worship fans, who just watch and read about celebrities (2002). Other types of fans are: those for whom following celebrities more keenly has a more "entertainment-social character"; those who manifest more "intense-personal feelings" with celebrities; and those "extreme" worshippers who "over-identify" with celebrities and who behave compulsively and obsessively toward them in a "borderline pathological" manner (Maltby *et al.* 2004).

In Chapter 2, we introduced the idea of a parasocial inter-action, which describes the relationship fans have with figures they have never met, and probably never will meet. Although it's a one-way interaction, this doesn't lessen its impact on the fan who may experience the relationship as genuine and just as valid as other kinds of social interaction. Every type of fan, even the ostensibly uninterested, has this kind of interaction with celebs, if only because it's unavoidable. Even if we wanted to insulate ourselves for a while, we couldn't escape over-hearing chats, glancing at newspaper or magazine covers, or resisting switching on the tv, even if only for the news. The cumulative effect is what the psychologists Horton and Wohl, who introduced "parasocial interaction" in the 1950s, called "intimacy at a distance" (1956).

Like it or not, we do get the feeling that we "know" celebrities. Think about anyone from any station along the alphanumeric scale that defines how prestigious a celebrity is. The probability is that you will either like or dislike someone from the A-list and feel progressively indifferent to those further along the scale. But what do you actually know about any of them? Only what you've gleaned from the media, which act as effective filters on information, and perhaps a few supplementary fragments sourced from sundry gossip. In other words, not really enough on which to make a judgment. We do the rest ourselves: we decide on how to interpret what is, after all, limited information about celebrities rather as we might choose how to watch a dvd of a film: we can change the sequence of the scenes, view one part repeatedly, slow down or freeze passages, explore how the special fx were achieved, or just watch outtakes. In other words, celebrities aren't just *there*: we create them out of the two-dimensional material presented on the screen. In the process, they become so real to us that we feel we know something about them – or, in the case of the Intense-Personal or the Borderline Pathological fans, feel we actually know them and have feelings that are reciprocated.

: ordinary people with extraordinary friends

In a revealing study published in 1991, Neil Alperstein wrote of "Imaginary social relationships with celebrities appearing in television commercials." The "artificial involvement," as Alperstein calls it, in the lives of people viewers have never met paradoxically helps them "make sense of reality." The other paradox of intimacy at distance features in the research, viewers expressing feelings of closeness, loyalty, or perhaps detestation about performers they know via their tv screens. In fact, they *know* them as they know a painting or a book: they have discerned, fathomed, read and, in other ways, made intelligible the figures they have only seen on television.

The screen might flatten the characters, but the fans "inflate that image – adding dimensions to the interaction – as evidenced in the descriptions of their attraction to celebrities" (1991). One viewer disclosed how she regarded Joan Lunden, who used to host the *Good Morning America* show, as "a trusted friend": "When she happens to be sick or on vacation, I miss her."

Another viewer described how Orson Welles, or more accurately, his perception of Welles, had shaped his entire life: his "maverick attitude," "his emphasis on quality at the expense of acclaim," the "grudging respect" frequently accorded him.

These helped the subject shape himself. So, it came as a shock to discover Welles endorsing wine in a tv commercial. "Seriously disillusioning . . . It was not a happy experience," said the fan.

Alperstein describes what he calls "a give-and-take with a multitude of media figures," with fans incorporating celebrities into their "imaginary social worlds." Far from dismissing his subjects as obsessive or even disillusioned, Alperstein credits them with intelligence, wit, and even skepticism. They enjoy "the confluence of information, gossip, and experiences" so much that they can suspend the last of these qualities whenever it suits them. Alperstein's study uncovers viewers entangled in a "complex web they weave through entertainment programming, news, sports and advertising" so that the complete experience is intricately satisfying. They're willing participants in the creation of "multiple realities"; so their lives are not constantly upset and their everyday routines disrupted. Their relationships with celebrities are seamlessly integrated into their daily lives, so that they remain a rewarding and, on this account, even enriching addition.

A later piece of research by Benson Fraser and William Brown yielded similar conclusions, though this time about one celebrity in particular. In their "Media, celebrities, and social influence: identification with Elvis Presley," Fraser and Brown wrote: "Fans develop self-defining relationships with celebrities and seek to adopt their perceived attributes, resulting in powerful forms of personal and social transformation" (2002: 196).

Like the Welles fan, the followers of Elvis in this study entered into a cognitive and emotional relationship that led to a "selective integration" of what they considered to be Elvis's key qualities with their own lives. As a result, they "changed substantially." Presley died in 1977. The fans in the study didn't take the *National Enquirer*-style approach and insist he was still living on a remote Pacific island or somewhere even weirder. As one fan testified: "I can feel him in my heart. I can see him in my dreams. I can see him on my wall in my posters, that's the stuff that's the real Elvis" (2002: 196). The *real* Elvis.

Fraser and Brown argue that the concept of parasocial relationship can't adequately cope with the bilateral or two-way character of this kind of fan–celebrity interaction: it precipitates affective and behavioral changes in the fan. Nor do they find the idea that fans model themselves on celebrities convincing "because it does not address the relationship between media consumers and media personae." They introduce a third possibility: *identification*, meaning that fans "reconstruct their own attitudes, values, or behaviors in response to the images of people they admire, real and imagined, both through personal and mediated relationships" (2002: 187).

The study's conclusions embrace all three possibilities: (1) "Ordinary people develop extraordinary psychological relationships with celebrities, whether living or dead"; (2) fans regard celebrities as role models; (3) fans adopt what they see as a celebrity's attributes, including his or her values and behavior. While it could be argued that Elvis was and, on the output of this study, is a singular celebrity, the fans' response appears to be representative in that they derived what they considered to be relevant to their own lives from mediated images. "The fabric of their self-identity is intricately interwoven with their image of Elvis, not only as an entertainer, but also as a friend, lover, husband, father, patriot and citizen," write Fraser and Brown (2002: 197). "The image of a celebrity can be more tightly held and more powerful than the real person on which it is based."

Both studies took place amid celebrity culture and both conveyed plausibly the manner in which contemporary fans immerse themselves in relationships that are both imaginary yet tangible in their consequences on the behavior and attitudes of fans. Any notions of the fan as a gullible dupe suckered by the wiles of artful celebrity-manipulators are blown away. Instead we view the fan as attentive and fully aware. Far from being a pointless and meaningless pursuit, following celebrities turns out to be a gratifying and significant activity that can and, on these accounts, often does prompt changes. But it's not Elvis or Jennifer

Aniston, or even Kylie Minogue, that's exerting the influence: it's the fans' interpretations of what those celebs are like, regardless of whether or not they're accurate assessments. What matters is that they are credible assessments.

A third study confirmed that celebrities influence attitudes and personal values, including work ethic and ethical stances. In "Admirer–celebrity relationships among young adults," Susan Boon and Christine Lomore were interested in the peculiar attachments fans have with celebrities. Part of the research required participants to list celebrities, or idols, they felt affected their lives (2001). Apart from Elvis, several other influential figures were long gone, Jim Morrison, Albert Einstein, and John Wayne included.

Again, the image of the fan as a hapless victim is exposed as flawed: the subjects interviewed were wide awake to the influences of celebrities and accepted that many celebrities had been inspirational in a positive way. They expressed strong feelings, suggesting that they had thought about what they believe some celebrities embodied, stood for, or exemplified. Boon and Lomore concluded that "as changing social and demographic patterns continue to weaken and fragment social networks," attachments are likely to become stronger. Perhaps so. This could mean more people's retreating into the solace of parasocial relationships with posters, dvds or other kinds of merchandise bearing celebrity images, like the character Jess in Gurinder Chadha's film *Bend it like Beckham*. Unable to confide in her parents or close friends, Jess has her feelings stirred every night by a poster of David Beckham on her bedroom ceiling and spends time confessing her deepest desires to the inert image.

The fictional Jess may have a lot in common with countless other worshipful fans of one of the world's leading celebrity athletes of the early 2000s. For her and maybe them, Beckham became a lifeline connecting them to resources that, at least in their eyes, weren't available to dilettantes or outsiders. Only they truly had access. To them, their relationships were singular, personal, and exclusive. Posters don't respect fans any more than dolls, or any other kind of celebrity merchandise. They simply exist.

The fans' attachment to them is not the result of desperate innocence, but of enthrallment. Not a sign of intellectual bankruptcy, but of emotional liquidity. The fans actually form the relationship, inflating the significance of the celebrity, with a well-meaning intensity that stimulates and inspires. The research cited here makes us realize that there's an invention that's often mistaken for inanity in the fans' relationship. It also reminds us that, while some fans develop personal, perhaps clandestine and, in their own eyes, privileged relationships, others itch to share their enthusiasm with like-minded members of their cohort.

: fragmentation

Simply by talking about celebrities, "we collectively define who we are and what we value as a culture." And, in case you think that grandiose claim came from some pompous professor of cultural studies, think again. It comes from the pages of that trusted purveyor of knowledge, wisdom, and facts *USA Today* (September 14, 2004: News section, p. 21a). In a short yet illuminating article, "What celebrity worship says about us," Carol Brooks (herself the editor of celeb mag *First for Women*) commented on the research of Lynn McCutcheon and her colleagues – which we touched on earlier in this chapter.

The original research paper "Conceptualization and measurement of celebrity worship" established that "parasocial interactions are part of the normal identity-development" (McCutcheon *et al.* 2002: 68). Those who are either "mild" celebrity worshippers, including introverts and those who are intuitively drawn to a celebrity without thinking about it too deeply, reported "fewer and less intimate relationships than they did before becoming a fan." So the *Bend it like Beckham* scenario rings true.

Brooks pulled out what she took to be an underlying proposition in the research: "Pointless conversation is one powerfully healthy social elixir." While the academics weren't explicit about this, Brooks detects that being a fan might involve more than worshipfully talking to posters. "Just by gabbing in the right way [about celebrities] you can expand your social circle, deepen your existing relationships, consolidate your sense of self and feel dramatically less stressed" (2004: 21a).

Even if the academic study was more circumspect in its conclusions, it provided the raw material for such an extrapolation. One of the joys of following the exploits of celebrities was and, of course, is being able to confer about them, what Brooks calls "using other people's triumphs and tragedies as fodder for discussion."

A major effect of modernity is the breakup of old-style communities in which the bonds people had with each other were organic, in the sense that they formed and grew like living phenomena. Industrialization, urbanization, and the multiple revolutions they introduced didn't exactly destroy communities, but they changed their character. One of the consequences was atomization: we lost contact with each other and became individualistic, like the fine particles that spray from those cologne atomizers, each headed in a different direction.

Several writers have pondered the effects of the end of old-style communities. The French nobleman Alexis de Tocqueville toured North America in the 1830s, reflecting on the individualism he saw developing around him and how religion and the family might act as counterweights to this tendency. In 1887, the German scholar Ferdinand Tönnies wrote about the replacement of *Gemeinschaft*, or community, with *Gesellschaft*, that is, modern society, and the indifference to others brought about by the latter.

One of the most influential statements on the subject in the mid-twentieth century included the concept of "other-directed" persons. According to David Riesman and his collaborators, the people whom de Tocqueville had observed in the nineteenth century were inner-directed by religious or spiritual principles, and therefore determined individualists. The typical American of the 1950s, by contrast, had become "other-directed" and wanted to be loved rather than esteemed. His or her mission was not necessarily to control others but to relate to them. Other-directed people needed assurance that they are emotionally in tune with people around them. *The Lonely Crowd* described a society composed of atomized individuals who interacted with each other but who had had no meaningful ties or obligations other than those arising from self-interests (Riesman *et al.* 1950).

So, while Brooks doesn't mention these ideas, she draws on a rich scholarly tradition when she observes: "Throughout our history, humans have generally lived in small communities in which the topic of 'social grooming' couldn't be more obvious – stories involving one's friends and neighbors." She goes on: "But in our current fragmented, fast-paced society, we all have multiple 'villages': where we live, where we work, where we vaca-tion, where we're from, even what chat rooms we log on to."

We're constantly shuttling from one "village" to another, striking up relationships – some fleeting, some enduring – with others with whom we share conversation. These aren't villages in the established sense, but portable or even cyber communities in which people can remain transient, yet still interact habitually, perhaps even changing identities as they shuttle between them. To do so, they need a "universal cultural currency" that extends across all villages. For Brooks, that currency is "celebrity chatter." Wherever we happen to be, we can always strike up a conver-sation about celebs. Try it next time you are, well, practically anywhere and with anyone: checking a book out of the library, standing at the supermarket checkout, getting served at a bar. "Far from being victimized by information about celebrities, we're using it for our own positive social ends," concludes Brooks (2004: 21a).

This is a persuasive argument and augments rather than contradicts reports of celebrity worship. Being worshipful carries no connotation of passivity, according to the original research. True, the researchers describe an "enthralled" population, which "reveres" celebrities. But Brooks stresses the activity of reaching out to people with whom we have little in common apart from an interest in celebrities, sharing information with them, and, in the process, strengthening a network of people we know, if only through a shared fascination with other people we don't know but with whom we still feel intimate. Something resembling genuine intimacy develops from the one-sided feelings of intimacy that derive from parasocial relationships.

This type of approach to fandom, as the collectivity of fans has become known, accentuates the positive. Celebrities have been the inspiration behind many social benefits, including a new propensity to connect with each other and the recreation of mobile or cyber communities. There is, however, a darker side and one that Brooks ignores. Fans chattering about so-and-so's new hairdo or wondering out loud about whether such-and-such is having an affair with you-know-who, all seems innocently wholesome. What about the fan who, in 1996, sent the singer Björk a package that, if opened, would have exploded with sulfuric acid and who videotaped himself committing suicide in a perverse supplication? The grim and tragic episode dispensed a reminder that the celebrity-worshipping fandom secretes dangers.

: in my heart, in my dreams, in the crosshairs of my gun

In 1949, baseball player Eddie Waitkus ensured himself a dubious place in history when a fan shot him while he was at a Chicago nightclub. The incident provided raw material for at least two films featuring passionate and vengeful baseball fans: *The Fan*,

in which salesman Robert De Niro, who gets his spiritual
nourishment only by following baseball, turns viciously against
his team's recently signed superstar after discovering the player
is motivated only by money; and *The Natural*, based on Bernard
Malamud's novel, in which player Robert Redford is shot by an
admiring *femme fatale*.

Celebrity athletes and musical celebs are worshipped more
intensely than other kinds of celebrities, according to
McCutcheon *et al.* Their fans sometimes evince "a mixture of
empathy with the celebrity's successes and failures, over-
identification with the celebrity, compulsive behaviours, as well
as obsession with details of the celebrity's life" (2002: 67).

Although they're labeled "borderline-pathological," these fans
are not necessarily dangerous to either themselves or to the
objects of their adoration, although, as Waitkus and many other
celebrities have discovered, they can be. In "A cognitive profile
of individuals who tend to worship celebrities," McCutcheon
et al. describe a typical borderline-pathological as someone who
might spend several thousand dollars on a napkin or a plate used
by a celebrity (2003). And yet, there is a point at which collecting,
reading, or other forms of pursuit from safe distance fails to satisfy
some fans. They seek a more active engagement in the lives of
their idols.

Günther Parche, an unemployed lathe-operator from
Germany, was obsessed with the tennis player Steffi Graf. He
followed her career with precisely the mixture of empathy and
over-identification reported by McCutcheon and her colleagues.
At his home, he built an altar in her honor so that he could
worship the object of his commitment. When Monica Seles
replaced Graf as the world's leading female player, Parche was
stung into devising a way of restoring his idol to her rightful
place. When Graf met her rival in the German Open of 1993,
Parche ran onto the court and stabbed Seles, putting her out of
action. During her inactivity, Graf resumed her place as the
world's number one. Seles eventually came back but without ever

capturing her irresistible form. Parche ended up in prison, but he accomplished his mission. Graf took the number one spot.

The case is unusual: fans who obsess over a celebrity typically reserve their immoderate behavior for him or her rather than an adversary. There are insights even so. McCutcheon *et al.*'s research indicated that "extreme" celebrity worshippers who inflict harm or pursue rapaciously might qualify for membership of a pathological fan club. Yet the study concluded that: "The distinction between pathological and nonpathological celebrity worship is somewhat tenuous." Broken into its component parts, celebrity worship involves, as we've seen, such practices as watching, hearing, and talking about celebrities, empathizing, perhaps even over-identifying with them, and compulsively collecting items, like pictures, souvenirs, or other artifacts. All celebrity worshippers do one or more of these, but "as celebrity worship increases, these behaviours increasingly occur together."

While the researchers urge caution, this is an interesting finding: fans often labeled obsessive-compulsives, stalkers, or even full-on headcases, do not, on this account, do anything that other fans don't typically do. Nor do they register any different items on the "celebrity worship scale." At lower levels of the scale, fans tend to worship either alone, or at higher levels, they reach out and connect to form what Brooks calls villages, and at the highest level, they revert to more solitary worship. Conceptually, they are all on the one scale.

What happens at the most extreme level is called *absorption*, which involves a total commitment of all available "perceptual, motoric, imaginative and ideational resources to a unified representation of the attention object" (motoric refers to movement; ideational refers to the capacity to form ideas). The fan might be motivated to learn more and more about their chosen celebrity, perhaps seeking out obscure sources of information that are not available to most fans. Harry Veltman was one such fan: he became fixated with the skater Katarina Witt, found out her home address and bombarded her with mail, some of which included nude pictures of himself. He then managed to discover her telephone number and called to profess his love.

At some point during his parasocial involvement with Witt, Veltman had presumably grown dissatisfied and sought to develop a two-way relationship, which, in an odd way, he did. In McCutcheon *et al.*'s terms, his need or capacity for absorption was so high that he wanted access to parts of Witt's life that other fans were denied. Crucially, he cultivated the deluded belief that he had a special relationship with Witt: he became convinced that they were married.

Erotomania describes a condition in which someone believes that another, usually of higher social status (sometimes older), is in love with them. Such beliefs when held by absorbed fans are resistant to extinction. Fans often actively create conditions under which they appear "true": they rationalize them, making them seem perfectly reasonable. In this sense, obsessive fans control their own destinies, though only with the unwilling cooperation of celebrities. Facing one such fan, Robert Hoskins, across a California courtroom in 1996, Madonna said of his trial: "I feel it made his fantasies come true. I'm sitting in front of him and that's what he wants" (quoted in Meloy 1997: 177). Hoskins had made three approaches onto Madonna's property and was shot twice by a security guard. (Celebrities are not the only recipients of erotomanic attention: research indicates that over 8.1 percent of all US females and 16.1 percent of British females have received unwelcome attention from "stalkers." See Wood and Wood 2002; Home Office 2003).

Sometimes fans remain engrossed for years. Mark Bailey broke into the home of Brooke Shields in 1985, seven years after her film début as a 12-year-old nymphet in *Pretty Baby*. He was put on five years' probation, surfacing again in 1992 when he made threats to Shields. Seven months' imprisonment did little to stifle him. A legal order in 1998 prohibited him from ever contacting Shields, though he continued to write to her, prompting his arrest in 2000. He was carrying a three-page letter for Shields, a greeting card, and a .25-caliber automatic. It's probable that this absorption will endure into its third decade.

Occasionally, fans threaten partners. Catherine Zeta-Jones, wife of Michael Douglas, was threatened by a fan who became convinced she stood between herself and Douglas. Dawnette Knight claimed she met Douglas at a party in Miami in 1999 and had a two-year relationship with him. In one of her letters to Douglas, she referred to Zeta-Jones: "We are going to slice her up like meat on a bone and feed her to the dogs." She was jailed for three years in 2005. Zeta-Jones herself had been the object of a fan who professed his undying love for her and harassed her with a stream of unwelcome email messages.

Even when there is no delusion of romantic reciprocation, a fan can still sustain the belief in a relationship – up to a point. This is why empathy turns to obsession: the delusion of the special relationship becomes harder and harder to preserve. It is the theme of Martin Scorsese's 1982 movie *The King of Comedy*. In it, another De Niro character, Rupert Pupkin, obsesses over getting his own tv show, creating his own mock studio, complete with cutout guests, at his apartment. Not only does he follow the stars: he uses them as his own, imagining he's with them, that he has what they have, that he can do what they do. It's a triumph of fantasy. He deludes himself into believing he has a close, amicable relationship with a real talk show host whom he buttonholes and later visits at his home, arriving unannounced and introducing himself to the maid as a personal friend.

The film finds an academic confederate in the research of Rense Lange and James Houran who report the existence of a "positive (self-reinforcing) feedback loop" among subjects who believe they have had paranormal experiences (1999). While far from exact, the parallels are there to see: fans who crave a special relationship with celebrities can tolerate ambiguous experiences or interpret events that buttress their personally held beliefs. Potentially damaging episodes can be neutralized, setting in motion a kind of irrefutable, self-perpetuating cycle.

This seems to have been the case with William Lepeska, who tracked Anna Kournikova to within three doors of her Miami Beach residence and settled down naked at a poolside to wait for her. When police apprehended him, he implored the tennis pro-turned-model "Anna, save me!" and later explained: "I had all kinds of delusional assumptions about Anna's feelings toward me."

Previously, Lepeska had written copious letters and posted messages on her webpage and though his communication was unrequited, Kournikova, like most other globally known celebrities made herself or, at least, her representations widely accessible. Once her sports career was over, Kournikova busied herself with fashion engagements, which guaranteed her visibility. Any internet search engine will still generate about two million results for Kournikova. Lepeska selectively screened the superabundant information about Kournikova and decoded it in a way that supported his own interpretation. Improbably, Lepeska was allowed to cross-question Kournikova when he defended himself during a hearing.

One wonders how many Kournikova fantasists were (maybe still are) out there, all with human fallibilities, all harboring forlorn yet expectant beliefs about her, all somehow expressing their allegiance to her, mostly in ways that escape public attention. Inadvertently perhaps, celebs supply sustenance: their sheer appearance is enough to keep some fans' faith alive. This went on for so long in the case of Dave Gahan who grew uncomfortable with a male fan who kept an all-night vigil outside the Depeche Mode singer's Hollywood home. Gahan ended up headbutting the fan who then sued, claiming brain damage. The fan ended up with $40,000 but, we presume, lost his faith (Dalton 2005: 22).

As I noted before, some fans develop a tolerance to behavior that at one stage satisfied their need for absorption and need to go one step further. Compulsive behavior and obsessional tendencies characterize addicted celebrity worshippers. The point to bear in mind is there may be much more psychological resemblance between this type of fan and those who enthuse over celebs but without expressing any thoughts or behavior that might be considered inappropriate.

Clearly, there are momentous exceptions. Recent history has thrown up the likes of Mark Chapman and John Hinckley Jr, both of whom believed they were acting as proxies for others when they embarked on their missions to kill John Lennon and wound President Ronald Reagan respectively. Chapman said he received instructions through J. D. Salinger's novel *Catcher in the Rye*, while Hinckley was motivated by his erotomaniacal fixation with Jodie Foster. Yet even these two extreme cases we can discern qualities common to most other kinds of fans, albeit taken to extremes.

Hinckley in particular shares much with the absorbed fans of Graf, Witt, and Kournikova, in both their spurious romantic attributions and in their delusion that they were responding to the caprice of others. "The obsessive fan who camps on the star's doorstep has the potential to become either a murderer or a marriage partner," David Giles reminds us. "The difference between the devoted admirer and the dangerous 'stalker' may be alarmingly narrow" (2000: 146).

: power over the lives of others

Fans have been around as long as there have been famous figures to admire, respect, and mimic. In Chapter 3, we charted the development of an industry geared to the production of stars, an industry complemented and indeed given *raison d'être* by responsive consumers. Without an audience, there was nothing. Yet, the late 1980s witnessed the emergence of the worshipful fans: Madonna wannabes, moonwalking Michael Jackson clones, and reverential Michael Jordan disciples included. Even as late as 1992, two scholarly books were at pains to point out that there was nothing socially dysfunctional or individually pathological about devoted fans. Henry Jenkins's *Textual Poachers: Television fans and participatory culture*, and *The Adoring Audience: Fan culture and popular media* edited by Lisa A. Lewis, both, in their own ways challenged the popular conception of fans as having immoderate tastes and abnormal likings. Most fans didn't fit into popular stereotypes, such as the "obsessive loner" who expressed the isolation and atomization of mass culture, or members of a "hysterical crowd," all of them victims of mass persuasion.

All the same, the fandom needed sense making of it. There seemed to be new resolution in fans' pursuit of celebrities, intensity in the way they observed them, and strength in the attachments they forged with them. There was also some abandon in the way they spent money: they were consuming fans. "How do we explain and understand the surprisingly intensified relationships created by a special category of audience – 'fans'?" asked Cheryl Harris, introducing her 1998 volume *Theorizing Fandom: Fans, subculture and identity* (co-edited with Alison Alexander). The book set out to make the "phenomenon of fandom" comprehensible.

The contributors to this collection try to move beyond the psychological makeup of fans toward their actual practices and how these were structured by the industrial apparatus often called (following Theodor Adorno and Max Horkheimer) *The Culture Industry* (1972). The premise of the book is summed up by Harris when she argues that fans "find empowerment in their consumption of popular culture." Yet: "At the same time, it is impossible to ignore the extent to which media industries may be said to engage in an attempt to economically *disempower* fans by encouraging heavy spending on artifacts and merchandise" (1998: 43).

Harris's reference to the media apparatus that we covered in previous chapters alerts us to the pitfalls of trying to make sense of fans by analyzing them as if they were compressed into their own tight clusters. They operate in a culture of consumption and are, as such, not joyless victims of commodification, but cheerful contributors in the process. The central insight of Harris and her collaborators is that being a fan leads to a sense of influence and control "in the face of a monolithic industry." In other words, it's empowering. Fandom is "a phenomenon in which members of subordinated groups try to align themselves with meanings embodied in stars or other texts that best express their own sense of social identity" (1998: 49–50).

This is consistent with the approaches of Gamson (covered in Chapter 3) and Brooks (earlier in this chapter) and helps broaden the analysis offered by McCutcheon and her psychologist colleagues. It also chimes with a case from 1991. A female fan of the multiple world snooker champion Stephen Hendry wrote him a series of letters that became progressively abusive and included a threat to shoot him. She claimed that her menace afforded her "power over people's lives . . . to know that you can cause such harm to people by doing something as simple as writing a letter" (quoted in the *Sunday Times*, September 29, 1996).

While Harris doesn't cite this or discuss obsessive fans, it fits into her framework. Following the exploits of others and perhaps displacing one's own perceived inadequacies in the process, fans can negate their feelings of powerlessness and replace them with a sense of influence. The influence may be limited to buying or not buying cds, whispering to posters on bedroom ceilings, or sending admiring letters. It might include committing suicide, sending parcel bombs, or shooting to kill. Seen in this way, the acts are all parts of one "spectrum of fan activities," as Harris calls it: "The ultimate payoff for fans has less to do with whether or not they get the ostensible goals they have articulated and more to do with the activity of being a fan" (1998: 52).

On this account, just doing the things fans do confers feelings of power onto people who are objectively quite powerless. It may sound like a rudimentary observation, but it helps explain the behavior of the "extreme worshippers," including obsessive and compulsive devotees, without marginalizing them to a pathological fringe. I can anticipate the challenge: how else do we comprehend the likes of the Goth fans who armed themselves to the teeth and killed 12 of their peers at Columbine High in April 1999? Or the besotted fan of actor Rebecca Schaeffer who shot her dead with a .357 Magnum and explained: "I have an obsession with the unattainable. I have to eliminate what I cannot attain" (quoted in Hooper 1995: 18)? These seem a universe away from the breezy enthusiasts who chat and collect.

But they are in the same spectrum: just at different parts. Schaeffer's killer, Robert Bardo, had written to her many times and watched her endlessly in *My Sister Sam*, which he taped. Her role in the CBS tv show was all sweet and virtuous. Bardo was upset when he saw her play a much juicier role in the sex comedy movie *Scenes from the Class Struggle in Beverly Hills*. Days later, he got the gun. In custody, he insisted that Schaeffer had his name and number in her address book; she hadn't (Merschman 2001).

None of the obsessive fans we've dealt with in this chapter just woke up one morning as predators. They all in some way progressed, often via circuitous routes, to a recognition that what they were doing was insufficient. Anything, literally anything, could prompt such recognition. As Charles B. Strozier writes: "The slightest hint of injury, as the disdain of a lifted eyebrow, can cause great emotional suffering among the socially disempowered" (2002: 240).

A different type of action is sometimes seen as necessary. Whether this is understood as an addictive craving for satiation or an attempt to neutralize feelings of helplessness, the feelings of power are undeniable – to the perpetrator. The fan can change the life of a celebrity in the same way as he or she might highlight a piece of text and hit the "delete" key on the computer. Such influence over the life of another, especially someone they worship, carries its own terrifying power.

CONSUMING/BEAUTY

: short cut to happiness?

Your name is Paul Newman and it's 1962. You're about as hot as any actor in the world. You've already triumphed in *Somebody Up There Likes Me* (1956) and *Long Hot Summer* (1958), but your pièce de résistance is Oscar-nominated *The Hustler*, in which you play the cocksure young pool player, "Fast Eddie" Felson. The character is years younger than you, but you always look as if you've come straight from a cosmetic makeover session. Are you really 37? Your skin is flawless, you have a full head of sleek hair, succulent lips and eyes like an unclouded vault of heaven. You could pass for 25 and a smolderingly sexy 25 at that.

Just one thing. A tiny thing, but, on close inspection, one or two frown lines are appearing on your forehead, probably because you have a low brow and tend to raise your eyes. Studio chiefs have doubtless assured you that they're nothing to worry about and, in fact, might add a little character to your otherwise wrinkle-free visage. On the other hand, those furrows will deepen with age and might spoil your otherwise exquisite looks.

Botox wasn't around in 1962. If it had have been, might Newman, a man of Apollonian handsomeness, have succumbed to a shot or two, just to smooth out the incipient brow lines? Its application is simple, practically as easy as waxing your chest and less hassle than having your teeth bleached. Newman might have opted for the latter to remove the stains left by smoking cigarettes. But Botox? Probably not. In the 1960s, being gorgeous was a valuable advantage, not a bounden duty of every Hollywood star. Now, as serial cosmetic surgery recipient Joan Rivers puts it: "We're in a business where it counts" (quoted in the *Independent*, May 11, 2005, p. 36). Actually, we all are.

Of the many dubious gifts brought to us by celebrity culture, perfection is simultaneously the most innocuous and pernicious. What's wrong with trying to improve your physical appearance? It's a fair question and deserves a straightforward answer. It's this: nothing – unless, the search for perfection becomes a dizzyingly compulsive fixation that translates into an intolerance of anything slightly less than faultless. It becomes additionally damaging if the inevitable consequences of age must be denied or rejected by whatever surgical means available. In other words, like most other human predilections, the quest for beauty can become an endless and fruitless pursuit that leads to discontent rather than satisfaction.

In 2002, *People* writer Michelle Green wrote "Those lips, that face . . ." which reported on a number of fans who had undergone cosmetic surgery in order to look like their favorite celebrity. In the spirit of the MTV show "I want a famous face," Green interviewed a devotee of Keanu Reeves who had paid $9,000 for two rhinoplasties (nose jobs) and an implant to fill out his chin. "It's cured my vanity problem," the fan confirmed, presumably meaning it had indulged his conceit (2002: 127).

Of the other fans interviewed, one had undergone gluteal augmentation to give her buttocks the J.Lo look. Another had breast implants that took her from a B- to a C-cup; not huge, but closer to Britney Spears' bosom. And, perhaps surprisingly, one had a gastric bypass that left her with loose skin, then needed 12 pounds of that skin removed before her body could resemble what she described as the "curvy and voluptuous" Kate Winslett. Green catalogs several other patients, or perhaps more properly, clients who had submitted themselves to surgical remodeling so that they could look like celebrities.

While Green records the usual caveats about "unrealistic expectations" and the "shortcut to happiness" cosmetic surgery offers but rarely delivers, there is conspicuous ethical neutrality about her tone. In the 1960s, before cosmetic surgery was as accessible as it is today, a story such as hers would have carried dire warnings about how invasive and potentially traumatic the surgery can be (duly noted by Green), but there would also have been disapproval. To have one's face or other body parts reconstructed just to look like a famous person, however admirable that person might be, would have been regarded as plain sick. In a sense, maybe mimicking celebrities still is. Cosmetic surgery in itself obviously isn't.

Year on year there has been a steady increase in the number of people opting for a nip, tuck, or enhancement of some order. In the USA, almost nine million clients have "work" done every year. The British are more reticent about it: 500,000 per year and growing. They're not all trying to look like celebs, though, looked at another way, they've all been influenced by the predominance of celebrities in contemporary culture.

In the 1960s and perhaps until the 1980s cosmetic surgery was a luxury reserved mostly for stars and elite white women. Now there is much more access. The surgery is still expensive, but many more people are prepared to pay whatever it costs to effect the modification. The reason for this is simultaneously simple and complex. People are increasingly unhappy, frustrated, or in some way discontented with their own bodies. Why otherwise would they want them changed? That's the simple part. What isn't so clear is whether they have become more – or less – dissatisfied in recent years and why they are opting for what can be discomforting procedures, which are usually followed by a painful post-op period.

: under the spell of Narcissus

James Ellroy's crime thrillers are fictional narratives punctuated by chunks of fact and biography. His *LA Confidential* is set in the 1940s and 1950s and tracks the lives of three Los Angeles police officers as they investigate a multiple killing at a café. One of the cops has a relationship with a prostitute who closely resembles Veronica Lake, the alluring 1940s star. She works at a high-end brothel where the employees have undergone cosmetic surgery to look like Hollywood stars. Kim Basinger plays a Veronica Lake look-alike in the 1997 movie based on the book.

The brothel has featured in other fictional accounts and has something of an iconic presence in Southern California folklore. Its premise is a powerful one: men who couldn't actually have sex with the stars could pay to have the next best thing – sex with someone who was a dead ringer for whoever they desired. Even in the 1950s, plastic surgery, as it was then called, was sophisticated enough to transfigure prostitutes into facsimiles of the stars.

The stars themselves probably had maintenance checks. Marilyn Monroe is thought to have had surgery to remove scar tissue on her chin. Elvis Presley was rumored to have had bags under his eyes removed in 1975 when he was 40. In the 1970s, cosmetic surgery was still the preserve of the rich and conceited But changes were afoot.

The Culture of Narcissism is the title of Christopher Lasch's book on the changes that began in the 1970s. It describes "the apotheosis of individualism," in which self-centered feeling or conduct reached its highest state of development. After the turbulent 1960s in which young people all over the world challenged and subverted traditional ideals, values, and norms, people saw the same problems: war, nuclear proliferation, structured inequality, persisting racism, political corruption, and ideological divergence. Their rebellious efforts changed hearts and minds, but not the material facts. So, they "retreated to purely personal preoccupations," according to Lasch, "getting in touch with their feelings, eating health food, taking lessons in ballet or belly-dancing, immersing themselves in the wisdom of the East, jogging, learning how to 'relate,' overcoming the 'fear of pleasure'" (1980: 4).

Lasch saw no harm in any of these pursuits in themselves, but he rued the break with history, the turning away from collective activity, and the switch from trying to change society to changing oneself. Personal well-being, health, and psychic security became the motivating goals for the generation that had earlier wanted to change the world.

Narcissus was the Greek mythological character who fell in love with his reflection in water. His name is used to describe the tendency to self-worship, developing an excessive interest in one's own personal features. Like Narcissus, we looked for our reflection and became absorbed by it. But this wasn't enough. What counted is what others saw. "The narcissist depends on others to validate his self-esteem," observed Lasch. "He cannot live without an admiring audience . . . For the narcissist, the world is a mirror" (1980: 10).

There were two dimensions to the culture of narcissism: on the one hand, swathes of people abandoned their collective endeavors and contented themselves with individual quests for satisfaction and happiness; yet, on the other, they depended on each other for confirmation that they were looking and feeling good. The cultural and moral climate became one of "self-absorption" and a generation progressively insulated itself from the very features of society that it once opposed, including military conflict, poverty, and injustice.

One of the most pronounced tendencies to emerge from this climate was "the therapeutic outlook," in which, as Lasch put it, "the individual endlessly examines himself for signs of aging and ill health, for tell-tale symptoms of psychic stress, for blemishes and flaws that might diminish his attractiveness" (1980: 49). (It will be obvious by now that, writing in the 1970s, Lasch used the masculine pronoun for both sexes.)

The harvest of this culture soon became evident. Health clubs and gyms, countless diets, a profusion of anti-wrinkle aids and any number of therapies, including colonic irrigation, acupuncture, hypnosis, and aromatherapy; all of them designed in some way to palliate the "stressful" consequences of self-absorption and delay the diminution of "attractiveness." And what diminishes attractiveness more than just about anything apart from disfigurement? Age.

"People cling to the illusion of youth until it can no longer be maintained, at which point they must either accept their superfluous status or sink into dull despair," wrote Lasch (1980: 212). Actually, there were ways in which that illusion of youth could be maintained. It was just that they were available only to the few privileged enough to afford them. Twenty years after Lasch's observation, there had been democratization: cosmetic surgery was not only available but also accessible to a wider distribution of people.

At some stage, probably in the late 1970s, the line between surgery to correct or ameliorate ailments or disorders and surgery for purely cosmetic purposes became less distinct. The word cosmetic is from the Greek *kosmetikos*, meaning adorn or beautify, and its current meaning is faithful to its source. But a related meaning is: to restore normal appearance. Surgery to remove stigmas or other kinds of natural marks or scars on the skin or to eradicate disfigurements was always cosmetic in the sense that it was designed to improve appearance without necessarily changing bodily functions.

Disfiguring injuries suffered by servicemen in World War I, 1914–17, occasioned restorative surgery. Techniques continued to improve in the interwar years, giving rise to the possibility of utilizing surgery for other purposes. Plastic surgery, as it was called, was completely synthetic and had no ostensible purpose besides altering appearance. Rhinoplasty might have improved breathing in patients who had broken their noses, but its principal purpose was to change the shape of the nose. A primitive, unsuccessful method of disguising wrinkles involved injecting paraffin into facial skin, the idea being that the odorless, oily substance would plump up the epidermal layer. The problem was that, after a while, the paraffin turned to waxy lumps, creating an uneven surface on the skin.

Fanny Brice, the showgirl who was played by Barbra Streisand in the movies *Funny Girl* and *Funny Lady*, had surgery to reshape her nose in the 1920s. She became famous in the lavish Ziegfield revues. Later, Hollywood stars such as Hedy Lamarr, Merle Oberon, Burt Lancaster, and even hewn-of-granite John Wayne opted for surgical enhancement. Purely cosmetic surgery remained the preserve of Hollywood stars until the 1970s. After that, as we've pointed out, the therapeutic outlook imbued it with new meanings. Changing one's appearance became more than a superficial pursuit of the vain and conceited: it enabled people to feel better about themselves. The culture of narcissism elevated appearance in importance. Lasch reminds readers that advertising as far back as the 1920s encouraged women (not men) to be self-critical about their appearance. He quotes the strapline of an ad: "Your masterpiece – Yourself" (1980: 92).

The ad enjoined people to divide themselves into subjects and objects, so that they could be both their body and an admirer of that body. The message may initially have had a commercial function, but the possibilities it raised were to be realized over the next few decades. We started to subject ourselves to regimes that promised to make our bodies resemble cultural norms of good looks. Like all the priorities of consumer society, this one was determined by ourselves: we chose – and were not impelled – to embark on body regulation. Such is the beauty of consumerism: conveying the impression of choice, while obscuring the influence of the directive.

From the 1970s, men were also included in the imperative to "project an attractive image." It was a new scope: "Outward appearances, in this view, involuntarily expressed the inner man" (1980: 92). So, it became necessary to study one's own image, not out of vanity, but in a critical spirit, to spot flaws, signs of fatigue or, worse still, aging. In the process we were encouraged to make objects of ourselves: treat our bodies as, to repeat the early ad, a masterpiece on which we should work, striving toward perfection.

It bears remembering that, if Lasch is to be accepted, this was part of a complete change in orientation. Turning in on oneself, becoming self-aware and self-absorbed has counterparts in the way we understood the world and our place in that world. There wasn't what psychologists call a Gestalt switch in which perceptions suddenly change completely: more of an accelerating tendency that had been around for decades, but, during the 1970s (and we should add 1980s) gathered even more momentum and left hardly anyone unaffected.

As the end of the twentieth century approached, baby-boomers – the demographic group born in the period after World War II, 1946–64 – began to hit 50. "They have long been obsessed with youth and vitality," observed Nora Underwood in her *Maclean's* article "Body envy." So, it was a happy coincidence that "the prospects for a longer, healthier life were increasing all the time" (2000: 36).

Underwood wasn't just referring to the advances in medical science and health facilities that lengthened life expectancy: she meant the all-round broadening of awareness of how to adjust lifestyles in a way that promoted health and fitness. And good looks. There was an almost natural correspondence between them.

So the culture of narcissism was not the result of some fiendish connivance to destabilize people, render them insecure about their appearance, and send them scuttling to the nearest gym, wholefoods store, or cosmetic surgeon. But nor was it a completely voluntary act of spontaneity done willingly and without prompting. Like everything else about celebrity culture, it emerged from a paradox: consumers are both active and passive, producers and products, controllers and the controlled.

: as if

How long before you will be looking at a screen? If you lift your head and there's a computer on your desk, seconds. Later, you'll probably stare at the television screen. Maybe tonight you'll catch a movie. Screens have become major parts of our lives. We educate as well as entertain ourselves by gaping at flat luminous panels. We rely on photographic imagery of one kind or another. The reliance has become so great that the distinction between the human and the two-dimensional has narrowed or even become disrupted. At least that's the view of one scholar.

"The beauty of images symbolizes what is now experienced as their essential lure, and plastic surgery is the cultural allegory of transforming the body into an image," writes Virginia Blum. In her 2003 book *Flesh Wounds*, Blum presents one of the most challenging arguments about celebrity culture and one in which cosmetic surgery is central. The issue of cosmetic surgery is embedded in a culture that has become indebted to the two-dimensional images, the ones we watch every single day, many of them digitally enhanced or created. According to Blum we have become "infatuated" with 2-D images to the point where we identify with them. By identifying not with living people but moving images, we have been drawn into an engagement with a kind of fantasy.

Images of beauty, both female and male, are ubiquitous. Even a visit to the supermarket implicates us in looking at the magazine covers at the checkout. It's impossible to watch tv for an hour before someone gorgeous appears, whether in a commercial or drama, or perhaps reading the news (even newsreaders have to look good nowadays). "It is no wonder that the identification with the image of beauty is so compelling," Blum remarks (2003: 19). But we're not identifying with actual human beings, but with mediated images of them. This finds qualified support in the research of Natalie King *et al.* who discovered that, while we can't escape the images of celebrities, we don't all identify or even see them in the same way. Specifically, "women who are concerned about their own body shape view thin women in the media as being even thinner than they actually are, whereas women who are unconcerned about their body view them accurately" (2000: 345).

If we link this finding to Blum's general observation, we're drawn to the conclusion that the more we're dissatisfied with our own looks, the more we tend to idealize or exaggerate the beauty of celebrities – which would tend to heighten our dissatisfaction without reducing our identification. Those who are less satisfied with themselves and who see celebs in an excessively favorable way would, on this account, be the ones who would be inclined to take action.

There is a self-imposed regulating function to this: we form judgments about ourselves by comparing our bodies against cultural ideals that are held before us – again, in only two dimensions – and modify ourselves accordingly. No one, on Blum's account, can escape this. We assess the bodies of others as we assess our own. So, while Blum refers to the "relentless coercion of a youth-and-beauty-centered culture," we don't experience it as coercion at all. In fact, we voluntarily aspire to what is culturally desirable. The images help us make up our minds about what is and isn't.

Beauty might be in the eye of the beholder, but unless that beholder has been raised as a feral child without human company, his or her evaluation will have been affected by the culture in which he or she operates. Obviously, culture is ultimately a human enterprise, yet we shouldn't underestimate the manner in which it provides everything that makes us human, including language. We learn to communicate from others. We also learn other uniquely human characteristics from others. Taste, for instance: this isn't something that spontaneously springs into our minds. We learn to discriminate, judge, and appraise. So, while there are those who rhapsodize about timeless beauty, there is no such thing. Standards and values change, often very quickly.

Take a look at a copy of *Vogue* from 20 years ago and you see immediately that the models, who were paragons of classy good looks, now appear to be beefier and a bit shorter. Go back even further to Rubens' seventeenth-century masterworks in which you'll find women that are plump by today's benchmark. We simply can't remain indifferent to cultural changes. There's nothing optional about it. Our conceptions of beauty and ugliness are shaped.

There's a scene in *Shallow Hal* where Jack Black's Hal haughtily reminds his critics which one of them is escorting a stunningly glamorous blonde: not them but him. The conceit of the film is that Hal, having undergone off-the-cuff hypnosis, is smitten by an ample, prosthetically enlarged Gwyneth Paltrow though he can only see her as the normal-sized Paltrow. Others look on incredulously at love-struck Hal and the corpulent object of his affections. In other cultures, at different stages in history, Hal's tastes wouldn't have been questioned. And Paltrow in her "natural" state might be seen as too stick-like to be attractive. But today Paltrow is seen as much closer to the cultural norm of beauty than, say, Roseanne Barr (at her heaviest) or Queen Latifa (either of whom could have posed for Rubens, by the way).

With the expanding presence of the media in the twentieth century came a new and unprecedented influence. It's difficult to imagine any single phenomenon with the kind of supreme power to influence not only behavior but thought and perhaps even feeling. Circulating with the endless supply of words was an endless supply of images, representations, or signs that indicated or suggested the direction of our taste. While the popular association between, for example, beauty and youth is seen as natural, there is really nothing natural about it. There's nothing immanently beautiful about leanness, white teeth, or the absence of wrinkles. These associations have been suggested so much that we take them for granted, as if they were exactly as they feel – natural.

In many other cultures, it's quite probable that people were just not aware of their bodies in the way we are. Perhaps they simply didn't think about the body apart from when they were sick or if they lost some part, as the work of, among others, Michel Foucault reminds us. So the kind of narcissistic grooming and modifying we're all habituated to just wouldn't be contemplated. "The body is nothing until it's jolted into being by the image of something it could become," writes Blum, adding the kinds of images she has in mind: "a movie star, supermodel, a beautiful body" (2003: 54).

It becomes a body only once we start thinking about it in comparison with other bodies, specifically those of exemplary subjects. We can't genuinely talk in terms of what Blum calls a "premediated body": she means that we are only aware of our own bodies through the medium of others. In a narcissistic culture, we are all likely to more vigilant about our bodies and this means we're likely to be vigilant about other people's bodies too. These are made available for our close inspection courtesy of a mass electronic media that has grown in importance in large part because of our interest in others.

From Hollywood in the 1930s came a new standard of beauty, one that drew near-unanimous agreement. As we've seen in Chapter 4, an industry geared to promoting and marketing stars ensured the widespread availability of airbrushed images. Collectively, they defined a kind of gold standard of beauty. It's unlikely that there had ever been such a standardization of taste. Cinema and its analogous publications made this possible.

Consumers' fantasies, like those of children, are delicate invocations: we might imagine that we had a Beverly Hills home, multiple Ferraris, a body like Paltrow, or eyes like Newman, but we realize that whimsy is no replacement for a life plan. Prior to the late 1980s, the Hollywood stars had an otherworldly quality. As we've seen, they were marketed in a way that perpetuated the idea that they were people with special talents that separated Them from the rest of Us. Blum observes: "Star culture, its beauty in particular, is dependent on a universal conviction of great beauty as special and privileged" (2003: 259).

The entrancement with the stars made us restless, yearning to be a little more like them yet never quite believing we could be. And then it changed. Celebrity culture brought with it an immediacy that was both enlightening and maddening. Enlightening because it showed that the celebrities were much more ordinary than previously thought. Maddening because the special privileges they enjoyed were probably less to do with talent and more to do with any number of other factors, including happenstance, or fluke, or tampering. "Once their beauty turns out to be surgical, something any of us can have for the purchase, then we are no longer in the thrall," writes Blum. "By ourselves entering the order of illusion, there is no longer any illusion as such, because there is no difference between them (the illusion of celebrity bodies) and us (real bodies)" (2003: 259).

It's as if we've internalized the two-dimensional images for so long, all the time believing that the celebrities lived on another plane, their conspicuously different status and lifestyles being the product of some sort of gift. The new celebrity culture brought with it an apparent openness and honesty. After the "rules of engagement," as we've been calling them, changed, so did the relationship we had with famous movie stars and the other kinds of entertainers who had joined them on their special plateau.

Blum captures this relationship in her phrase "as if lives." She takes the phrase from the psychoanalyst Helene Deutsch, who, in the 1940s, used "as if personality" to describe individuals whose "whole relationship to life" was lacking in genuineness and yet outwardly ran along "as if" it were complete (Deutsch 1986). In idealizing and modeling ourselves on celebrity, we are identifying with subjects whose very living depends on continuously shifting identities. While Blum doesn't elaborate, she must have in mind actors, who transfer from role to role, rock stars who change chameleon-like so that fans never get bored (Madonna being the supreme example, David Bowie being another), and athletes who switch teams or essay new ventures. Identifying with fast-changing models means "our experience of identity is made not only insubstantial but also . . . transformational" (Blum 2003: 147).

Remember Blum's premise: our identification is not with people but with 2-D images. She likens them collectively to an "ever-unfolding pageant," a spectacular procession of figures that never stops. And, like characters in pageants, celebrities have an allegorical purpose: "They represent for us both what we are and what (and where) we long to be" (2003: 147).

This close and forever incomplete identification with representations works as both cause and effect of cosmetic surgery. While the distance between stars and fans was closing, cosmetic surgery became more accessible and affordable. Fans learnt about how the fabulous looks of the stars they saw on screens and in magazines were not as special or as god-given as they might have supposed. So their quest to identify with them took on what Blum calls an "aggressive" character. If stars could have themselves surgically changed to look beautiful, so could fans. Anyone could have good looks.

In the early 1980s, only seriously big stars would have used surgery to modify normal, functioning features. Now, anybody can do it. They may have to save for a while. But most things of value necessitate a little belt-tightening. What would a consumer want more? asks Blum rhetorically. "A new car? A sleek new jawline?" There are always choices; they give the consumer sovereignty. At least that's the preferred impression. Another interpretation is that we, the consumers, are the ones being bought and sold.

And, if there is still a missing link between cosmetic surgery and celebrity culture, it is this: all problems have solutions that can be bought. Everything is potentially soluble, as long as the consumer has enough money. As we know, consumer society generates problems of a particular kind: the ones that have their sources in insecurities, anxieties, cravings, greed, and desires.

Cosmetic surgery has become a buyable solution to a problem that starts in identifying with mediated images.

In Blum's vision, cosmetic surgery is no mere byproduct of a culture driven by vanity, but an experience that distills the raw materials of celebrity culture. It's as if the imperatives of consumerism, its narcissistic excesses and its media-promoted visions of the good life were heated into vapor, condensed by cold air then re-collected in the form of what Blum calls a "cult of the surface."

There is something both liberating and oppressive about this. Proponents may point to the boosts in self-esteem or confidence brought about by cosmetic surgery. Opponents may deplore an enterprise founded on superficiality and surface appearance. Someone sitting in a locked car in which the doors are jammed may turn the ignition and drive to wherever they want. Those standing outside the car may pity the poor soul trapped in the metal conveyance.

One thing is for sure: cosmetic surgery is a perfect complement to a consumer culture predicated on the principle that anything – *anything* – can be bought in the market. Even good looks.

Every ingredient of what we've come to regard as the good life arrives at our senses through the media. Think about what would make you happy. They probably involve either having or appearing. Possessing cars, clothes, or homes, for example. Looking better than the most drop-dead celeb imaginable. We know things can be bought. Increasingly, so can looks. The urge to improve ourselves, again brought to us courtesy of the media, involves commodities – commodities without utility, apart from their image value. We desire things not so much for appropriation, but for presentation: to stimulate ourselves by projecting ourselves in a certain way.

Celebrity culture has brought with it new possibilities: the endless novelty of new commodities disguised as people with images that titillate and inspire emulation. Their distinctive manner of living, their enviable belongings and, just as importantly, their attractive appearance make us restless. We want to be more like them. How can we resist figures with whom we identify so closely?

: changing

Before closing this chapter, I need to consider two more questions: why don't more celebs come out and admit they've had work done, and would it make any difference if they did? Joan Rivers insists: "Look at any actress over 60 who doesn't have jowls. They say they've done nothing, but they're lying" (in the *Independent* story cited above). When it comes to cosmetic surgery, Rivers vaunts: "I go to my surgeon once every two years, like you service your car or repaint your house." She made fun of other celebrities who denied having work done. Eyebrows have been raised metaphorically at the manner in which other facial features have been literally raised. While Rivers and the other famed cosmetic surgery aficionada Cher talk as openly about their surgery as they might about their clothes, the vast majority of celebs, young and old, treat their surgery like a dark secret. It's almost as if they're embarrassed to reveal that their looks are not entirely natural. Or that they live in fear that their professional careers are contingent on their physical looks and that a disintegration of one will lead to a disintegration of the other.

If their motive is to preserve their specialness, they should think again. Fans, as we have seen, are both participants and voyeurs: they are astute enough to see through the subterfuge of the celebrity industry. Anyway, on the account presented here, it wouldn't matter. The whole point about cosmetic surgery is that it is the highest development – or, to use one of Lasch's words, the apotheosis – of celebrity culture. So, when Melanie Griffith appears in three Revlon advertising campaigns between 1995 and 2001 and, as Blum puts it, "looks like three different women" it doesn't matter at all. The shifting, transitory character of celebs is central to their appeal. We might suspect that Griffith's age-defying transition is more attributable to surgery than moisturizer, but neither her status nor Revlon's suffered.

As nature abhors vacuum, celebrity culture abhors stillness. Change, novelty, surprise are prerequisites. The enduring celebrities are transformational, changing appearance and identity in a way that keeps consumers stimulated and refreshed, though not always with comparable results. Contrast Clint Eastwood and Burt Reynolds. Eastwood's early roles created for him two alter egos, "The Man with No Name" from the *A Fistful of Dollars* series and Harry Callahan from *Dirty Harry* and its sequels. Eastwood diversified into different roles in different genres, directing as well as acting and, at one point, taking an elected mayoral position in Carmel, California. His appearance ripened as his professional personae expanded. In contrast, Reynolds seemed to strive painfully to retain the dark, mustachioed macho looks for which he became known in such movies as *Deliverance* and *Smokey and the Bandit* in the 1970s. As his looks matured, so the roles disappeared and his celebrity waned. His face seemed to reflect heroic efforts to make time stand still. In the 1990s, he reappeared in *Boogie Nights*, but in a role that seemed either to echo or parody his former self.

Celebs are allowed to age. What they're not allowed to do is stay the same. Even Britain's ever-youthful sexagenarian Cliff Richard, whose musical career spans five decades and whose looks seemed resistant to age, changed considerably in choice of music, as well as in physical appearance. The secret of his longevity lay in his adaptability. Were he to opt for cosmetic surgery, his considerable fan base would suffer no damage at all. It would just be a further signal of his intention to keep changing.

The fans' pleasure is in possessing celebrities just like they possess all the other articles of expendable and obsolescing merchandise. Celebs who are prepared to keep changing present themselves just as possessions that can be upgraded. Obviously, there's a qualitative difference between being a devotee of someone and desiring a new Audi. There's also a similarity. If Audi produced the same models as it did in 1990, we would go off them and turn to a make of car that cycles in new models every few years. We want change. We want celebs to change. How they change, with what methods, and with what results is of secondary importance.

COMMODIFYING/RACE

: the other hierarchy

What do the following have in common: Anna Nicole Smith, Beyoncé Knowles, Donald Trump, Eve, Gwen Stefani, Jessica Simpson, Lil' Kim, Missy Elliott, Nicky Hilton, Pamela Anderson, Serena Williams, Steve Harvey? There are no doubt several answers, though the one I have in mind is this: within a few weeks at the start of 2005, they all launched their own fashion lines.

Notice anything else? Out of the twelve, six are African Americans. This may not be headline news, but it's revealing. Black designer labels have for long had a presence in the fashion market, with the likes of Willi Smith, Carl Jones and T. J. Walker developing successful lines in the 1980s and 1990s. But the black celebrity lines are much more recent. Rap entrepreneur Russell Simmons, movie director Spike Lee and the Wu-Tang Clan all branched into clothes with their own labels. A slew of rappers joined them: Jay-Z, Master P, Busta Rhymes, Ice T and, perhaps most famously, Sean Combs/ Puff Daddy/ P.Diddy (take your pick). Now, it seems that anytime an African American approaches the A-list, there is a new line ready to hit the racks. This would have been unthinkable as recently as the late 1970s (though Smith launched his WilliWear men's range in 1978). By the early twenty-first century, it was clear that black celebrities could shift merchandise; they were bankable commodities.

On one level, this was because of the associations between blackness and style. As urban or streetwear became *de rigueur* among young people of all ethnic backgrounds, black celebrities acquired a kind of crossover status that enabled them simultaneously to earn fortunes while acting like card-carrying members of the ghetto. That's at one level; it's the other levels that are more interesting, though. It's here that there have been changes that have turned a handful of eye-catchingly successful and often ostentatious ethnic minorities into celebrities while leaving the structure of what some call the "racial hierarchy" essentially intact (Louis Kushnick used the term effectively in a 1981 essay).

There have been signs of change for decades: civil rights in the USA and race relations legislation coupled with equal opportunities in Britain have combined to destabilize older-style ranking systems in which whites stayed on top while ethnic minorities tried to claw their ways out of an underclass. On both sides of the Atlantic, groups that have been historically denied the chance to excel have fought for and won those chances. There have also been diversifying influences that have changed what was once thought to be a melting pot, then a mosaic and then a salad bowl into something more like an mp3 player that stores disparate, miscellaneous tracks from different genres that can be played in any order, randomly if required; new items can be added, older ones thrown away, so that the collection is never actually complete. It's always a work-in-progress. Some of the tracks might have been mixed, using samples from other works, giving the impression that they're fused. So, how come researchers still insist that the hierarchy persists?

Clearly, it doesn't. At least, not in the way it did as recently as the 1980s, when young blacks rioted in Britain's inner cities and America struggled painfully with racially charged incidents, such as the cases of the Central Park jogger, Tawana Brawley, and Charles Stuart, all of which threatened wider repercussions. In fact, the events that impacted the racial hierarchy most powerfully came in the next decade. In 1992, a predominantly white jury acquitted four LAPD officers who were brought to trial after brutally beating Rodney King. The verdict was a catalyst for widespread, often violent protests by African Americans across the USA. The "Rodney King riots," as they were known issued a reminder that assumptions that racism had disappeared were ill founded.

Seven years later, the conclusions of an investigation into the police's handling of a murder of a black youth in London prompted a similar recognition in Britain. The report condemned the police, citing the presence of institutional racism and the failure to accept the murder itself as motivated purely by racism.

Both events stimulated long, probing investigations and soul-searching, though the palpable improvements in ethnic relations that many suspected would follow weren't immediately obvious. In fact, it could be argued that the experiences of ethnic minorities on both sides of the Atlantic were affected at least as much by the effects of the September 11 attacks. White racists, it seemed, changed focus, singling out anyone who faintly resembled a Muslim and treating them to a dose of violent discrimination. Islamophobia may not have been an especially helpful term in understanding the hostility against just about anyone who looked as if their origins or ancestry lay east of zero degrees longitude, but it somehow captured the shifting mood of the times.

The race issue seems to have run like a plot from *Prizzi's Honor* in which a mafia hit-man falls for a woman who, unbeknown to him, is also a hired assassin, albeit a freelance (*Mr and Mrs Smith* recycled the story). Racism might not have been as debilitating as it was in the late twentieth century but it persisted and continued to affect the lives of the majority of blacks, Asians, and other ethnic minorities. But, almost independently of this, another, smaller yet still visibly ethnic group appeared to surpass racism, or at least zip by peers en route to celebrity status. With that status came a certain credit that served to neutralize what might otherwise be the corrosive effects of racism. In other words, while most blacks and other ethnic minorities struggled against the diminishing though still considerable forces of racism, some were elevated to the stratospheric heights of celebritydom, from where the impact of racism was barely felt, if at all. Each group knew of the existence of the other but never actually felt their presence or the consequences of their actions. But there *were* consequences.

You don't get to have your own line of fashion wear if you are a marginal celebrity: you have to be central and influential enough to be able to persuade consumers to part with cash. The expanding group of ethnic signatories to designer labels hardly suggests a reliable measurement for social science, but it does suggest an important change in status for ethnic minorities and not just those who lend their names to the products.

: insect or monster?

In 1985, Clint Wilson and Félix Gutiérrez wrote "advertisers promote consumption of their products as a shortcut to the good life, a quick fix for low-income consumers" (1985: 128). Their book *Minorities and Media* was an analysis of how and why the media's portrayal of ethnic groups has changed. "The message to their low-income audience is clear," they wrote, referring to the manner in which advertisers had begun to take notice of previously ignored segments of the market: "You may not be able to live in the best neighborhoods, wear the best clothes, or have the best job, but you can drink the same liquor, smoke the same cigarettes, and drive the same car as those who do" (1985: 128).

Wilson and Gutiérrez's cautionary study arrived just as markets were segmenting and advertisers were recognizing the distinct consumption patterns of certain ethnic minorities. The authors showed that there had been "dramatic changes in the relationship between advertising and racial minorities" since the 1960s and that, by the mid-1980s, advertising agencies understood that the ghettos and barrios were waiting to be exploited. Minorities were urged to remain mindful that they lived in "a system of inequality that keeps them below national norms in education, housing, income, health and other social indicators" (1985: 130).

More significant changes lay ahead: markets segmented further, enabling a tv channel like MTV to offer large, demographically desirable audiences to advertisers wishing to target specific consumers. MTV, as we've seen, both reflected the change in the market and, as a powerful medium in its own right, catalyzed further changes. One of the more important ones was the proliferation of entertainment-centered media. In his book *Mass Media*, Pierre Sorlin makes the point: "Unlike information, entertainment can be advertised; conversely, advertisement becomes at times entertainment" (1994: 90).

In the 1980s, it may have been possible to tell where the program breaks and the ads begin. Today, product placement (in which advertisers pay to have brand names spoken or seen in films or tv shows), program sponsorships, magazines that puff people and products (praise or exaggerate their value), and any number of other symbiotic connivances have effectively ruled such a task out of the question. Can we ever know for sure when we are not exposed to advertising?

As the market-driven media sought to target specific groups of consumers, so the market underwent fission, splitting into new cells, some defined by ethnicity, others by age, education, gender, geography, income, and any number of other markers. The cross-hatching that characterized the new markets taxed advertisers even more. A 25-year-old Latina store assistant from Miami might seem to have more in common with a 30-year-old woman with Mexican parents living and working as a receptionist in Carson City, California, than a 23-year-old white male software worker from Liverpool. But, their consumption patterns might reveal something different.

Did this mean that the traditional fault lines of race and ethnicity were no longer relevant? They certainly were when it came to examining the racial hierarchy: blacks and other several other ethnic minorities, including American Indians, occupied lower tiers when it came to education, income, wealth, and home-ownership, and poverty continued to be a feature of African American life in particular (unemployment often rose to two or three times the rate of white unemployment even in times of prosperity). But they were not such reliable indicators of consumer preference. The days when malt liquor ads showed only black drinkers and stir-fry sauce was aimed at Asian shoppers vanished with the twentieth century.

Coinciding with the diversification of the market came the rise of ethnic minority celebrities. But, of course, it wasn't mere coincidence, or, for that matter, kismet, or the unfathomable randomness of life that coupled the two. Ethnic minority celebrities were both agents and effects of the new heterogeneous marketplace, as well as an expression of a world in which racism was supposedly going or gone. In his *Blacks and White TV: African Americans in television since 1948*, J. Fred MacDonald dismisses those who believed the arrival of more ethnic minority television characters in the 1980s was the result of principled tv execs with righteous minds: "TV had to serve black Americans because it financially needed them, not because it was morally supposed to be fair" (1992: 245).

The media dealt with this coexistence. On the one hand there was an emerging group of affluent ethnic minorities with enough spending power to make their presence felt as consumers. On the other, study after study revealed that, despite all attempts to defeat or minimize the effects of racism, patterns of racial inequality persisted stubbornly. Affluent ethnic minorities had managed to surmount the traditional obstacles. They gave evidence that, in Shelby Steele's terms, racism, while once a monstrous threat to black people, had diminished to the stature of an annoying insect – which just needed to be swatted. As long as ethnic minorities in general and African Americans in particular continued to labor in the role of perennial victims and squander their energies on fighting the mosquito-like irritant, they would not "progress" as individuals, argued Steele in his *The Content of Their Character* (1990).

Was there ever a better emblem of ethnic achievement than the celebrity? Typically, the black celebrity coursed through society from a dysfunctional family in a poor part of town onto a fast track to fortune. Famed, often throughout the world, the celeb usually had more money than he or she knew how to spend and commanded the quality much sought after but often denied ethnic minority people: respect. Honored, admired, perhaps even approved of, the celeb enjoyed respect in abundance. There weren't many clearer proofs of how effective society had been in ridding itself of racism and the discrimination it fostered. Ethnic minority celebrities emerged from a meritocracy in which coming from an ethnic background was no longer an impediment to progress. Anybody could become rich and famous.

If you lived in the 1980s, you would know that there were many distinguished and well-known artists and athletes from ethnic minority backgrounds. Black singer/songwriters like Bob Marley and Stevie Wonder had global fame, as did athletes like Muhammad Ali and Pelé. Movie actors, such as Sidney Poitier and Diana Ross, who also had a distinguished singing career, were internationally recognized. Before them, the likes of Nat King Cole, Lena Horne, and Louis Armstrong had all received acclamation from around the world. Perhaps more revered than any other black entertainer, Ray Charles, in 1958, released an album entitled *The Genius of Ray Charles* and no one accused it of hyperbole.

Yet, their fame was also a form of imprisonment. Imprisonment in a six-star hotel's penthouse suite maybe, but still a form of confinement. They were among a tiny minority of abundantly gifted performers who were permitted by white society to succeed in either entertainment or sports. Jan Nederveen Pieterse extends the idea of granting permission in his book *White on Black* (1992). He argues that white society accepted, even rejoiced in the brilliance of these and other illustrious blacks. But only on the condition that they did not challenge the paternity of a white society that produced them and gave them their big chance. Ali, unlike the boxer Joe Louis before him, did exactly that and was, for a while, ostracized before rehabilitating himself in the eyes of many whites. In a sense, he was turned into a martyr retrospectively, so that, by the end of the twentieth century, he was seen as a courageous standard-bearer of human rights. In the 1970s, he was a virtual outcast.

In Nederveen Pieterse's view, black stars were welcome only if they were prepared to toe the line. Any breach of conditions was subject to punishment. So, for example, when Paul Robeson expressed communist sympathies, he was denounced and frozen out of parts. It was as if the contract that enabled them to cross over into the mainstream rather than purely ethnic market stipulated that they should express no political views, refrain from challenging the status quo, and remain deferential. After desegregation had made it possible for blacks to stay in the same hotels, eat in the same restaurants, and live in the same neighborhoods as whites, there was still a sense in which even the most celebrated black people were confined.

Nederveen Pieterse is one of a number of scholars who have fretted over the tragicomic history of ethnic minorities in popular entertainment. Even after the liberation brought about by civil rights in the 1960s, age-old stereotypes were still in use. If blacks didn't approximate one of those stock images, their careers were limited. Female black artists, in particular, were often forced into the roles of asexual mammy-style figure, or lusty temptresses. The title of Donald Bogle's book summarizes the full range of role: *Toms, Coons, Mulattoes, Mammies, and Bucks* (1998).

The black comic occupied a special place, perhaps because the role was so congruent with the sambo stereotype: amusingly stupid and without a care in the world; someone to be laughed at. In the USA and Britain, there has been a tradition of black comedians stretching right back to the nineteenth-century minstrels who were allowed into the mainstream. Some of them used their position to mock the conditions under which they'd been allowed entry to the mainstream. The minstrels themselves would often do this, poking fun at how whites saw black people, yet without causing offense. After all, comics were not to be taken seriously.

: the acclaim of whites

On the night the Rodney King riots broke out, NBC aired the 198th and final episode of the most popular television sitcom in history. *The Cosby Show* featured Bill Cosby as the benign patriarch of a well-ordered, professional, black family living in fashionable Flatstone. It started in 1984 and was the first show featuring a predominantly black cast not to depict its subjects as dim, oppressed, or in some way marginal to the main action. Cosby's character was affluent, educated, secure, and very main-stream. Above all, he seemed quite ordinary.

The last show made a perfect counterpoint to the riots. In the comedy, the fictional Huxtable family faced the same kind of predicaments as any other family. No one grumbled about racism or how tough it was for members of the black middle classes. The teenage children weren't crack-users or gangbangers and suffered none of the pathologies typically attributed to young African Americans. In fact, the family could have been a Norman Rockwell figurine come to life – if they hadn't been black.

The show propelled Cosby to the A-list. He became one of the richest African Americans and featured in a series of movies, though none of them received the same kind of praise as the tv show. He also wrote books and involved himself in public speaking. Cosby the actor was synonymous with the Cliff Huxtable, his urbane character, and, in this sense, he was a standard-bearer. The image of a black man who was neither an object of ridicule, a possessor of great physical gifts, or a social fatality was hailed by critics who had assailed television for its reliance on stereotypes. Yet there were questions. Did the Huxtables present a realistic portrait of black family life in contemporary society? How representative were they? Was racism genuinely so insignificant that it never intruded on their coziness? The show's answers might have been designed to appease those who wondered if the King riots hinted at more widespread unease. And in this we find a clue as to why black celebrities have been so enthusiastically accepted by white society.

The Cosby Show could have been designed to disabuse anyone who thought racism was still as potent as it was 20 years before. Here are the Huxtables, well-mannered, well-appointed, and happily well-heeled. Here is the head of the family: wise, successful, always stressing the value of education. Here are his wife and kids: reassuringly ambitious. They were exemplary. If they could make it amid the enterprise culture promoted by President Ronald Reagan, why couldn't the other 15 million or so blacks?

For this reason, critics, like Sut Jhally and Justin Lewis, believed that the show secreted "a new and insidious form of racism," which, as the title of their book suggests, is *Enlightened Racism* (1992). "The Cosby Show, by demonstrating the opportunity for African Americans to be successful, implicates the majority of black people who have, by the Huxtable criterion, failed," assert Jhally and Lewis. "They [the Huxtables] also prove the inferiority of black people in general" (1992: 94–5).

As the show became an advertisement for how blacks could and perhaps should live, so Cosby himself became a living ad, not just for the good life portrayed in the show but for, among others, Coca-Cola, DelMonte, Ford, Kodak, and, most famously, Jell-O pudding. Staying in character, he smirked his way through one of the USA's most popular, long-running campaigns. The Jell-O commercials played no small part in his ingratiation: he became a kind of symbol not so much of how middle America saw black men, but how they would like them to be – manifestly trustworthy and not the least bitter. In fact, Cosby/Huxtable seemed incapable of anger.

If there was a lesson in Cosby for advertisers, it was that they could no longer afford to exclude African Americans from their plans. Remember MacDonald's point: tv "financially needed" black people; by the early 1990s, they constituted a consumer market worth over $200 billion (1992: 268). While Cosby might have been in Ford commercials, many other blacks were driving Bentleys. People on both sides of the Atlantic might have referred to the "black community," but the sharedness and homogeneity implied by such a term was largely a fiction. The black population had the same kind of divisions and echelons as the rest of society. It was segmented.

By the time of *The Cosby Show*'s disappearance, other ethnic minority entertainers had emerged, partly in emulation of Cosby, partly in response to the shifting market and perhaps partly in satisfaction of the deal. The deal was this: we'll invite you to see the world through the eyes of a black family, which will not only amuse but reassure you. The droll Cosby and his hilarious family painlessly removed any uncomfortable thoughts about the failure of civil rights to reduce racism to an irrelevance. Viewers became guilt-free peeping toms watching the private goings-on of a typical black family. *Typical?* Maybe the Huxtables were actually representative of a tiny fraction of the African American population. This was easily forgotten amid the laughter.

In 1994, with reruns of *The Cosby Show* still being screened around the world, Whoopi Goldberg declared: "I am not an African American, I am an American." Goldberg had risen to prominence in 1985 when she memorably played the "poor, female, ugly and black" Celie in the film of Alice Walker's Pulitzer Prize-winning novel *The Color Purple*. The remark brought a stinging rebuke from Ron Walters who used his column in the *Washington Informer* to launch an attack, not only on Goldberg who, he argued "spent considerable effort to distance herself from her African-origin identity," but on Morgan Freeman, O. J. Simpson, Pelé, and Michael Jackson (1994: 17).

Walters' critique had two prongs. "They are the stock in trade of the neutered black" in that, they either occupied or chose roles that were the "stuff of deep racial stereotypes." Goldberg was "a modern day Aunt Jemima," while Freeman often played a servile "stop-and-fetchit" character. The sports heroes were loved for their thrilling athleticism, but for nothing more and, as such, carried the stigma of the "Black jock." Since the mid-1990s both Goldberg and Freeman have broadened their character tableaux and Simpson and Jackson have been involved in unforgettable scandals (which we will come to in the next chapter). But, even if Walter's first prong appears blunter than it did in 1994, his second remains sharp.

The celebrities in question had all reached the level of the "cultural pantheon where race is irrelevant, or where although race may at times be relevant, it carried an altogether different meaning for them" (1994: 17). Walters argued that the "denial of black identity" is a common operation among people who have gained an acceptance to the elite, whether of movies or sports. Were Walters able to anticipate the rise of Colin Powell, he would have to include him in his criticism: Powell famously refused to prefix his status with "black."

"Attempting to transcend race and become something they can only be at the sufferance of someone else . . . is the classic condition of a slave," wrote Walters, notifying readers that, stripped of celebrity status, his subjects would be urgently reminded of what it means to be black. As they have risen, they have given the impression of transcending race. What's more, as Walters puts it: "Whites would be willing to join with them in the façade that they had all transcended race, as long as Whoopi, Morgan, O. J. and others did not threaten their status and as long they continued to make them feel good, make them laugh" (1994: 17).

Perhaps surprisingly, Bill Cosby evaded the salvo. Walters took issue with "Black conservatives" who played not the race card but the "race neutrality" card in a way that "brings them the acclaim of whites." By this, he means that many celebrities from ethnic minority backgrounds, in their efforts to stay audience-friendly, downplay the significance of racism in contemporary culture. In 2004 Cosby appeared on CNN and berated and blamed black parents for allowing themselves to remain victims and suffering in poverty. While the ideology was consistent with that of Huxtable's, it was delivered with a rumbling gravitas that was quite at odds with the more familiar Cosby of the 1980s.

Do all ethnic minority celebrities become blissfully unaware of their compatriots as they rise to fame? Or do they deliberately stifle their comments to avoid the kind of controversy that could ruin their careers? Do they become conservative and "race-neutral" as they draw the "acclaim of whites"? Or do they draw the acclaim because they are conservative and race-neutral? These are not exactly options, of course. The reality is that all these are, in some measure, true, some celebrities succumbing more easily than others to the inevitable pressure toward race neutrality.

: Oprah's glamorous misery

The Color Purple's cast also included Danny Glover who would probably have drawn Walter's wrath for playing Mel Gibson's sidekick in *Lethal Weapon* and its offspring. But what would Walters have made of Oprah Winfrey, who played Sofia, a role Bogle reckons is "precariously close to the mammy of old days" (1998: 293)? Winfrey was the host of a Chicago tv station's talk show which went national in 1986, the year after the movie's release. It soon became the nation's premier show of its kind. Within two years, she had set up her own company, Harpo Productions, to make *The Oprah Winfrey Show*, as well as several other projects in which she both acted and executive-produced.

Over the next several years, Winfrey involved herself in myriad enterprises, starting with a campaign to establish a database of convicted child abusers. The "Oprah Bill," as it became known, provided for such a database and was passed into law in 1993.

The talk show became globally famous, attracting about 30 million viewers worldwide. Oprah published her own magazine, started her own cable station, and founded her own charities, including Oprah's Angel Network. This helped build rural schools in at least ten underdeveloped countries and raised about $30 million. It was but one of dozens of philanthropic projects with which she was associated. By 2003, she was valued at over $1 billion on the *Forbes* list. She also joined Elvis and Marilyn at that level of Christian name-only fame: they existed at a level somewhere above the usual layer of celebs where the mention of one word provokes instant recognition. A sort of A★ list.

The phrase *transcending* race has cropped up several times in this chapter: all ethnic minority celebrities have, by some means, surpassed the restrictions of race and the limiting range of experience it imposes by becoming popular with multicultural audiences. Even in this company, Oprah was different. Often voted the most influential woman in the world, she changed everything from people's reading habits to their perceptions of victimhood.

Winfrey's ascent coincided perfectly with the rise of celebrity culture. Making the ordinary extraordinary and the extraordinary ordinary could have been an epigram of the times. Daytime talk shows, confessional shows, like Jerry Springer's, and reality tv, disclosed everyday people with mundane lives as exceptional individuals with remarkable lives.

Eva Illouz's book, *Oprah Winfrey and the Glamour of Misery*, examines the renowned talk show in terms of what the author calls "the culture of pain and suffering." The "glamour of misery" of which the Oprah Winfrey show is said to partake is part of a larger cultural phenomenon by which victimization and the power to transcend suffering provide the basis for Winfrey's enormous popularity. En route to her global fame, Oprah had overcome manifold problems: she had been a victim of abuse as a child, rape, and depression. Being a black woman was but one of the hurdles she had to cross. In some ways, she was the "ultimate victim." Instead of narrowing her focus, she broadened it to show how harrowing problems often attributed to racism were often more generic than suspected. They were also more soluble than suspected. Like Cosby and indeed the many other black celebrities emerging in the 1980s, she served as evidence, in her case of recovery. As she had recovered from a troubled past, so she encouraged others to do the same.

Can we diminish the impact of Oprah by invoking the kind of criticisms leveled at Cosby and any of the other black celebrities who emerged in the last two decades of the twentieth century? It seems mean-spirited when we consider that she built much of her reputation not by sashaying around Hollywood but in championing causes, challenging prejudices, and confronting many of the big problems faced by people – including black people. She never appeared to concern herself about becoming unpopular and somehow managed to stay tough and softhearted, cynical and maternal.

She was certainly an advertisement in that she measured up handsomely to the Huxtable criterion: from lowly beginnings – in her case a farm in Kosciusko, Mississippi, where she was raised by her grandmother – to become successful: spectacularly so. But, in the process, she refused to mirror racist or sexist stereotypes; instead, she took a hammer to them, challenging and subverting rather than conforming to expectations.

This makes David Krasner's complaint that she is a "cliché" unconvincing, though his other criticism that she "profits from the desires of her guests" has merit. Of course, all celebrities benefit from the wishes and fantasies of fans. That's why they're celebrities.

In reviewing Illouz's mostly appreciative book for the Fall 2004 edition of *African American Review*, Krasner argues that Winfrey's childhood abuses and battles with obesity were "recycled" publicly over and over to sustain the idea that celebrity status had not affected her ordinariness. There's something of a balancing act in being a celeb: convincing fans you are like them, while keeping the aura of being special. For all her supposed ordinariness, Oprah, in June 2005, led her entourage to the Hermès store on Paris's upscale rue du Faubourg Saint-Honoré after closing hours, presumably in expectation of special treatment (though she didn't get it and was refused admission).

When the first edition of Bogle's history of black people in film was published in 1973, black people were admitted into the mainstream entertainment industry on the condition that they conformed to one of the traditional stereotypes. "Permission," to use Nederveen Pieterse's phrase, had to be sought. Those who challenged were denied, while those who played the game enjoyed a modicum of success. The second edition was published in 1989, in the midst of significant changes that guaranteed that the third edition would need additional material on figures who played a different game. During the 1990s, the conditions of entry were radically revised, releasing actors such as Halle Berry, Eddie Murphy, and Wesley Snipes to take more demanding roles. They were joined by singers and musicians who strayed out of the soul and r&b genres that had been traditionally reserved for African Americans. In fact, the whole concept of black culture was conferred with new validity and respectability, as if it had been discovered, or rediscovered rather than simply put together for marketing purposes – a point we will return to shortly.

Recent history reveals a sharp turnaround in the fortunes of ethnic minorities in the late 1980s. As well as the showbusiness celebrities referred to so far, the rise of politicians like Colin Powell and Condoleezza Rice, of high-powered lawyers like Johnnie Cochran and Alton H. Maddox, and scholars like Henry Louis Gates and Cornel West signaled progress. But progress can sometimes be an illusion: a kind of antidote to despair. The despair in question would be at the failure of contemporary society to have purged itself of racism. It's a fallacy that racism continues unabated: studies since the 1960s have recorded a diminishing though still significant impact. The point is: every so often an incident explodes onto our tv screens to remind us that it is still there. So, how do ethnic minority celebrities figure in this? One in particular can serve as a case study.

: perfect dreamgirl

Let's eavesdrop on a lunch meeting that might have happened at a Hollywood Boulevard restaurant in 1996. "Whitney is history and Mariah is soon going to be. We need a new megastar," says a Sony Records exec. "Well, Britney Spears is coming along," his New Line Cinema producer friend responds. "We'll be able to find a vehicle for her soon." "Britney works with a white audience, though we really want someone who appeals to the widest ethnic spectrum," the music exec completes his thought. The film producer nods: "Rap is getting so big; imagine if we could find someone who has a street vibe but looks as if a nice white boy could take her home to meet his parents. I'm hearing that Fox is going to put that Latina – what's her name, Marquez or Lopez or something – from *Money Train* into a Jack Nicholson movie next. I hear she can sing a little too: Fox will try to make her into a big crossover artist."

Their colleague, who works at McCann Erickson advertising, chimes in: "That's my ideal demographic too – someone I can use to sell anything from moisturizer to military fatigues and to all ethnic groups." "And once she's big enough in music, I could cast her straight into starring roles without the trouble or cost of promoting her," adds the movie producer, recalling an eighties film. "Remember *Weird Science*, when the two guys computerize their perfect woman and she comes to life with great looks, does the housework, and cooks for them? Think we could get their software?" They didn't need to.

Like every great entertainment act, Destiny's Child reinvented a wheel. Not *the* wheel, but a new one that looked in all significant respects like any other, but was different in one detail: it was spinning now, as opposed to when TLC's and the Supremes' were turning. In 1997, Destiny's Child recorded their first major success with "Hot, Hot, Hot," a single that set their wheel rotating. Originally a duo comprising LaTavia Robertson and Beyoncé Knowles and managed by the latter's father, Matthew, Destiny's Child added Kelly Rowland, then, in 1993, LaToya Tuckett. Having signed with Columbia, the band followed up their initial success with more hit records from a second album. Robertson and Tuckett tried to drop Knowles as their manager amid rumors of favoritism and in 2000 left to form their own group Anjel. Two new members, Michelle Williams and Farrah Franklin, replaced the pair, before the release of the globally successful track "Survivor" in 2001. Later, Franklin left. As lead singer, Beyoncé occupied most attention. Make that *all* of the attention: her two colleagues became little more than backup singers, as Mary Wilson and Florence Ballard and, later, Cindy Birdsong, were for Diana Ross.

Cast as Foxxy Cleopatra in the 2002 film *Austin Powers in Goldmember*, Beyoncé cut a glamorous figure, with a fixed smile and coiffured Afro hairdo. Still, there was that touch of hardness and enough slur in her diction to remind fans of the adage "you can take someone out of the street, but you'll never take the street out of the person." With some celebrities, at some points in history, this has been a shortcoming. With Beyoncé in the early twenty-first century, it was a huge plus.

In 2003, Beyoncé, then aged 21, made a declaration of intent: she released her first solo album *Dangerously in Love*. It sold six million copies. The single "Crazy in love," featuring her boyfriend Jay-Z, was a global success. And so began her assault on the likes of Britney Spears and Christina Aguilera for the position of premier female singer. As with Cosby, her appearance in commercials benefited her as much, if not more than the products she advertised. Pepsi, renowned for splashing out big money but only on high-end endorsers, persuaded Beyoncé to join its esteemed stable of spokespersons, which included, over the years, Madonna, Michael Jackson, and David Beckham, as well as Spears and Pink.

The process of converting Beyoncé the woman into Beyoncé the brand continued with endorsement deals with McDonald's, Tommy Hilfiger and L'Oréal, the latter earning her $4.7 million over five years from 2004. A contract with the Tarrant Apparel Group produced the fashion range mentioned at the start of this chapter. It was called House of Dereon, named after Beyoncé's grandmother, Agnes Dereon. And, with an eye on the 5- to 13-year-olds (who make up a significant chunk of record buyers), Mattel, the children's toys maker, in 2005, unveiled a Beyoncé doll.

By the time of the re-formation of Destiny's Child in 2004 (they announced their breakup the following year), Beyoncé had completely eclipsed her colleagues to the point where she effectively *was* Destiny's Child. She'd already added a second movie in *The Fighting Temptations* and was working on two more, *The Pink Panther* and *Dreamgirls*. Short of running for President, there was no way to improve her commodity value. She sold, well, practically anything: cds, movie tickets, makeup, toys, clothes, and (it almost goes without saying) burgers. In a way Beyoncé offered a new variation on the old melting-pot idea. It was possible to separate out the ingredients – singer, movie star, endorser, designer – but, once stirred together and left to simmer, they all mixed to create a commodity that was, at once, intriguing and obvious. Beyoncé's ascent was not easily explained. She was, after all, an African American and, while there have been plenty of black singers who have transferred to the movies and enjoyed success in both media, none have deliberately turned themselves into advertisements. Not simply advertisements for the products Beyoncé was paid millions to endorse, but for the culture in which she demonstrably, palpably thrived. Yet the reason she was able to do this is obvious.

She, perhaps more than any other individual, convinced us that racism was outdated: her very existence was evidence of this. Any global celebrity is both unmistakably of his or her time and historical. Beyoncé was an innovation, but she also fitted comfortably into a tradition that stretched back to the 1920s, when Josephine Baker scandalized the American and European stage with her taboo-breaking theatrics. Artists such as Dorothy Dandridge, Lena Horne, and Eartha Kitt extended the tradition of the striking and talented black female entertainer. But these artists and Beyoncé's most obvious predecessor, Diana Ross, were around during times when either racial segregation was either legal or customary. Beyoncé appeared at a time when all vestiges of America's sorry past were supposed to have gone.

She also emerged amid a propagation of celebrities, any number of whom soared and sank so quickly they barely made an impact. Beyoncé had the kind of longevity that eluded many of her contemporaries, though a very notable exception was Jennifer Lopez who also hailed from an urban ethnic enclave – the Puerto Rican section of the Bronx, or "the block," as she described it in one of her tracks. Lopez's featured in Fox sitcoms before acquiring international visibility with parts in the movies *Blood and Wine* and *Selena*. She was then cross-promoted as a singer and from there the plot became predictable: a string of massively publicized, frequently ill-starred and usually momentary romances – some with rappers – that shaped her impact as a celebrity. Like Beyoncé, J.Lo was able to use her ethnicity to good advantage, a strategy that wouldn't have been possible before the 1990s. "I have a very American way of thinking," she told Rene Rodriguez for *Hispanic* magazine in 2002. "But I also feel very Puerto Rican . . . People ask me all the time how do I stay connected, and I always tell them 'How could I not?' It's who I am and it manifests itself in everything I do" (2002: 37).

: a different kind of white

If we view Beyoncé, Lopez and the many other celebrities from ethnic minority backgrounds as billion dollar advertisements disguised as human beings, we can understand how immaculately the race issue has been solved. "Solved" might not be the word, though neither alleviated or concealed quite does justice to the manner in ethnic minority celebs effected a resolution to the so-called "race problem."

Actually, there were two problems. The one was to how to exploit the newly affluent market of African American and Latino consumers; the other was how to tackle the more abiding issue of racial inequalities. Ethnic celebrities couldn't flatten the racial hierarchy. But they could undermine beliefs in its unshakeability. And, better still, they could distract. Talk of the endurance of racism and the injustice it reproduces seemed oddly out of tune with the new order of things.

Three celebrities, emerging over three decades and in different cultural and historical contexts. A spate of incendiary incidents in the 1980s offered a background to the newly affluent generation of professionals personified by Cosby. Bill Clinton's 1990s indexed the kind of liberal values that were perfect for an independently minded female who had no truck with the stifling old prejudices of previous eras. Beyoncé soared transcendingly into the celebrity firmament like a luminescent motif of the new millennium. They weren't anomalies plucked from obscurity, though neither were they representatives: at least, not of black people. They were, however, key players in a kind of game of chutes (or snakes) and ladders, in which the former had been obscured and the latter had been replaced with those glaze-paneled scenic elevators in which you can see the passengers. And, as they were all global phenomena, the upward moving passengers were visible to the world.

Maybe my argument appears too neat, too structured, and perhaps too thought-out. After all, the dining executives I visualized earlier didn't actually exist. No one actually dreamt up Beyoncé as a convenient simulacrum – someone who resembled, though actually wasn't, any other black person. In fact, critics might argue that her pale skin (which she was born with) and coppery blonde hair (which she probably wasn't) helped endear her to white consumers. So, even if Beyoncé was not contrived, she may as well have been.

There are many celebs who resisted being pressed into the pattern cut for Beyoncé. Take Missy Elliott. When her *Supa Dupa Fly* was released in 1997, hip-hop was just about to transfer to mainstream pop. Rap entrepreneurs such as Russell Simmons, Suge Knight, and Sean Combs had shown corporate America how much money there was in what was once thought to be a minority music. In 1994, Simmons had sold half of his Def Jam records to PolyGram for $33 million. Knight's Death Row Records could boast the world's best-selling rap artist in Tupac Shakur, who had been killed the previous year and whose death perversely raised awareness of the genre. Combs had just come to the end of a three-year $10 million deal with Arista and BMG (owned by the giant corporation Bertelsmann) and was poised to become not only the world's most instantly recognizable hip-hop practitioner, but a suitor of J.Lo.

Elliott's single "Get ur freak on" from her 2001 album *Miss E . . . So Addictive* has been acclaimed as a classic of its genre, even though its genre is indistinct, fusing rap with r&b, Bollywood samples, and a chorus. This sounded edgy at first, though it wasn't long before it could be heard on a zillion ringtones. Hailing from the ghetto herself, looking very unlike a supermodel and staying in a genre associated with black people helped Elliott retain the kind of credibility that eludes many black artists. But was she any less – or perhaps more – effective in advertising, if not the end of racism, at least an end in sight of racism?

While embracing US artists, Britain produced its own signifiers of "inclusion," which was its buzzword for all things culturally diverse and prejudice-free. Like Elliott, Ms Dynamite grew up in the inner city – in her case, of London – and held on to her credentials with lyrics that appealed for a cessation of bloodshed among black youths. Britain's version of gangsta culture drew opposition from another black celeb of the 2000s: Jamelia's words were made the more believable when one of her relations became embroiled in a gangland murder and her efforts to distance herself from it involved speaking out against violence.

Neither Ms Dynamite nor Jamelia discovered the formula that made earlier black British artists Seal and Sadé globally famous. Actor Adrian Lester, who seemed to submerge rather than elevate his blackness, and *Bend it like Beckham* star Parminder Nagra, who went on to play Dr Neela Rasgotra in *ER*, found their understated qualities more transferable and became internationally renowned. Perhaps the difference was that the singers were essentially facsimiles of established American acts disguised as originals. In a landscape teeming with living advertisements for the all-inclusive, culturally diverse society, the need for more of the same was limited.

"Industry research suggests that among White teens, who are considered the most desirable audience, crossover stars such as Jennifer Lopez, Lucy Liu and Halle Berry are not perceived so much as minorities but as 'a different kind of White person,'" wrote Wiley A. Hall (2002: A2). The comment invites comparisons with some ideas presented by David R. Roediger in his 2003 book *Colored White: Transcending the racial past*. Today we observe celebrities operating in a culture that has rendered whiteness plastic, melting, stretching, and shaping it in a way that accommodates new meanings. The ethnic minority celebrity may be seen in this light: as part of a new type of whiteness that makes the racial hierarchy invisible or at least opaque.

Disregard the improbability of ethnic minority plutocrats boasting of their street credentials and their associations with the ghetto. Even the most ingenuous consumer realizes that this is, as Gamson puts it, "the key to the celebrity industry's ability to sustain itself while revealing artificial manufacturing processes"

(1994: 195). We accept the reasons for this. Disregard also the unending catalog of commodities and merchandise endorsed, designed, or modeled by people who would never use let alone buy the products they promote. Again, consumers are in on the trick. But regard this: the most unlikely effect of newly whitened ethnic celebrities is that they have applied a salve to one of the West's persistent sores.

Celebrities comfort rather than challenge. That's what they're for. They may occasionally be charmless, egotistical, and sickening; but they are always persuasive. We listen, take note, act on, and remain receptive to them. The conspicuous success of a few celebs from ethnic minorities may not convince everyone that racism has disappeared or that the inequality we see all around is just a vestige, a remnant of a bygone age. But it sends out a question: why take one step down when you can make two up? Ethnic celebs have made those steps, or perhaps they were leaps of faith; after all, startlingly rapid progress through a system that's supposed to be weighted against you is liable to affect your perception of that system. Their cred still intact, they serve as proof of the possibilities available for those with enough talent, willpower and perseverance; and for those who want to see an insect where others see a monster.

THRIVING/ON SCANDAL

: not guilty, but condemned anyway

Imagine you are the managing editor of the *Vigilance*, a hypothetical regional newspaper in a medium-sized city. One afternoon, a colleague bursts into your office waving a dvd, which she tells you features Skye Roquette, a premier football player who is black, having sex. Roquette is known for his extravagant rock 'n' roll lifestyle and his all-night parties have frequently upset his neighbors in the affluent and exclusive part of town where he lives. He's the part-owner of an independent record label specializing in hip-hop music.

You ask your colleague from whom she obtained the disc but her source wishes to remain unknown at this stage. It's a known fact that Roquette recently had a big fire at his place and so many people, including fire-fighters, police officers, and insurance investigators must have had access to his private belongings.

You play the dvd and, sure enough, there is someone who looks a lot like Roquette, together with someone who is almost surely his wife Bombôn, a well-known photographic model, and an unidentified female who looks as if she's about 14. They are having sex.

"This is going to be uploaded onto the net in three days," she tells you. "Shall we run the story?"

You tell her she must get more facts before it becomes a legitimate story, so she sets about the task. Two days later, she has nothing to add. Roquette is out of the country and not contactable. Bombôn agrees to a conference call in the presence of her agent and divulges that she and her husband occasionally tape their sexual activities. But, beyond that, she refuses to comment. The dvd has still not appeared online.

"OK, what do we have?" you wonder out loud. "A recording of what seems to be a three-way sex situation. There's a guy who looks and sounds a lot like and might even be Roquette and someone else who is a dead ringer for Bombôn. And then there's this young girl; and she really does look like no more than a girl and could be under-age. We just don't have enough to run with this. I know you don't want to disclose your sources, but, off the record, where did you get this?" She prevaricates, then tells you: "A police officer."

You call a staff meeting. "Is there a backstory here?" enquires the newspaper's features editor. "I don't see this as a page one news story, but an investigative piece that asks how a cop came into possession of the dvd in the first place and why that officer has been unusually cooperative in giving it to us."

Your colleague reminds you that: "Roquette has a giant-sized rep. Remember that time he boasted that he spends more on a bottle of champagne than a police officer's take-home pay for a week? His record label has artists who rail against the police on their cds. And let's not forget he's black."

Another colleague chips in: "He and Bombôn have a pretty explosive relationship too. She's told some of the tabloids that he's slapped her about on more than one occasion. Perhaps she's trying to get back at him by releasing the disc."

"I don't think the dvd itself is the story," another colleague responds. "But the events surrounding it are. Think of the context in which everything afterwards has happened, like his status and the status of his wife and the well-documented tension between them. Would we be in possession of this disc if the principal subject was a white non-celebrity, or even a white celebrity athlete without the colorful reputation, or even a white celebrity athlete with the same kind of reputation?"

Time is against you. The recording could appear on the net at any time, or perhaps not at all. You might have the scoop of the year in your grasp, or you might fall prey to the hoax of the decade. What's your call?

While the newspaper is fictitious, the narrative is pastiche – made up from fragments of actual events rather than entirely invented. Whatever happens to Roquette and Bombôn, one thing is for sure: their fame will grow if either the paper publishes the story, or the recording goes online. Such is the nature of celebrity culture: whether the social response is one of condemnation or compassion, repugnance or approval, the subject or subjects typically loom large in the public imagination. Athlete-turned-actor O. J. Simpson was well-known in the USA but not far beyond before 1994, His generously covered murder trial ensured that his renown became global. Presumably fearing his presence in a film would mean the kiss of death, studio chiefs disregarded him and he was forced to auction his estate for less than $4 million in order to pay debts. (See also Bechtel *et al.* 1999.)

In contrast, Mike Tyson was able to resume his boxing career after three years' imprisonment for rape. For his first fight after his release in 1995, he earned $10 million and went on fighting for another ten years. His earnings capacity (ranging between $4 million to $17 million per fight) reflected public fascination with him, not in spite of but because of his infamy. Either boxing promoters are more inveterate risk-takers than film-producers or they are more used to offending sensibilities in their quest for material rewards. Probably the latter. Whatever the reason, there is at least inferential evidence that suggests Simpson could, given an opportunistic studio, have prolonged his film career if his trial had taken place ten years later. Simpson, in case readers forget, was found *not* guilty.

So was Roscoe "Fatty" Arbuckle, though again he was condemned anyway. One of the eminent silent-film stars of his day, Arbuckle was arrested in 1921 for the sexual assault and manslaughter of a female actor at a party in San Francisco. His films were withdrawn and Paramount cancelled his contract.

Even though he was acquitted at his third trial, the media had already ensured that a stigma was burned into him. Studios ignored him while creditors pursued him. He turned to drink and died destitute aged 46, in 1933. His fate served as an advisory notice to any popular entertainer. There was no uncertainty about the effect of scandal, especially sex-related scandal, on a showbusiness career. The famous violated or were seen to violate the law or social mores at their peril. After all, Arbuckle was cleared: his innocence mattered far less than the media's evaluation and subsequent treatment of him.

As the media's influence grew, so did their ability to shape, make, and break popular entertainers' careers. Even at a time when the Hollywood industry had a close and cozy relationship with the media, it was possible for someone to get swept to an untimely doom by a media wave. Mary Astor, who had played the duplicitous siren Brigit O'Shaughnessy in John Huston's 1941 version of *The Maltese Falcon*, was scandalized by three divorces, alcoholism, and an attempted suicide. She appeared in only five minor roles during the whole of the 1950s, underlining how important it was to maintain a wholesome image.

But today we credit a celebrity with inadvertent ingenuity for becoming involved in a moral indiscretion that manages to outrage and delight in such proportions that it creates rather than destroys their careers. Media indignation serves only to spur us into taking more notice. Take Paris Hilton's *succès de scandale*.

: guilty as sin, but so what?

The great granddaughter of hotel chain founder Conrad Hilton and heiress to a fortune, Paris claimed no talent apart from possible photogenicity: walk-on parts in minor movies seemed the limit of her dramatic prowess. Still, her party-going ventures and A-list connections kept her in the gossip columns and generated enough buzz for Fox to feature her in *The Simple Life*, a reality tv show shot on an Arkansas farm. Days before her début in 2003, *Us Weekly*, the celeb magazine, was shown excerpts from a video featuring Hilton having sex in an hotel room three years before. Marvad Corp., a porn company, planned to sell the full version over the net. The *New York Times* reported that an anonymous source was offering samples to media outlets. In spite of Hilton's parents' threat to sue anyone who helped make the tape public, excerpts appeared on the net and tabloids reported on it, often in explicit detail. Hilton became a cover story. Then the story migrated to other media. As Cynthia Cotts, of the *Village Voice*, wrote: "Serious new outlets were scrutinizing a celebrity who had done nothing to merit their attention . . . two points emerged: Why do we care, and how exactly has the tape hurt this girl's reputation?" (2003: 32).

The answer to the first question is implicit in Cotts's own article: because media of every variety afforded it coverage; this helped draw 13 million viewers to their screens for the first episode of *The Simple Life*. The second question is invalid because, far from damaging her reputation, it actually made it. Hilton went from a rich kid socialite to the "must-have" celebrity of the season. The Fox show was a hit, her memoirs were published as *Confessions of an Heiress* and film roles beckoned. Every reader of this book has probably heard of Paris Hilton, though how many can name her film roles? Between the 2003 scandal and 2006, she appeared in eight movies, including *House of Wax, Pledge This!* and *Bottom's Up*.

Notoriety is a resource for those who crave fame, whether as an entrée to a showbiz career, a route to martyrdom, or a means of securing the abhorrence of society. But it was studiously avoided up to the late 1980s and, even then, was sometimes a short cut to oblivion. For example, in 1989, the year in which Madonna's *Like a Prayer* was released, Rob Lowe, then 25, underwent a transformation. Having established his credentials in films like *About Last Night* and *St Elmo's Fire*, Lowe became a reluctant star of a porn video. In an episode comparable to Paris Hilton's, Lowe had engaged in hotel room sex in front of a videocam. Bootleg duplicates of the video began circulating; if the net had been up-and-running then, it would surely have gone online. The allegations of exploitation and extortion and the settlement that followed were incidental to the main action: the media had been animated by the scandal of a young star – a princely one – and video'd sex.

The media lined up to kick the corpse of Lowe's once-promising career. Today, critics might even have dismissed it as a vulgar and transparently obvious publicity stunt. Lowe's next film was *Bad Influence*, in which he played a manipulative Beelzebub-like character who films his impressionable friend's sexual encounters. But the movie, though opportune, did poor box office and Lowe found himself yanked off the front covers of magazines, such as *Teen*, which immediately spared its four million readers' blushes by spiking a feature on him.

One of the more honest pronouncements came from Jeanne Wolf of *Entertainment Tonight* who seemed less concerned about the act itself and more about the self-inflicted career harm it occasioned: "The [Hollywood] community looks down on Rob's bad judgment for doing something that would put his career in jeopardy" (quoted in *USA Today*, June 26, 1989: 1D).

Viewers of *The West Wing* will know what happened next. The penitent Lowe donned the sackcloth and traipsed forth into the celebrity wilderness, cropping up in unlikely places, like *Wayne's World* in 1992, and in *Mulholland Falls* in 1996 (an uncredited role). His appearance at the White House, albeit television's version, was providential. By the time the multi-Emmy-winning and globally watched tv series premiered in 1999, Lowe's misdemeanors seemed not exactly harmless, but nowhere as shocking as they looked ten years before. So when Hilton's contribution to the video sex genre came into view, there was prurient interest, displeasure with its poor taste, but no wide-spread condemnation.

When Lowe was given his own tv show *The Lyon's Den* in 2003, the moral censure that had followed his sex tapes had long since abated. In the interim, Madonna, who had been breaking sexual taboos as a career-advancing tactic since the late 1980s, had helped redraw the lines of decency. Sexual mores too had changed in a way that not only permitted the famous to be riskier, edgier, and altogether more venturesome, but often rewarded them for doing so.

Hugh Grant, for example, was fined and put on two year's probation after pleading no contest to charges of lewd behavior with prostitute Divine Brown on Hollywood's Sunset Strip in 1995. Over the next ten years, Grant made fifteen films, including blockbusters like *Bridget Jones's Diary*, *About a Boy* and *Love Actually*. His notoriety, though short-lived, enabled him to exchange his image as an ersatz Cary Grant and suitor of Estée Lauder's golden girl for that of a rakish libertine. Like a rebranding exercise, an indiscretion that might have ended a career in earlier times offered the chance to adjust the public image and renew fortunes.

Occasionally, there was a kind of defiance, as in the case of r&b artist R. Kelly. Again, sex tapes were the source of a scandal, though Kelly's alleged appearance with an under-age female complicated the affair. After a series of lawsuits and dropped charges, Kelly faced fourteen counts of child pornography. Kelly kept producing cds, including a series of five singles linked by a narrative about Kelly's waking up with a woman and having to hide from her husband, who then discovers them and later reveals himself as a pastor who is also having a relationship, in his case with a man! The whole suite was called "Trapped in the closet." More self-consciously and resourcefully than any other celeb, Kelly exploited his sexual imbroglio by creating his own opus.

George Michael also turned a potentially embarrassing and maybe ruinous incident into an opportunity following his arrest for lewd behavior in a public lavatory in 1998. Fined and ordered to do community service, Michael was virtually forced into coming out and declaring that he was gay. The video accompanying his next single following the arrest, "Outside," featured kitsch s&m scenes with characters dressed in burlesque police uniforms. As if this didn't generate enough publicity for the single, the arresting officer later tried to sue Michael for causing him humiliation and emotional distress by "mocking" him in the video. (In 2005, Michael suggested he was retiring from being famous because "the business of media and celebrity" was "unbearable." At the time he was worth £65 million, or $110.5m, according to the *Sunday Times* "Rich list.")

Compare the experience of Shakespearean actor John Gielgud, who was arrested in 1953 for a similar offence in a public convenience in London, to which he pled guilty and was fined. At that point in his career, he was predominantly a stage actor, though he'd just finished making *Julius Caesar*. He had appeared in only the occasional film, such as *The Prime Minister* in 1941 (he would later appear in Laurence Olivier's acclaimed 1955 *Richard III*). One wonders, had Gielgud been part of the protective Hollywood system, whether his dalliance would have ever been publicly known. Only later did Gielgud embrace Hollywood: he won an Oscar for his supporting role in *Arthur* in 1981.

His fellow thespian Alec Guinness improvised with own evasive technique when he was caught soliciting for sex in a public toilet in 1948: he gave the name Herbert Pocket, the Dickens character he had recently played in David Lean's *Great Expectations*. It's doubtful whether such a ruse would have worked in the 1970s, by which time Guinness was featuring in Hollywood films. How many police officers would believe a suspect named Ben Obi-Wan Kenobi? (Britain didn't decriminalize homosexual acts between consenting adults until 1967; the USA began repealing its sodomy laws in 1971.)

"The rules are changing because of a whole new cultural climate created by the media," according to Maer Roshan, an editor at *New York* magazine, who suggests that the protections once afforded celebrities have vanished: "As with everything else, their sexuality is now on the table" (quoted in Kirby 2001: 56).

But is it? Even in the twenty-first century, celebs remain reticent about their sexuality, perhaps fearing they might douse consumers' ravishment desires should they reveal their true inclinations. If so, it's an irrational fear. All may not have been what it seemed when Michael's case became known, but it did no lasting harm to his reputation. Despite the number of celebrities who have declared that they are gay without detrimental consequences, seemingly invulnerable celebs such as Tom Cruise and Robbie Williams have sued those who have alleged they are gay and, in so doing, effectively validated a long-standing stigma. Ironically, Williams enjoyed a large gay following and told the *Advocate* interviewer Larry Flick: "If I meet a man I fancy enough to have sex with, I will" (2003).

If Roshan is referring to the media's longing to disclose sexual preference, he is right. But celebs themselves show no enthusiasm for tabling their predilections unless they have a reason for doing so, or no alternative. And yet, as John Morgan Wilson observes: "In recent years a number of closeted stars have uttered 'no comment' to questions about their private lives, without any visible damage to their lucrative careers" (2006). Admissions, whether coded like this ("When was the last time a straight person told you 'It's none of your business'?" psychoanalyst Cindy Kasovitz-Sichel is quoted by Kirby 2001) or stated flatly are less terminal than they used to be.

Roughly the same kinds of misdemeanors or suspected misdemeanors that once brought an abrupt halt to careers can now be occasions for rejuvenation. For today's celebs, the most terrible, vile, awful experience, and the experience they strive continuously to avoid is being overlooked. Once the media fail to notice a celeb's presence, their status as a celeb disintegrates. A scandal, by definition, fires up interest. There is no chance of being disregarded. The media attention may be for the wrong reasons; but there again, the precise reasons are of secondary importance. Of primary importance is the attention.

Then what happens when a celebrity has all the attention he needs and has had it for 35 years? When the media has praised, glorified, and honored him as the king of his genre? When his precocious genius has been acknowledged as both genuine and unique? When his often-puzzling idiosyncrasies have been pored over, examined, analyzed, and evaluated time and again? And when what was once the whiff of wrongdoing becomes a pungent odor?

: walking free?

If Michael Jackson's life was a movie scripted by publicists, this is how the plot might unfold: the world's premier male pop star of the late twentieth century reclines on his laurels and his personal fortune in the privacy of his own Neverland ranch in California. His albums no longer sell in their dozens of millions, but, combined with his back catalog, royalties provide him with a prolific income. His personal life meanwhile continues to be a kind of self-replenishing fountain of whispered secrets, hearsay, and innuendo. Despite two marriages, stories of his companionship with young boys circulate. People remember how, in 1994, Jackson agreed to pay Jordy Chandler, then 14, an undisclosed sum, thought to be over $25 million, to stop a sex abuse lawsuit ever reaching court. Jackson was never put under oath for a civil deposition that could be used in a criminal trial.

For reasons known only to himself, Jackson agrees to an interview, which is aired on February 6, 2003 on ABC's *20/20*. Jackson discusses sharing his bed with children. After the telecast, Jackson moans that his interviewer, Britain's Martin Bashir, has betrayed him and files complaints with British media watchdog groups. Then, he helps produce a rebuttal entitled *The Michael Jackson Interview: The footage you were never meant to see*, which is shown on Fox two weeks later. Meanwhile, over the course of the year, rumors have it that Jackson has money troubles, compounded by the multiple lawsuits filed against him. Several suits remained unresolved. Jackson's former financial adviser sues him for $12 million in unpaid fees and services; he countersues and the matter is settled out of court for an undisclosed sum.

A German concert promoter sues him for dropping out of concerts and is awarded $5.3 million; both sides appeal. A design firm claims that Jackson didn't pay for $78,000 of work on a proposed theme park, Neverland Estates: the case is settled on undisclosed terms. But worse is to come: in November, Jackson is arrested for allegedly molesting a 12-year-old boy, who was, at the time, undergoing treatment for lymphoma. Jackson contracts an illness that attorney Brian Oxman calls a "reaction to lawsuits."

In June 2005, after a trial that dominates headlines for four months, Jackson is cleared of the charges and walks from court a free man. Within a month, his record company Sony/BMG – presumably subscribing to the R. Kelly/G. Michael scandal → sales theory of causation – release *The Essential Michael Jackson* compilation double cd.

If this had been a script, and if Jackson were not a mortal human but a dramatic construct whose publicists are forever trying to dream up ways of maintaining his position as one of the most famous people on the planet, it's unlikely that any focus group asked to read over the script and adjudicate on whether it should go into production would think it tenable enough.

The Jackson trial of 2005 was the first *cause célèbre* of the twenty-first century. Who better to star in this wonderfully over-the-top piece of melodrama than a man who had matured from child virtuoso to the world's greatest pop singer and then became an inscrutable, color-changing recluse?

Child stars rarely develop in a straightforward manner. Drew Barrymore was in dope and alcohol rehab by the time she was 13, slipped into obscurity, then re-emerged as one of *Charlie's Angels* in 2000. *Home Alone* star Macaulay Culkin was commanding $2 million per movie in the early 1990s, but fell out of favor, argued with his parents, and dropped out of showbusiness completely before he was 20. Jackson, by contrast, appeared to go through untroubled rites of passage. By 1975, he had been performing and recording for four years with his brothers, collectively known as the Jackson 5. Still only 17, he moved from the Motown label to CBS. Motown, the now-legendary business created by Berry Gordy, had enjoyed success since the mid-1960s and could boast the likes of Stevie Wonder, the Supremes, and Smokey Robinson and the Miracles. While Jackson had begun a solo career at Motown, his father and manager Joe sensed better prospects with a big corporation. Reborn as the Jacksons, the band continued to make successful records, though it became little more than a showcase for the young brother. He emphasized his independence by appearing in the Motown-backed movie, *The Wiz*, in which Diana Ross starred.

Few, if any, black artists have conquered all segments of the market as accomplishedly as Jackson. His *Off the Wall* album of 1979 was produced by Quincy Jones and was, as Barney Hoskyns calls it in his *Waiting for the Sun: The story of the Los Angeles music scene*: "a triumph of studio-crafted miscegenation . . . the first real mass-audience black/white album" (1996: 301).

Sales exceeded six million and spawned four hit singles, establishing Jackson as a genuine solo artist. The album cover was revealing, featuring Jackson in white tuxedo as a black sophisticate. His face in particular was revealing if compared to images of him at his trial in 2005. Shortly after the release of the album, Jackson had two rhinoplasties following an accident in which he broke his nose. The result was a narrower job in which the nostrils took on a pinched appearance. He also abandoned his Afro hairdo for a then-popular Jeri-perm and, later for a chemically straightened look. His facial skin began to blanch; some suggested this was due to a condition known as vitiligo, while others supposed it was induced.

In Chapter 3, we examined the crucial role of MTV in the development of celebrity culture. Even by 1983, within two years of its start-up, it had assumed the power to make or break acts. Typically, a record company would send MTV a video for the tv channel's consideration. Acceptance onto the playlist virtually guaranteed high sales. Duran Duran benefited greatly from liberal airplay on MTV and, as we noticed earlier, Madonna had the clairvoyance to make videos that were controversial but usually not too shocking for MTV's target demographic – that is, young, white, and with disposable income.

When MTV rejected Jackson's "Billie Jean," CBS was furious enough to threaten a boycott of all its artists. MTV relented and included the video on its playlist. No one will ever know how far MTV's change of heart affected sales, but the album from which "Billie Jean" was taken went on to sell 57 million copies. Was MTV's initial refusal motivated by racism? Very few black acts had appeared in its first two years of operation and the occasional exception, like Herbie Hancock, was squeezed into a box in the corner of the screen when his "Rocket" played. Remember the point made in Chapter 7: advertisers were only just waking up to the idea that ethnic minorities, the largest group of which was African American, constituted an exploitable market segment in the early 1980s. MTV was funded by advertising revenue. Maybe showing a black artist seemed too risky at the time.

Whatever the reasons for MTV's change of heart, the effects were undeniable. The music channel discovered that, far from prompting viewers to hit the remote control button, Jackson glued them to their screens. The promotion offered by MTV airplay pushed sales of the single and album upwards and paved the way for another video that had historic importance. *Thriller* had a kind of epic quality: longer and costlier ($600,000) than the usual videos of the time, it had a narrative-within-a-narrative and was packed with special fx; it was granted a special tv première in December 1983. The video helped turn the *Thriller* album into the highest seller ever and Jackson into arguably the leading male artist in the world.

Jackson's career then veered toward a new domain. He began to assume a mysterious, almost occult, air; his stage presence was interesting, but the really interesting aspects of him were the ones outsiders couldn't see. As the media's glare became more incessant, Jackson seemed to recoil, hiding away and becoming protective about his private life. Nothing whets the media's appetite more than a secluded celebrity who either doesn't want or pretends not to want their attention.

The interminable stories of Jackson's odd behavior began just after *Thriller*'s release. He insisted on including a disclaimer on the video release following protests from Jehovah's Witnesses. Most artists would probably have laughed off the complaints. Then his accident when filming a Pepsi tv commercial started a world media circus. Pepsi paid him a reported $700,000 to endorse its product. Rumors of his weird fascination with the skeleton of Joseph Merrick, the "Elephant Man," and his habit of sleeping in an oxygen tent began to circulate. Every public appearance became an opportunity to inspect the results of his latest cosmetic surgery. And whatever the skin condition was, it continued to whiten his complexion. So much so that it persuaded Don King, who promoted one of his tours, to conclude: "It doesn't matter how great he can sing and dance . . . He's one of the megastars in the world, but he's still going to be a nigger megastar" (quoted in Taraborrelli 1991: 377).

Jackson's transmogrification did nothing to hurt his record-selling power. *Bad*, his follow-up to *Thriller*, was a comparative failure, moving only 20 million units! The tour to promote it in 1987 was watched by a total of 4.5 million people. The video of his single "Black or white" was simultaneously shown to an estimated 100 million tv viewers in 27 countries in 1991. The six-album deal he signed with Sony, which took over CBS Records, was worth up to one billion dollars and included a royalty rate of twice the industry standard. King was perhaps too reserved when he described him as *"one of* the megastars in the world."

Of all the questions asked of Jackson – and there were many, many – the one asked too often was: "Why does he like the company of young boys?" The settlement with Jordy Chandler in 1994 to stop a sexual abuse lawsuit reaching court was but one of several episodes that had ended unhappily. Children and young men were often invited to Jackson's Neverland ranch in California for "sleepovers." Disclosures were still making the news in 1995, a year after the settlement, by which time Jackson had made a double album *HIStory Past, Present and Future, Book 1* containing two tracks that seemed to challenge his critics. Jackson later apologized for "They don't care about us," which had lines that might have been construed as anti-Semitic; Chandler's father and attorney were both Jewish.

Jackson had cut an unusual but unthreatening image. In this sense he was like the countless other black male entertainers who had been admitted to mainstream entertainment. His fads and foibles were freaky yet somehow suited to the times. His quirkiness endeared him to millions. Still, there were telltale signs that he might not be so safe after all. Some of Jackson's behavior seemed like damage limitation. A surprise marriage to Lisa-Marie Presley, daughter of Elvis and devotee of Scientology (the marriage was succeeded by a second, this time to a nurse who worked for one of his cosmetic surgeons). An interview, accompanied by his wife, with Diane Sawyer on network news. A "chat" with his fans via the internet, believed to be the first time a celebrity had turned to the information superhighway to communicate with followers. A whopping $60 million marketing campaign for *HIStory*. It was as if Jackson was trying to appear like an "ordinary" pop star. Certainly sales of the double album were ordinary: less than a million in the US market.

By the mid-1990s, fascination with Jackson had started to evaporate, leaving him to watch his sister Janet score a series of commercial successes with *Rhythm Nation 1814*, which was the world's top-selling album of 1990 with six million, and *Janet*. (When her own status began to falter, she "accidentally" exposed a breast while singing at the Super Bowl halftime show in 2004 and garnered media reportage around the world.)

A new generation of self-aware youth of all class and ethnic backgrounds sought expression in the swearing, sexuality, and criminal glamour of rap. By the start of the twenty-first century, Jackson seemed a forlorn character, a once-great sovereign, now deposed and idling his time away in the privacy of his personal fiefdom. Maybe agreeing to do the *20/20* interview was designed to enliven public interest in him. If so, it worked like a charm.

Diana Ross Presents the Jackson 5 was released in December 1969. JACKSON WALKS FREE was the front-page headline of innumerable newspapers on June 14, 2005. Do the dates define the beginning and end of an epoch? Jackson's longevity as a worldclass celeb was due to his mutability: he changed from a child prodigy to the pop monarch who ruled the MTV age before becoming an engaging eccentric and then a man-child with an unwholesome interest in boys. Maybe news of his acquittal didn't define the epoch's end so much as the start of another transition. Jackson could reach his fiftieth birthday (on September 29, 2008) a broken man, his finances in a mess and his career finished. But celebrity culture, as we've seen, nurtures success from scandal.

: winds of change

Reactions to scandal, especially sex scandal, form four main categories: condemnation; indifference; resentment; and approval. Whichever of these dominates depends more on the context than the outcome. As we've seen, for most of the twentieth century prior to the arrival of what we regard as celebrity culture, unsparing efforts were made to suppress news of Hollywood transgressions. The fear – and a well-founded fear – was that they would be damaging. Widespread condemnation, disapproval, and censure could ruin careers. Elizabeth Taylor's indiscretion, as we saw in Chapter 2, was arguably the most publicized and, therefore, "biggest" scandal to date.

Swirling forces of conflict were gathering in the early 1960s: civil rights protests, the decolonization of Africa, and the rebellious rhythms of rock music added to the growing sense of emancipation. It was as if entire nations were involved in collective rule-breaking. Despite the furor in conservative Catholic Italy, Taylor's deviance hardly qualified for moral turpitude elsewhere. In a way, it seemed in accord with the times. Swinging-age liberation had arrived and, while some might have found her action imprudent, others would have admired and perhaps longed for her ability to disobey convention.

The dawn of the celebrity age in the late 1980s opened new vistas for both media and the aspirant celebrities. As we saw in Chapter 3, Madonna refined rule-breaking into a method of career advancement. While the 1989 film *sex, lies and videotape* wasn't actually about video'd sex (the videotapes feature women *talking* about their sexual experiences) the title's linkage was tantalizing. So, Rob Lowe's vcr exploits in the year of the film's release occasioned questions about whether it was such an awful wrongdoing and would it finish his career? The fact that Lowe emerged – eventually – unscathed and, 16 years later, was commanding a leading role in London's West End indicates that he had been swept safely by the winds of change.

The first big scandal of the 1990s involved William Kennedy Smith, the nephew of Senator Edward Kennedy and member of the illustrious extended family. He was acquitted of rape, the thrust of a successful defense being that his accuser wasn't credible, having had abortions and been abused as a child. There was also the matter of the skimpy black underwear she favored; this was interpreted by the defense to signify intention. Kennedy Smith was white and of what might be called "good stock."

Mike Tyson was black, a product of a dysfunctional family in the Brownsville slum district of New York. He wasn't the first black athlete to have made the headlines for off-field offenses. Darryl Strawberry rarely seemed out of trouble in the early 1990s. Nor the last: Jamal Lewis was sentenced to four months following a drugs case.

Again, context was all-important. In a sense, Tyson's guilt or innocence of the myriad violations of which he was accused at some point or other was less relevant than times, places, and personnel. America in the 1990s was a time when celebrity subsumed culpability. And yet his case, like those of Simpson and later Jackson, dramatized the relative values of celebrity.

In their study "Famous or infamous? The influence of celebrity status and race on perceptions of responsibility for rape," Jennifer Knight and her co-researchers discovered that "being a celebrity had distinct advantages for white defendants, whereas for Black defendants, being a celebrity was a liability" (2001: 183).

While they were concerned mainly with rape cases, the psychologists broadened their conclusions to include other types of cases in which sex has been involved. "Social attractiveness" describes a quality attributed to celebrities, particularly by jurors who adjudge sex violations as "out of character" for high-status defendants. In other words, celebrities can often receive a lenient verdict simply because of the esteem they enjoy.

But not all celebrities. According to Knight *et al.*: "Aversive racism theory proposes that although most people today are not openly racist, a subtle form of prejudice emerges when people feel safe to express themselves" (2001: 184). This kind of racism thrives in the courtroom, leading to the study's conclusion: "Black celebrities were perceived more negatively than were Black noncelebrities, whereas White celebrities were viewed more positively than were White noncelebrities" (2001: 187).

This is plausible, especially when set against the cases of Charlie Sheen, Winona Ryder, Christian Slater, Martha Stewart, Robert Downey Jr, and the previously mentioned Kennedy Smith and Lowe. It could be argued that where sex is absent from the offense – Ryder was caught shoplifting, for example – forgiveness is easier to come by. Supporters of Tyson, who included Jesse Jackson, Al Sharpton, Spike Lee, and Don King, speculated how his trial might have gone differently had a prominent white athlete been in the dock.

The picture is further complicated by polls collected during both the Simpson and Tyson trials. The majority of African Americans believed Simpson and Tyson to be innocent, while a majority of whites thought they were guilty. In their *Contemporary Controversies and the American Divide*, Robert Smith and Richard Seltzer explain the differences in terms of distinct historical and social experiences and the disparity in economic circumstances between blacks and whites. And, to confuse matters even more, we should remind ourselves that "negative perceptions" don't necessarily impair a celebrity career. Tyson continued to sell out arenas and move pay per view buys for ten years after his release. Sales of Michael Jackson cds spiked for the first time in years after his acquittal.

Throughout this book, I've argued that, while the media's influence is great, it's far from total. We, the consumers aren't like children who can be persuaded into believing in magic by a few conjurors' tricks. At the height of the Simpson trial, Lexis/Nexis, the online news service, asked the question: "Which sports figure is the undisputed champ in generating the most negative media coverage for off-the-field incidents?" After surveying print and broadcast media, the research showed that, up to August 1994, the media had reported 9,906 stories about Tyson, comfortably more than the widely disparaged Simpson (6,754) and Ben Johnson (6,688), whose use of steroids in 1988 earned him universal opprobrium (*Business Wire*, August 29, 1994). Yet, we remained absorbed in Tyson. Had comparable research been done during early 2005 with all celebrities included, would Jackson have headed the list? And, if so, would it have made much difference to his status?

The findings so far appear as fragmentary and possibly contradictory. Scandals that once killed careers now boost them: unless the celebrity is black, in which case their status doesn't enhance perceptions of them in the same way as it does for whites. That is, until the asymmetry between blacks and whites is taken into consideration: then scandalized black celebrities are perceived more positively by black people, while whites see them in a negative light. But, even then, black celebrities often have a kind of post-scandal renascence, suggesting that actual popularity isn't a necessary prerequisite for celebrity. Interest in them is. Two final cases will help us see the arterial connections between these points and enable us to understand why and how some celebs have risen while others have fallen in the aftermath of scandals.

: unable to see straight

Celebrity culture is prismatic: it enables us to see something but its refractive surfaces ensure that what we see depends on the angle from which we look. One of the least surprising survey results was that of a *CNN/USA Today*/Gallup poll conducted in July and August 2003. About 63 percent of black people felt sympathetic to Kobe Bryant, at that time facing charges of sexual assault, compared to 10 percent of whites. The consistency with similar polls taken at the time of the Simpson and Tyson cases is striking yet predictable. Whereas 68 percent of blacks believed the charges against Bryant were false, only 11 percent of whites saw it that way.

Bryant, the Los Angeles Lakers' guard, was found not guilty of sexual assault. He had been accused by a white woman of raping her when she was 19 and, if convicted, faced four years to life in prison. His widely reported reply was: "I didn't force her to do anything against her will." The case against him collapsed in 2004 when she refused to testify against him the day before the criminal case was due to start. Bryant later settled a civil lawsuit with the woman, though the terms were never disclosed.

Bryant was, in many ways, the antithesis of the stereotype black sportsman. Raised in Italy and in the suburbs of Philadelphia, he progressed through basketball without any of the histrionics that typically accompany a black athlete's ascent. No fights, drugs, wild parties, or any of the usual revelry associated with topflight athletes. If anyone could take over the mantle of Michael Jordan, it was Bryant. His clean-cut image made him a favorite with advertisers: he had contracts with adidas, McDonald's and Sprite. But the accusation left grubby fingerprints and, while Bryant continued to play for the Lakers, his image was soiled. His Sprite ads were pulled by Coca-Cola and McDonald's announced that it would not be renewing its contract with Bryant. As with Arbuckle and Simpson, being cleared of all charges proved of less significance than the initial smear.

While Bryant's destiny unspooled, a remorseful Martha Stewart was serving twelve months behind bars. British readers may not be familiar with Stewart; so think of Delia Smith crossed with Dame Judi Dench, but with the kind affection typically reserved for Mother Theresa. Then imagine what might happen if such a figure were found guilty of illegal dealing in stocks and shares. By the time she left prison (complete with electronic tag) in her private jet in March 2005, her company's share price had trebled, taking her personal stake's value to $1 billion (£575m). Two tv shows awaited her, including *The Apprentice*, for which she was paid $100,000 per episode. Her prison memoirs were likely to earn her another $5 million. And she continued to draw her $900,000 per year salary. The then 63-year-old convicted felon emerged considerably richer and more fascinating than when she went into prison.

NBC Universal's ceo Robert Wright, when explaining his decision to sign her to *The Apprentice*, likened Stewart's rise, fall, and redemption to a drama: "Americans are waiting for the next act. They want to see a happy ending" (quoted in the *Independent on Sunday*: BusinessWeek, February 27, 2005, p. 8). There may be some truth to this, but there wasn't too much curiosity about how Simpson fared and, while Bryant continued to play basketball, he lost much of his celebrity luster. Of course, Stewart's sin was monetary, rather than sexual or homicidal. But she was, after all, found guilty, prompting the thought that her whiteness and perhaps her gender had some bearing on the response to her.

Kate Moss, who lost a big chunk of her modeling portfolio after a cocaine scandal in September 2005, played out a similar parable. By December, she had been in rehab and returned with an estimated £12 million ($20 million) of work lined up. Longchamps, Roberto Cavalli, and Calvin Klein seemed unembarrassed about being associated with her.

Recall the injunction of our fictional journalist at the start of this chapter: "Think of the context." The circumstances surrounding an event, the conditions under which it happens, and the situations that precede and follow it fix its meaning. As we've seen, scandals that once damned the famous have become opportunities for replenishing a celebrity career. Our relationship with celebrities becomes judgmental only when certain criteria are met. The most important of these is that the victim or casualty or party injured by a violation of some sort must be valid. Another is that the wrongdoing is indisputable. The wrongdoing in this sense is not necessarily the offense for which the suspect is charged, but rather the less visible though no less real transgression as interpreted by a wide constituency of consumers.

Who was Stewart's victim? Of course, there were victims: thousands of stockholders whose fortunes were adversely affected by her trading activities. But, the stock exchange is an anonymous abstraction without a human face. Who got hurt by Lowe's misadventures, or Hilton's injudicious conduct? Was Saks Fifth Avenue in Beverly Hills going to miss the few thousand dollars' worth of merchandise lifted by Ryder in 2001? Where there is no tangible victim, the offense becomes an embarrassment rather than a catastrophe. Forgiveness isn't even needed.

In any scandal, consumers focus on the actual offense itself. Simpson was cleared, so was Bryant. They both negotiated civil suits, though these were, in a way, postscripts to the main narratives. The widespread assumption following the Simpson verdict was that he remained "guilty" in the eyes of many and was condemned accordingly. Many didn't share the reasonable doubt discerned by the jury. The question is: was the murder of his wife and her friend in 1994 Simpson's real offense? Nicole Simpson was a white woman. As was the woman who had sex with Bryant.

Earlier, I offered the metaphor of celebrity culture as a prism through which we look at the world, the angle from which we look affecting the image we see. Race works as another refracting lens, according to Alton H. Maddox. "Whites are naturally unable to see straight about Black male/white female sex," he wrote in the *New York Amsterdam News*. "Black wealth has no chance against white power" (2003: 12).

Maddox likened Bryant's predicament to those of Emmett Till and the Scottsborough Boys, who were punished for their purported behavior toward white women (2003). Maddox might have added Dick "Diamond" Rowland whose alleged misconduct started a riot in Tulsa in 1921. It was a challenging argument and it implied that, even today, a taboo hangs over relationships between black men and white women. The days when black men were lynched, as Till was, because of a casual remark to a white woman, have passed. Yet there is still discomfort occasioned by the notion of a black man getting together with a white woman.

One hundred and ninety-nine years after Emancipation and 40 years after civil rights, Bryant was cleared of rape, but remained culpable of one of the most culturally sensitive and perhaps unpardonable improprieties. Tyson became a wretched totem of a people linked unendingly to a natural primitivism. Would he have so easily absolved and applauded in his futile pursuit of redemption had he raped a white woman instead of Desiree Washington, the black beauty pageant contestant? We can only surmise, though, on Maddox's account, it is unlikely. The aversive racism found by Knight *et al.* and the negative perceptions it encourages adds weight to this.

So, to Jackson. A black male whose alarmingly variable appearance gave many the impression he was trying to divest himself of his blackness, Jackson was Wacko Jacko to detractors and the King of Pop to admirers. He married white women and, in the absence of evidence to the contrary, consummated his relationships. It could be argued that the taint of an unhealthy interest in children is colorfast – no amount of washing would remove it. But Jackson simply doesn't fit into any coherent pattern. Of course, he was an African American, but was he perceived as black? Perhaps not in the same way as the other black male celebrities we have discussed in this chapter. He was what Nederveen Pieterse would call a symbolic eunuch: someone who is valuable though not threatening. The penchant for children, harmless or not, functioned as proof of this. Married to a white woman, he seemed more joyful in the company of children. This, I stress, was a *perception*; but perceptions are part of the context.

From the time of his appearance as an artist, Jackson has magicked innocence from what might otherwise be seen as certifiable weirdness. He could do this because of his disinclination or perhaps inability to fit into established categories. Instead, he appeared at the thresholds between several, a borderline or liminal figure. He was a black person with white skin, an adult with childlike characteristics, a man with feminine mannerisms. His near-treble voice and naive giggling helped make it possible to believe a reclusive millionaire's inviting children into his personal wonderland was not as unwholesome as it might be had anyone else been the millionaire.

Like other celebrities that have resurfaced after being submerged by the media deluge that accompanies a scandal, Jackson found his fans attentive, many of them still worshipful. What might at another time been a nightmare denouement was, in fact, a happy ending.

It is the anomalous nature of Jackson's scandal that alerts us to how the very categories he avoided dictate the kind of fall-out from all other celebrity scandals. Even in an age when dishonor and outrage bring their own rewards, a black male can expect indignity at best and oblivion at worst if the "offense" – as popularly perceived – involves a white female as "victim." We doom innocent parties to cultural bankruptcy, leaving them stripped of their most basic asset – interest – while granting malefactors with new leases on their celebrity lives.

BUYING/SALES

: the product, or the people promoting it?

The advertising industry pays little attention to the laws of time and motion. The evidence of our senses tells us that, as we get older, so our bodies start to wither: skin gets wrinklier, waists get fatter, and hair gets thinner. Ads are always surprising us with news about how we can resist nature with anti-aging cream or age-defying moisturizer. To convince us that the products work, they adorn advertisements with images of the likes of Halle Berry or Elizabeth Hurley. It might strain logic and credibility to suggest that, by using a particular product, the consumer can look like this pair, or any of the other beauties that endorse cosmetics. But their decorative visages are there to set up a connection: to start potential consumers linking exquisite images with a commodity.

Lauren Bacall may have stopped traffic with her looks during the 1940s, but she didn't get endorsement offers as an 80-year-old. Advertisers are more likely to opt for women who represent what consumers want to look like rather than those whom they most resemble. Celebrities, being instantly recognizable, are well suited to advertising. As we saw in Chapter 6, people are often prepared to go to great lengths to emulate celebrities. Buying products seems modest compared to undergoing surgery. This is why advertisers are happy to pay celebrities to be their shill: someone employed to entice others. But not all advertisers.

In 2004, Ogilvy & Mather got together with Dove's marketing team and came up with the idea for "The campaign for real beauty." Spurning the trend for featuring gorgeous, waiflike celebrities or even lesser-known models for the ad campaign, Dove used women who looked "ordinary": some had freckles, some were middle-aged, most had bodies that were more Roseanne Barr than Elle Macpherson.

"I personally think it is risky," said Richard Kirshenbaum, of the ad agency Kirshenbaum Bond & Partners to New York's *Daily News*. "I've often found using real people to be problematic" (July 31, 2005). Leaving aside the question of whether or not celebrities are "real people," the strategy was undeniably risky, though not without precedents. The Halifax Building Society plucked one its managers from obscurity and dropped him in a series of ads, only to see Howard Brown become a celebrity in his own right in Britain.

But the gamble on "real" women, with abundant cellulose and cutaneous imperfections, reaped rewards. In Britain, where the campaign was initiated, sales of Dove rose 9 percent in the year to £120m ($68m), while sales of its firming lotion rose 700 percent. Unilever, which owns Dove (and spends over $3 billion a year on advertising), didn't release US sales figures, though there's no obvious reason to suppose the campaign didn't meet with a similar response.

This encouraged some writers, like Katy Guest, of the *Independent on Sunday*, to pronounce: "We have had enough. The automatic association between a famous face and a successful product is over" (February 20, 2005, p. 16). She didn't mean that we would all start poring over consumer guides like *Consumer Reports* or *Which?*, though our fatigue was beginning to show: "Shoppers are bored with endorsements and actually finding fame a turn-off."

Guest cited market research conducted by Mintel, which discovered that 20 percent of shoppers were actually "celebrity-resistant," 60 percent were "bored with celebrities" and only 8 percent indicated that they would buy a celebrity-endorsed product and even then only if the celeb was someone they "admired or trusted."

Elsewhere in the very same publication, a report by Steve Bloomfield might have been written expressly to embarrass Guest. Analyzing the roles played by Kylie Minogue, or Scarlett Johansson, Bloomfield quoted a 16-year-old woman: "Your mind doesn't look at the product being promoted but at the people promoting it. You don't consider whether it's meant for your skin. Celebrities have a lot of influence and we believe them when they say these products work."

So, whom do we believe? Despite the Dove experience, advertisers flock to celebrities in an effort to maximize their market share. Bloomfield's interviewee sounds like an advertiser's ideal: suggestible to the point of idiocy – seemingly incapable of rational thought. Does anyone else in the world believe celebrities are sincere when they advocate or recommend for a product? Is anyone in the world unable to spell out the motive behind celebrities' behavior (clue: five letters beginning with "m")? Is anyone so utterly gullible that they are prepared to accept the word of a well-paid mercenary when they part with their hard-earned cash? We'd probably like to say the answer to all these is an emphatic *no!* On inspection, though, we probably conclude that it's *no-ish.*

Whatever the pitch or the spiel, the consumer appears to get only one thing – merchandise. Having the approval of a celebrity may convince some consumers that they are buying something authentic, substantial, or even profound. The product may be promoted as desirable and "real." And the consumer may walk away from the store feeling like they have acquired something of genuine value. They may even believe they have taken another step toward being the person they want to be. That doesn't alter the fact that they have bought a commodity, plain if not simple.

Value doesn't exist in any pure form: products are invested with value. Think of the countless items discarded by celebrities and endowed with great value when circulated on eBay or some other exchange system. An old toothbrush, a used tissue or a worn sock become exceptional items. Kylie donned a floaty apple-green dress while in Cannes in 2004 and immediately fashionistas across Britain turned to eBay to get their hands on an affordable version. Such was the demand that used garments that sold in the supermarket Tesco for £45 ($78) were going for twice that on the auction website.

Most shoppers are aware that endorsed products are, essentially, the same as the generic ones. An M3Power razor endorsed by David Beckham may incorporate a blade-stacking feature patented by Gillette and the profits from Paul Newman's range of foods may go to good causes, but the majority of products are functionally indistinguishable. Advertising agencies are as aware of this as consumers; which is why they get paid to make those indistinguishable products distinguishable. M3Power sales surged by 13 percent in 2005 following the Beckham campaign. (Gillette is owned by the world's biggest spender on advertising, Procter & Gamble, which splurges $4.5 billion per year.)

The task is made harder by the fact that advertising, especially television advertising, isn't as helpful as many assume. In response to the question, how effective are tv commercials? Jib Fowles writes: "The answer is both *not very* and *quite a bit*, depending on how the situation is perceived" (1992: 209). This isn't quite as useless an answer as it first appears. While his book *Why Viewers Watch: A reappraisal of television's effects* was published in 1992, some of its insights are timeless. Fowles rounds up evidence to conclude: "Not only don't commercials make an impression on us, but as strange as it may seem, no experimental evidence exists that they get us to buy anything" (1992: 209).

Strange indeed, especially as companies like Unilever and General Motors regularly spend $3.3 billion per year on advertising, over 40 percent on tv commercials. The size of the audience is, as Fowles puts it, the key. "All but about 10% of the money spent on television commercials is wasted," records Fowles

(1992: 209). Only that percentage of tv viewers retains product knowledge after watching an ad. Even then, only 10 percent of that sub-group might actually go out and buy the product. But that percentage is from a total population of millions. Some sports events, such as the Super Bowl, which draws about 200 million viewers, or the World Cup Final, which gets 1.7 billion – that's a quarter of the world's population – are spectacularly huge and untypical. Finales of popular sitcoms are also great viewer magnets: 52.5 million US viewers were glued to the last episode of *Friends* (8.6 million Brits watched). Even a modest show can draw, say, 15 million in the USA, or three million in Britain. When a five-times weekly soap like *Coronation Street* can bring 11 million viewers to their sets for every episode, then an advertiser might be swayed by the prospect of 110,000 potential buys.

Michael Schudson opens his book *Advertising, the Uneasy Persuasion* bluntly: "Advertising is much less powerful than advertisers and critics of advertising claim," but qualifies this with "advertising helps sell goods even if it never persuades a consumer of anything" (1993: xv). He argues that a self-fulfilling prophecy operates, with key personnel tending to believe advertising works. In other words, if retailers and sales staffs think advertising works, they tend to push one product rather than another. For an ad to work, it must be seen to work.

So, if an advertiser can design some way of not just distinguishing a product, but distinguishing it in a way that enables both vendors to stock it and consumers to confer extra value on it, then they have something like the goose that laid the golden eggs. This is, of course, where celebrities come in. Advertisers are always on the lookout for a "face of . . ." some product or another, that is, someone who personifies a product or a range or products or perhaps even an entire brand. That someone may be the right match or fit for one type of product rather than another. Elizabeth Hurley was the spokesperson for and hence the face of Estée Lauder for ten years up to 2005. Presumably Lauder – which owns, among other lines, Bobbi Brown and Clinique – felt she radiated the kind of values it wanted associated with the brand. That is, until she hit 40, when they replaced her with Gwyneth Paltrow, seven years her junior. Budweiser, Castrol Motor Oil, Snickers bars or thousands of other products would have found little use for Hurley. Unless Budweiser decided to reposition its beer in the marketplace: for example, it might follow the example of Häagen-Dazs ice cream which was marketed by its owner Pillsbury as a seduction fuel rather than dessert or sugary junk food for children. As Bud is the world market leader in beers, this is about as unlikely a scenario as we might imagine. Budweiser also knows its demographics, which is why the company often uses celebrity athletes who are easily identifiable and embody the kind of values typically associated with an uncomplicated blue-collar beer. But do celebrity endorsers present value?

: . . . because they're worth it

Gillette's double-digit sales growth in 2005 was testimony to the appeal of Beckham, whose endorsement portfolio also included Pepsi, adidas, Brylcreem, Marks & Spencer, the British retail chain, and Police eyewear, which was one the first companies to profit from the soccer star-turned-marketing phenomenon. Silvia Nanni, the managing director of Police, renewed the original 2001 contract with Beckham, tripling his fee to $5 million and justifying this by citing a doubling of sales figures, which was "due in no small part to David" (quoted in *Sunday People*, February 17, 2002). By 2004, when he signed with Gillette, Beckham's fee for a three-year deal had increased sixfold to $30 million.

As endorsers go, Beckham was in the same league as Michael Jordan. In the June 1998 issue of *Fortune* magazine, Roy Johnson and Ann Harrington analyzed what they called "The Jordan effect," which described the celebrity athlete's impact on the overall economy of the US. Nike developed the Air Jordan line of footwear and apparel and, over the 1990s, it was worth, in terms of sales, $5.2 billion, or over £3 billion (more on Jordan in Chapter 12). Nike, which spends over $400 million a year on advertising, still dominates the world market in sportswear, claiming 34.1 percent of all sales. It has invested in people as much as product: before Jordan, there was Steve Prefontaine, the middle-distance star of the 1970s, then John McEnroe, the tennis player and Bo Jackson, the American football player. After Jordan, there was Tiger Woods, whose first contract with Nike in 1996 earned him $40 million. His second was estimated at $125 million, the biggest endorsement contract to date. In return Nike saw a $50 million revenue growth in golf balls and the overall golf line gross $250 million in annual sales.

Nike's market leadership encouraged rivals toward what seems profligacy. Reebok splashed out $100 million on Allen Iverson, but made such little impact on Nike's leadership that it was taken over by adidas in a $3.8 billion deal in 2005. Earlier, Reebok had signed Shaq O'Neal for $15 million over five years, but passed on a renewal when the contract expired in 1998. Just signing a celebrity athlete is no guarantee of sales. Nike's judgment has been near-faultless, while its rivals' has been hit-and-miss. So, when Nike closed arguably its most audacious endorsement deal in 2003, there was less surprise but not shock: LeBron James was a high-school basketball player, unproven either at college or NBA levels when Nike signed him for a reported $90 million.

Such is the confidence of advertisers in the added value brought to a product by the imprimatur of a celebrity that Chanel No. 5, in 2004, bought the services of Nicole Kidman for just one television commercial. The commercial reunited Kidman with director Baz Luhrmann with whom she had worked on the movie *Moulin Rouge*. The one-off advertisement was estimated to have cost $32 million (£18 million), Kidman's fee for four days' shooting being, at its lowest estimate, $12 million (£7 million) (*Independent*, April 26, 2006). No sales figures were released in the aftermath of the transmission.

Advertising has moved away from the utilitarian approach in which product information was at the forefront. Many global brands avoid even mentioning products in an attempt to create synonymy between their brand and the celebrity endorser. Of all the endorsers used by L'Oréal, Andie MacDowell was most closely associated with the brand and its signature tagline ". . . because I'm worth it" (a slogan dreamt up by Ilon Specht, of McCann Erickson, in 1973 and which is now recognized by 70 percent of consumers, according to Lewis and Bridger 2001: 39; L'Oréal spends over $1.7 billion per year on advertising to maintain this kind of brand recognition).

There is a business adage: "Anybody can buy sales." It means that, if you spend enough on advertising and marketing, your merchandise will move off the shelves. Let's say a satellite/cable television company needs to meet sales projections in order to impress prospective advertisers for the forthcoming season. One way of doing it would be to recruit the services of a celebrity, run a new campaign, and watch the sales figures rise. But profits will be squeezed by the overall cost of the campaign. There may be a quixotic motive at work: the advertising revenue that pours in over the next several months and years will more than offset the cost of the celebrity. This is why celebrities who can kickstart the process can command what seem to be exorbitant fees.

The fee Joe Montana received for his Diet Pepsi commercial during the 1991 Super Bowl was never revealed. We can assume the then top-rated quarterback did not come cheap. Fowles, in another book, *Advertising and Popular Culture*, quotes market research on the efficacy of the ad: a healthy 70 percent of the television audience recalled that Montana had appeared in the commercial, but only 18 percent remembered the product he was endorsing (1996: 125). Not all geese lay golden eggs.

If a person who is endorsing a product is believable, what he or she says is likely to be convincing. The source of a statement has a bearing on whether or not it's believable. When advertisers scan for likely endorsers, credibility is uppermost in their minds.

If consumers regard the celebrity as credible, they're more likely to take notice of the message. If they don't, there opens up a credibility gap: a seeming difference between what's being said and what's seen as the truth.

Ford, for example, thought a credibility gap had opened up when Eminem released his single "Ass like that" in 2005. Encouraged by the way young people appeared to take notice of Eminem and afford him respect, Ford, which spends $2.4 billion a year on advertising, was offered what seemed an ideal opportunity to shed its staid image when the rapper asked to feature one of its new models in his video. There seemed to be a good fit: Eminem, or Marshall Mathers, was born in Detroit, the home of the car manufacturer and had a huge following among the demographically desirable young adults.

Earlier the conservative American Family Association had urged consumers to boycott Ford on the grounds that it had a "pro-gay" agenda, having offered to donate $1,000 to Glad, a gay and lesbian rights group, if requested by customers buying a Jaguar or Land Rover. (Pepsi had earlier felt the wrath of conservatism when Madonna, with whom it had a $5 million contract, released the "Like a prayer" video in 1989; as we saw in Chapter 3, a furor ensued.) Eminem could hardly be described as "pro-gay," of course. He was edgy, though, being white, not as threatening as many black rap artists.

All the same, there was a credibility problem: would potential Ford buyers consider Eminem believable? After all the lyrics to the track in question included a plea to Gwen Stefani ("Will you pee-pee on me please?") and his previous cds received as many criticisms as accolades. Ford may have done a cost-benefit calculation and decided that the possible harm done by association outweighed the advantages of attracting the attention of a young market, which would collectively ask itself: would Eminem really drive a Ford?

Similar questions could be asked about any celebrity endorser. But the answers might be different. Did Michael Jackson drink

Pepsi? An 8 percent rise in sales in the first year after he appeared in ads suggested consumers thought he did; in fact, he didn't. Beckham may have been paid millions to appear in M3Power ads, but his gleaming stubble-free chin indicated that he probably used the razor (a clause in his contract stipulated he had to be clean-shaven at all times. Brylcreem failed to include a comparable clause about hair-length in an earlier deal and was embarrassed when the footballer cropped his hair, after which it suffered a 25 percent drop in sales). Beyoncé and Andie MacDowell may have actually used L'Oréal products in the past and possibly still do. And the numerous endorsers of fragrances probably availed themselves of the products every so often. While consumers may be aware that endorsers are rewarded financially, there is still the issue of whether they see them as potential users. Jordan and Nike was the gold standard in this respect.

: competing for the consumer's soul

In the age of celebrity, market researchers are forever trying to establish the exact properties that make some celebrities fit advertisements and others seem like audiocassettes in a cd player. Source credibility sits at the top of a hierarchy of properties that affect whether consumers will take notice of the endorser. This is far from straightforward: credibility is, according to Rajan Nataraajan and Sudhir Chawla, a "multidimensional variable," the main dimensions being "expertise, trustworthiness, and attractiveness" (1997: 120). One of their conclusions was that "celebrity endorsed ads are perceived to be significantly more credible than ads endorsed by non-celebrities."

Fowles adds another dimension when he writes: "As the star's image cycles back into popular culture, it does so with the new accretions of inferences from the commercial detour" (1996: 131). The very fact of appearing in a campaign can add credibility, which then enhances a celebrity's popularity. Bill Cosby's "detour" with Jell-O had this effect, as we noticed in Chapter 7. Gary Lineker's lackluster image was given panache by his appearance in Walker's snacks commercials on British tv. So there is a kind a feedback loop in which credibility built in one medium transfers to another, which then transfers back and so on.

Michael Basil's research uncovered another factor. "Identification occurs when an individual adopts an attitude or behavior from another person when that attitude or behavior is associated with a satisfying self-defining relationship with that person" (1996: 479). In other words, buying something "being advocated by that celebrity can be seen as a way of 'hitching your wagon' to the star." We discussed identification in Chapter 5 when we saw how some fans develop "self-defining relationships with celebrities and seek to adopt their perceived attributes."

So, if consumers believe celebs are credible and they identify with them, then they are likely to be persuaded. This still doesn't tell us exactly why. In their analysis of what they call *The Soul of the New Consumer*, David Lewis and Darren Bridger provide an answer: "New consumers are really seeking to discover themselves. Not the people they feel themselves to be at this moment, but the kind of men and women they aspire to be and feel it within their power to become" (2001: 28).

I alluded to this in Chapter 4 when I pointed out that, from the mid-1950s, we became aspirational consumers, buying not just to subsist, but to make statements about our progress in the world. The "new consumers" were shaped by the social changes that ensued in the 1960s, particularly the "exponential growth in power and wealth of corporations" which has mirrored the rise in consumer influence and power. Previously, manufacturers and suppliers dictated all major aspects of transactions with "old consumers." But, as the balance of power shifted, so consumers were increasingly able to dictate not only what they wanted, but how, where, and even how much they wanted to pay for products. Schudson puts it plainly when he writes that commodities are not "foisted unwillingly upon defenseless consumers" (1993: 16).

Many might respond that this so-called power of the consumer is largely illusory and the more tangible power of corporations is ultimately decisive. Lewis and Bridger, by contrast, suggest that the new consumer is armed to the teeth with more accessible information than at any point in history and uses that information, if necessary to undermine corporations. They give the example of copyright-defying file sharing. The boycott of Nestlé products would also support their argument: Nestlé's aggressive marketing of baby food undermined breast-feeding, especially in developing world countries, argued consumers. Many of the corporations mentioned in this chapter, including L'Oréal, Procter & Gamble and Unilever have been embarrassed by consumer groups, which have exposed and, indeed, forced them to change animal testing practices. Chunks of their advertising budgets – nearly $10 billion combined – go toward repairing damage done by active consumers.

The same changes we tracked in Chapter 3, leading to global media and the proliferation of entertainment, were responsible for diffusing information to new consumers. It equipped and enabled them to exert their influence over the marketplace. This kind of approach is consistent with the image of the consumer at the center of this book: aware, discerning, and judicious. Corporations have been catalyzed into restoring a new order in which they have needed to respond in kind – treating consumers as well-briefed subjects who knew that corporations and their ad agencies were always trying to anticipate their next move. They were, advised a corporate head to fellow executives, "watching you watching them in order to figure out how they act" (quoted in Schor 2004: 50).

Competing for their "soul" has put corporations and their advertising agents on their mettle. Using celebrities as today's equivalent of sandwich men is integral to the response. The challenge to advertisers and the corporations they served, according to Lewis and Bridger, was that, unlike traditional customers, new consumers tended "to reject mass-produced and mass-marketed commodities in favor of products and services that can claim to be in some way authentic" (2001: 4).

The "quest for authenticity" drives new consumers to pay $10,000 for a Leica lens that lacks many of the features of most Japanese equivalents, such as auto focus and power winder. Leica products have the "aura of authenticity" that derives from their founder who was a German mountaineer in the early twentieth century. While Lewis and Bridger don't cite them, we might also include Nike's Air Jordan IV, produced in 1989 and regarded by many as the quintessential piece of footwear. Pairs fetch $1,000 or more on today's market. There's actually a collector's guide-book on this subject: *Sneakers* by Unorthodox Styles (2005). It's the same quest that motivates consumers to spend inordinate amounts of money on some designer handbags even though there are knockoffs that look almost the same at a thirtieth of the price. Even then, only *some* designer handbags: usually ones that have what Lewis and Bridger call "a subtle demonstration of uniqueness" such as a Chloé Silverado (at $1,900, or £1,086; Chloé took British retailer Kookaï to court for producing one that was too similar and retailed at £35).

While I proposed earlier that people wouldn't be scouring consumer reports magazines prior to purchase, we should remember that such magazines are very much in business and have wide circulations. Still, at the end of the quest, there is no Holy Grail: just merchandise, in all probability, produced by a global corporation that spends billions on advertising designed to persuade consumers that they are actually buying something that has that aura of authenticity – when they are still getting merchandise.

So, authenticity is the theme, according to this theory. In buying something that has it, or at least its aura – a quality that emanates subtly – a consumer steps closer to being the person they want to be. That's what makes them aspirational consumers. When we buy products, we don't take to the store a rational, calculating mentality. We remain judicious, but appeal to emotion as well as logic when we make purchase decisions. Buying is affected behavior: it's influenced by feeling, sentiment, sensation, even passion. Cornel Sandvoss may not have buying microwaveable meals, or sports gear in mind when he writes in *Fans: The mirror of consumption* that popular icons "are appropriated by fans as meaningful resources in their everyday lives" (2005: 13). But it barely needs explication: when consumers buy, say, food or footwear endorsed by celebrities they admire, respect, or like, they are appropriating "meaningful resources" too.

In making the purchase, they give their pleasurable assent to both the celebrity and the product he or she is supporting. At this point, the motives that spurred the endorsers to lend their services seem less important than the appropriation that's made possible by the simple transaction. Consumption requires us to be discerning: we desire to buy certain products. Marketing generally and advertising in particular influences our choices, as do our status in society, our income, and many other factors. Yet we still do the choosing; and we do it in a manner that is intended to communicate inwards and outwards. Put another way: we buy products that are congruent with who we think we are, our sense of self or identity; the way we use those same products expresses this to others.

Whether wearing, driving, drinking, or just filling space in the fridge with products, we are using them. Anything at all we do with the products we buy suggests something about ourselves. This sounds uncomfortably like an ad man's pitch, though Madison Avenue execs are unlikely to want to acknowledge whether they see their products as being appropriated by the consumer or the consumers being appropriated by them. After all and as Deborah Root reminds us in her *Cannibal Culture*: "Appropriation occurs because cultural difference can be bought and sold in the marketplace" (1996: 68).

While Root is writing about the manner in which the artifacts and images of different cultures have been turned into commodities, her point is resonant: aspirational consumers are actually striving to be different when they make their purchases. Lewis and Bridger make the point that new consumers "devote more time, effort and energy to closing the gap between their real and ideal selves" (2001: 29). They may be just buying merchandise, but they're buying into the prospect of making a difference to their lives.

Lewis and Bridger suggest that a "striving for self-actualization" fuels the quest for authenticity Even this is for sale. Root again has a salient remark: "The apparent seamlessness between culture and the marketplace means that anything can come under the purview of capital" (1996: 86). So, while self-actualization, or the process of becoming all that one is capable of being, may be a long, laborious, painstaking, and possibly tortuous process, buying products is not. Commodities make the entire project more manageable. Everything is for sale. Where once we defined our ambitions and selves by the work we performed and what we produced, we now consume to be who we are and who we want to be.

: who's exploiting whom?

In Chapter 7, we noted how, in the 1980s, analysis of market segmentation revealed the exploitable potential of the African American market. Ethnicity, like age, gender, income, occupation, and location, was a variable that enabled advertisers to target populations according to their demographic profiles. Celebrity culture, or, to be more precise, the conditions under which it developed, changed the ways in which markets segmented, taxing advertisers to find new ways of reaching potential consumers. The same technology that brought us unlimited entertainment also brought us boundless information. The same curiosity that made us privy to the private lives of celebs made us inquisitive about the products we were expected to buy.

Consumers checked on the ethics of the manufacturer, studied labels, read guarantees, compared prices, and weighed up options. The market segment, a concept that had been a functional servant of the advertising industry practically since the advent of mass society in the 1920s, looked suspect. Segments were still there, but groups moved between them, defying a consistent, stable categorization. The boundaries between segments are now continually broken as we move between positions. In this sense, the market reflects the way in which we understand ourselves. Identity was once seen as essence or core that remains with us through the life course: nowadays it's conceived as an assembly or moving configuration of different, often temporary, ways of imagining ourselves. We may move through several dozen different identities during a day, changing with changing contexts. Identities exist only in relation to everything else in the surrounding environment.

Picture the consumer at the center of a spider's web, each filament around him or her representing tastes in products: one for music, clothes, food and drink, gadgets, and so on. Each strand takes the consumer to different groups of like-minded consumers in whose company he or she thinks about the self differently. As the consumer move across the strands, he or she encounters new groups and adopts new identities, without ever needing to stop and think about any fixed foundation of qualities or properties that constitutes a unique identity. Instead the consumer has several identities, all based on consumption.

While they don't discuss it in exactly these terms, Lewis and Bridger depict their new consumer in a broadly compatible way. "The mass market is disintegrating," they argue, offering the "taste web" as an alternative. This allows for a more flexible conception of consumers as capricious, inconsistent, erratic, and unsettled – though not entirely unpredictable. After all, if they believe some figures, identify with others, like even others, and find some attractive, then they can be persuaded to follow those figures.

There aren't many Pied Pipers, who can command obedience as well as respect and due deference: though Nike's sales figures suggest that Jordan came close. And, in any case, there's no such thing as obedience in celebrity culture, though, in previous eras, advertisers had an easier time in persuading consumers to submit to their directions, mandates, prescriptions or other kinds of injunctions. Several psychological experiments showed how relatively unproblematic it was to create conditions under which people could be made to do things even when they didn't want to.

In 1936, for instance, Muzafir Sherif took subjects into a darkened room individually and asked them to make judgments about how far and in what direction a beam of light was moving. The evaluations were wildly diverse. When the subjects were taken back in, this time in a group, the judgments converged, indicating that individuals tended to conform to the judgments of the group regardless of their personal perceptions. Later, in 1955, Solomon Asch asked subjects to decide which of a number of lines was longer. Although the correct answer was obvious, Asch planted subjects who'd been instructed to guess way off the mark. When the genuine subjects agreed with the phony estimates, Asch concluded that forces to conform to others overpowered a person's ability to make simple sensory judgments.

Such studies highlighted the influence of collectivities in affecting both the thought and behavior of individuals, even in the face of often bizarre, conflicting evidence. Individuals were more comfortable when conforming to group norms than they were in challenging majority views. The study that brought out the more ominous implications of these findings was Stanley Milgram's 1974 *Obedience to Authority*, in which subjects were told they were participating in learning experiments: "learners" were fastened into an electrically wired chair and had electrodes attached to their bodies. The subjects were told to test the learners and, if they got an answer wrong, administer electric shocks.

Actually, the learners were in on the experiment and didn't receive the shocks; they just reacted dramatically to convince the subjects.

The subjects were prepared to keep upping the electric jolts, even when the learners were thought to be in excruciating pain. Each time the subject would object, a researcher would snap back: "Please continue" or "You *must* go on." Milgram found that 65 percent of the subjects obeyed, progressing all the way to the maximum voltage of 450 volts. Subjects surrendered their autonomy to the experiment, believing it to be conducted in the spirit of science.

The unsettling research disclosed plasticity in the human makeup. The advertising industry had a more pliant and less skeptical population to woo, cajole, torment, and occasionally intimidate into action ("is your bad breath letting you down?"). Authority figures, in particular, could exact compliance. But, as we noted in Chapter 3, "We have forsaken our traditional heroes and replaced them with actors and athletes," as Sherman puts it. And, while many celebrities may have the moral authority once wielded by politicians, church leaders, or military heroes, it's not certain whether they have the suasion.

Yet celebrities and the advertisers who hire them are always trying to make us do things. Whereas once advertisers would badger us with reminders that next door has a better car, whiter washing, and maybe fresher breath than us, they now offer us the chance of being that bit more like someone we like, admire, identify with or just believe. But there's more. Sandvoss's work offers a way of understanding the relationship fans have with the objects of their adulation or even just admiration (2005).

Recall how earlier we acknowledged that identification with a celebrity yields a "satisfying self-defining relationship" that advertisers can exploit. Sandvoss reveals: "The relationship between fans and their object of fandom goes beyond mere identification" (2005: 102). Being a fan often means appropriating the celebrity as "part of the publicly performed self" (2005: 111).

And that fans are "shaping a sense of self through the object of fandom" (2005: 157).

In other words, the object of adoration, whether an individual celebrity, a team, a tv show, a track on a cd, or whatever, is seen as more than a possession. It can "become an integral part of their [the fans'] identity, vision of self, as much as their perception by others" (2005: 163). Sandvoss isn't referring only to the kind of people we discussed in Chapter 5, like Rebecca Schaeffer's killer who taped the tv show in which she appeared and the Steffi Graf fan who built a shrine around her. He means anyone who enters a transaction in which they form an emotionally significant relationship with a celebrity or something he or she represents, appears in, or produces. Buying shampoo does not implicate a consumer in such a relationship with whoever is endorsing the product, but, like it or not, it means they are involved in the same social practice, albeit at a different level.

My earlier remark about having echoes of an ad man's pitch bears repeating here. On Sandvoss' account, the emotional relationship often dismissed as marketing verbiage is actually the crucial nexus that helps explain why most of us, not just those marginalized as devotees, are awed – and I mean impressed rather than frightened – by celebrities. It's because they have become resources when we think about ourselves, position ourselves, and reflect on how we would like others to see us. The seemingly mundane act of shopping actually involves us in "actively shaping a sense of self" as well as acquiring possessions.

Schudson's position is companionable: he views the buying of goods as an attempt to build what the anthropologist Mary Douglas once called "an intelligible universe" (1993: 160). An empirical study by Steven Kates provides evidence of what he calls "identity projects": "Consumption is reflexive," he concludes, meaning that products are used to achieve status and "consumer practices are read and displayed with interpretive frameworks that incorporate explicit concerns about inclusion, exclusion, social meaning, classification of people and objects, and the privileged status of this knowledge" (2002: 399).

Robin Andersen suggests that some advertising styles acknowledge this, promoting a kind of social organization for like-minded shoppers: "Lifestyle messages promise a sense of group membership, but membership earned through commodity consumption" (1995: 120). Once in the hands of consumers, the commodity becomes a resource, perhaps a valuable one in constructing group identity and even "a sense of belonging," as Andersen puts it in her *Consumer Culture and TV Programming*.

Andersen despairs at this, as she does about the entire cultural shift that started in the 1980s. "A narrow view that telescopes all problems into personal faults" is the way she captures the prevailing outlook and the one that informs contemporary advertising. Celebrities are brought in simultaneously to high-light those faults and to signal a relatively easy way to fix them. Hence the term retail therapy.

Advertising coaxes consumers into vainly pursuing a lifestyle that's tantalizingly within reach yet forever beyond their grasp. The merchandise it offers might supply consumers with the raw material to shape personal and group identities, but there's still only merchandise on the counter. Or is there? David Luna and Susan Forquer Gupta are two among many scholars who believe that the merchandise is loaded: "Culturally-constituted meaning first moves into the persona of the celebrity. Then, the meaning moves from the celebrity into the product. Finally, it moves from the product into the consumer" (2001: 48).

We need to modify this in the light of the arguments presented in this chapter: the meaning doesn't just "move" into the consumer. The consumer originates the meaning. All the corpo-rate power in the world can't put meaning into merchandise. Affixing it with the signature of a Kidman or a Beckham plays if there is a receptive population of consumers who read the celebrities in a way that makes them attractive, credible; or invests those celebs with the right kinds of meaning. Meaning isn't just transferred: it's created.

Among the many criticisms of celebrity culture is that it's turned us all into zealous idolaters, who not only follow the exploits of irrelevant characters, but clamor to buy the products we suspect they use, or at least like. The imperative to acquire is never far away from celebrities. Yet, in this chapter I've presented various arguments that resuscitate the consumer from what many writers imagine is a comatose state. Consumers are engaged in what might pass as a creative process: the endorsed products, even the menial items you pick up in a supermarket, are resources and, as such, usable. I can anticipate the incredulous response: so when I grab a bottle of shower gel that's endorsed by Heather Locklear or somebody, I'm actually shaping my identity? It sounds a heady and implausible proposition. But think of the manifold ways in which celebrities affect us.

Every morning, newspapers, even the most sober broadsheets, hum with news on celebrities. Radio and television programs don't so much feature celebrities as provide virtual showcases for them. Many of the internet sites we visit exist because of them. This is before we even consider the advertising that has been the focus of this chapter. Whether buying groceries, a new car, house, vacation, pharmaceuticals, stocks, almost anything, we are forced to accept that, if it can be exchanged for money, it can bear the mark of a celebrity, sometimes several. Politics is fast becoming a favored territory of celebrities eager to exploit their profile for higher purposes (as I will discuss in Chapter 11). Our speech is affected by what we hear celebs say and even how they say it. Our children unwittingly copy them. Our colleagues gossip about them. We sense their presence.

There is a kind of celebrity pulse beating through society. No matter how we try, we can't fail to feel it. It's either specious or illogical, or both, to suggest that the way we think about ourselves and present ourselves to others *is not* influenced by celebrity culture. Consumption has replaced work as the heart that regulates this pulse. So much of who we are and what we do depends on it. The proliferating appearances of celebrities have made it harder than ever to spot where the advertising stops and everything else starts. And this shows no signs of letting up.

Advertising, as we know it, is approaching its end. Television's dominance has already been undermined by the internet and its power to communicate to billions is compromised by its inability to nail viewers to the screen during commercial breaks. We watched tv in the same way for thirtysomething years before the video cassette recorder made it possible for us to organize our viewing around our own priorities. The fast-forward button allowed us to race through the breaks, avoiding the advertising. In the early twenty-first century, the personal video recorder, incorporating a hard drive that stores programs, introduced even greater consumer freedom: viewers could effectively co-ordinate their own channels, watch them at their convenience and, if they wished, edit out the commercials. While some channels, such as HBO, which is funded by subscriptions, and BBC, which draws money from license fees, were largely unaffected, the vast majority of broadcasters are driven by advertising revenue.

Celebrities provide a solution of sorts. In 1982, the movie *ET: The extra-terrestrial* featured a scene in which the eponymous character was lured out its hiding place with Reese's Pieces, a confectionery which was then used extensively in various cross-marketing initiatives. The script had originally included M&Ms, but Hershey's, the makers of Reese's Pieces, pitched successfully for what became a classic piece of product placement. Audiences are now inured to commercial products being surreptitiously – and sometimes blatantly – exhibited in movies and tv shows. The Austin Powers series were effectively 90-minute ads for global brands such as Virgin and Starbucks. Ray-Bans and Nokia phones were integral to the Matrix movies. Virtually every movie features branded products being worn, used, driven, flown, drunk, or eaten by recognizable celebrities.

Television is no slouch in this matter. Fans of the early *Hawaii Five-O* cop show might have wondered whether there were any other vehicles apart from Fords on the island. More recently, we may ask whether the judges on *American Idol* had a thing for Coca-Cola; that's all they ever had in front of them when they gave their assessments. Often crude, product placement has given way to brand integration, in which identifiable characters, whether in drama, news, documentary, or reality television, either utter the name of or exhibit a consumable product. Showing Simon Cowell slurping from a glass of Coke may not seem effective advertising; but advertising is most persuasive when it's not seen as advertising.

At its coarsest, brand integration can take the form of a group of characters swigging Budweiser and talking about how they once drank it by the crate, as they did in scene from sci-fi show *The 4400*. It seems a short step from this to Britain's perennially most popular soap *Coronation Street*, where patrons of the Rover's Return pub drink the fictitious Newton & Ridley's beer. It's conceivable that some characters could switch allegiances and start ordering Heineken by name. This is neither old-style product placement nor straightforward endorsement: it is an integration of commercial content and dramatic content. It's impossible for viewers to avoid.

Even the celebrities who emerge from reality television – which we consider in the next chapter – have the resources to influence our consumption patterns. Celebrities have for long been living commercials, though for a conception of the good life we should all aspire too. Now, even those without endorsement contracts are co-opted into an arrangement whereby they are coupled with products they may neither abominate nor adore, but which producers have deigned necessary for the survival of the medium.

 **TELEVISING/REALITY**

: a hit of disposable fame

"Superficial celebrity culture was over," wrote Thomas de Zengotita, of *Harper's Magazine*, "A new age of seriousness was upon us" (2002: 33). After September 11, 2001, many people swore they could already see the vapor trail of celebrity culture. The dizzy days of frivolity and froth were surely over. Who wanted the shallowness and inconsequentiality that had been served up in the previous decade? The trivial lives of celebrities may have amused us when there was nothing better about which to concern ourselves. But everything was different in the aftermath of the attacks. Solemnity, self-reflection, and earnest analysis were called for.

Things did change, of course; though not in this way. "The spotlight never wavered," de Zengotita remarked, "It went on shining." And in its beam, a new type of celebrity emerged. If we considered the rock/movie star/model celeb inconsequential and shallow, the next generation didn't so much plumb new depths but stayed even closer to the surface. Its natural habitat was not drama, news, sport, or even documentary – but reality.

In the early twenty-first century, just as in any other period, television attracted critics. "One new category of entertainment programme was particularly under attack," write Asa Briggs and Peter Burke in their *A Social History of the Media*: "So-called 'reality

TV' shows such as *Castaway 2000*, *Big Brother* and *I'm a Celebrity . . . Get Me Out of Here*, which exploited melodramatic settings, and which critics considered morally repugnant" (2005: 262).

While Briggs and Burke don't specify why critics thought reality tv morally repugnant, as opposed to aesthetically, informatively, educationally, or just plain repugnant, one such critic, Brian Johnson of *Maclean's* shed a little light when he described it as "a mongrel genre that lets us pass judgment while indulging in some safe, Disneyfied voyeurism" (2001: 56).

Reality television tended to turn its characters' vices into virtues, so that people who displayed ignorance, dishonesty, or some kind of depravity became praiseworthy. Many of those who appeared in reality tv shows were well rewarded with endorsements, record contracts, and other kinds of profitable assignments. Several of them became celebrities for no other reason than that they were recognizable. Reality tv made it possible for someone working at a supermarket checkout one week to be nationally famous the next. Or someone serenading commuters with a guitar on streetcorners at Christmas to be a best-selling recording artist by Easter.

Prior to reality tv, it was usually assumed that the decisive fact of celebrity status was that those in possession of it were famous. Being famous without having accomplished anything of note was commonplace as celebrity culture went into its post-9/11 phase. "Of note" is a relative concept, of course: what's noteworthy in one era may not look so remarkable in another. And vice versa: unremarkable events can take on a significance that would have seemed ridiculous ten years before. The kind of event I have in mind is appearing on a reality television show. As such shows became showcases for a new type of celebrity, so an appearance became a valued resource.

The criticisms of reality tv are comprehensive, though most of them are easily discounted. Boring: then why do so many viewers watch them? Passive: then why do millions vote? Demeaning to participants: then why do so many clamor for a chance to appear on television? Patronizing to viewers: then why don't they switch channels? Scarcely believing critics have been astonished by the popular appeal of reality tv, which has influences in fly-on-the-wall documentaries, *cinéma-vérité*, talent contests, game shows, *Candid Camera* and *Lifestyles of the Rich and Famous*. Shows like *Survivor* and *Big Brother* incorporated features of all these, turning the viewer into a guilt-free peeping tom with power over the destinies of those they were peeping at. Interactive television, instant text-messaging and the internet made it possible for consumers to decide on whom they wanted and whom they didn't want to remain on the show.

Two shows, *An American Family* and *The Family* carried the virus for contemporary reality tv. Airing on PBS in 1973, the former chronicled the everyday life of a nuclear family in the throes of a divorce. In the following year, the British series focused on another family, this one happily united. The dialogue between family members in both cases resembled bad acting with dialogue that could be either spirited or lifeless. There was no commentary or intrusive interviews: just a naturalistic recording of family life. At a time when cop shows like *Cagney and Lacy* and *The Sweeney* and epic documentaries such as BBC's *The Ascent of Man* were in vogue, a faithful register of family life should have worked like a sedative on any viewer without boundless patience.

Remember, though: this was a time when, as we noted in Chapter 9, psychological studies by, among others, Stanley Milgram were probing the reasons behind our seemingly rule-following behavior. The advertising industry was trying to understand how to reshape our habitual patterns. At least two intelligent films – *The Manchurian Candidate* (the original) and *The Ipcress File* – had already dramatized methods of bringing people's actions under control. And the idea behind the family documentaries eventually found its way into a couple of movies, *Network*, in 1976, and much later *The Truman Show* in 1998. The point is that there was a general interest in the plasticity of people. Did they act the way they did because of freewill or were they determined or influenced by something? And, if they were determined, could we identify the determinants and change them? These were big questions and they were not about to be answered by a couple of tv shows. Yet there was a sense in which a wall-residing housefly's perspective on the everyday goings-on in most people's idea of an ordinary home complemented the overall line of enquiry.

If there was a single academic study that presaged reality tv in intent and format, it was Philip Zimbardo's prison simulation in 1971. Twenty-four subjects were randomly split into two groups, "prisoners" and "guards" and instructed to act out role-appropriate behavior in a specially constructed prison at Stanford University. Those playing guards were given suitable uniforms and accessories, while the prisoners were assigned numbers and made to wear muslin smocks. The experiment soon edged toward catastrophe as guards tormented the captives, imposing punishments cruelly and arbitrarily. They took away basic rights, such as a mattress, food, and washing facilities from the prisoners, one of whom went on hunger strike in protest at the callous treatment. Zimbardo aborted the experiment, though this in itself was a more interesting conclusion than he might have hoped for (Haney *et al.* 1973; see also Insight Media 1990).

Expectations of normal behavior went awry: closeted away and commissioned with the authority to behave in unfamiliar ways, some guards swiftly adopted conduct that bordered on the sadistic. Even in its incomplete state, the experiment disclosed how human behavior is susceptible to quite dramatic change by adjustments to situational contingencies. The lesson: put people in unfamiliar environments and assign them with unusual power and instructions and their behavior changes, often in a way that seems "out-of-character." Questions about the ethics of this type of research effectively prevented a replication – at least, in an academic setting.

The two shows responsible for the rapid spread of the reality format seemed like the televisual offspring of Zimbardo's experiment. *Big Brother* and *Survivor* were both based on European ideas, the former's name inspired by George Orwell's all-seeing sentinel in *1984*. They took the observational format of shows like *COPS* and MTV's *The Real World* and added the contrivance of enclosed environments and new tasks. Were the results as dramatic as the experiments, viewers would probably have looked only through their parted fingers. In the event, they proved fascinating rather than repellent.

Writing shortly before the shows were aired in 2000, David Giles wrote about Maureen Reece who appeared in a BBC documentary called *Driving School*, which was a kind of visual diary of Reece's learning to drive. "Maybe she represents the next-door neighbour, or the woman you see regularly in the bus queue or at the supermarket checkout," pondered Giles as he tried to unravel the reasons for her sudden popularity. "Someone *so* ordinary that a real relationship might be a distinct possibility" (2000: 70).

It was an interesting insight and one that led Giles to suggest: "The television viewing world is a bottomless pit of potential celebrities . . . Perhaps the democratization of fame is still not complete" (2000: 71).

A combination of relatively low production values and high viewing figures alerted the television networks to the possibilities of democratizing fame. And Giles's "bottomless pit" was seething with volunteers seeking to satisfy their appetite for fame. Why? In the 1970s, people were not noticeably animated by the prospect of becoming subjects of television shows. Fame, recognition, and distinction were usually attendant on achieving something of value. The arrival of celebrity culture changed that. "A certain shift has taken place in the whole concept of fame, which, it must be assumed, corresponds to a shift in the nature of ambition more generally," conjectured Philip Hensher, of the *Independent* (November 24, 2004, p. 33). *Maclean's* Brian Johnson thought that the people whose ambitions had changed collectively made up "a service industry of brave souls willing to risk humiliation for a crack-pipe hit of disposable fame" (2001: 56)

But the availability of would-be television performers lacking in anything resembling training and motivated only by their craving to be seen on tv didn't necessarily make them watchable. And it certainly didn't make them the raw material of celebrity. What was it about them – and I mean everybody who ever appeared on a reality tv show for more than one episode – that made them attractive? What did they have that offered pleasure to the viewers? What did they do to warrant being celebrities?

Years before the advent of reality tv as we know it, Richard Dyer wrote about *Stars* and speculated that they embodied both the properties of extraordinariness and ordinariness. "They act out aspects of life that matter to us," Dyer argued (1979: 49). He was writing in the 1970s before the many changes that have made celebrity culture, as we understand it, happen. The near-voyeuristic inclination we associate with today's celebrity culture was not in evidence, nor was the ravenous pursuit of insubstantial morsels of information about private lives. And, while the purveyors of such information already existed, the word "paparazzi" wasn't in common use. Dyer couldn't have predicted the changes that lay ahead, but his central point remained – the characters who strolled into reality tv mattered.

In Hollywood terms, it was as if extras had been upgraded to headline players: people that would previously have gone unnoticed were promoted to a status comparable to movie stars and rock singers; occasionally they actually became movie stars or rock singers. Reality tv didn't exactly start this: the genre itself was made possible by a wider dispersal of interest in areas of life that were once classified as personal. In two decades, the stars had descended from their exalted positions and become recognizable human beings, their foibles and fantasies, strengths and weaknesses, loving and loathing all paraded in full view. And all bearing resemblance to the kind of properties shared by everybody.

Once the Them and Us distinction started to melt away, reality tv provided a scope on people who were not celebrities but whose lives seemed every bit as interesting. Their overlapping relationships with people they hardly knew, their attempts to get to grips with often taxing challenges, and their facility for adapting to unusual circumstances were evidently captivating. This led to an irony – if indeed reality tv did have a different outcome to the one intended – and it was that the individuals whose appeal lay in their genuine ordinariness became just as gaze-worthy as bona fide celebrities. In some cases, as we will soon see, they went on to become celebrities in their own right.

One thing is certain: reality tv was the dominant genre of the early twenty-first century. From the moment ten volunteers moved into a custom-built house cut off from the rest of the world to live under the constant gaze of hidden cameras, consumers and advertisers showed their affection for a format that required others to grapple with unusual situations and discard their dignity. In the process, those "others" became celebrities.

: objects of desire and spectacular freaks

Watching reality tv – and I am referring to the genre in its widest sense to include any unscripted show involving non-professionals as its centerpiece – can be like staring uninterestedly at the wallpaper of a house you're renovating in Holland, then peeling it off to discover a sketched self-portrait of Van Gogh daubed beneath it. One layer holds more fascination than the other.

The top layer may appear tedious: human beings, unknown or moderately famous, interacting with each other in an artificial environment and compelled to perform pre-structured tasks. Judged on their ability to perform the tasks they, the players, are involved in a survival of the fittest, fitness in this instance being based on their appeal to the viewers. If their singing or their appearance or just the way they conduct themselves in their daily interactions entertains the viewers, they vote for them. "Celebrity culture represents a process of social levelling," writes Jessica Evans, condensing the view of "media proprietors, journalists or editors who want to defend their interests"(2005: 14). This is even more democratic than Giles anticipated.

The democratic element of reality tv extended to many of the participants too. Those who came to the fore via *Big Brother*, for example, were not even famous in the first instance. Many of the contestants, especially those who were voted off early in the shows, never actually became famous. And several more enjoyed the most evanescent type of fame before returning to obscurity. For instance, the winter 2004 season of British television's *I'm a Celebrity . . . Get Me Out of Here!* featured Fran Cosgrave, whose main qualification for inclusion was that he had been out with a member of the girl band Atomic Kitten. He later appeared in some advertisements before completing his elliptical route back to ordinary life.

Others like Jade Goody remained popular after her fourth-place exit from Britain's third season of *Big Brother* in 2002. She was all but executed by the press for being loud, fat, and dim. Death threats were taken seriously enough to warrant police protection. Goody was almost an object lesson in contrariness: critics panned her mercilessly, while viewers found her irresistible. Bizarrely, the media antipathy ensured her a kind of afterlife, so that she came out of the house to a plethora of lucrative assignments that kept her busy for years and lent permanence to what might have been ephemeral renown. So much so that she was distinguished with her own entry in Wikipedia (http://en.wikipedia.org/wiki/Jade_Goody).

There is no divine right to fame. Nor any commandment that says you must have talent to be a celebrity. It could be argued that many showbusiness celebrities and the Hollywood stars that preceded them possess sparse talent, anyway. And, as we've seen in previous chapters, the interest in their private lives that we accept so matter-of-factly today is actually the product of a recent combination of design and circumstance. So there is no intrinsic reason why people should be more concerned with Keira Knightley's private life rather than that of Jade Goody. On the contrary: Knightley's artistry is properly appreciated through her dramatic performances, while Goody's worth is only grasped by observing her everyday routines. Knightley may be more than a match for Goody when it comes to looks or acting, but she was easily outscored in the ordinariness contest. Perhaps KK was one of several exchangeable blondes who would appear, either in the guise of a Jane Austen heroine or an improbable bounty-hunter; but there was something indisputably unique, something authentically gauche, something ingenuously commonplace, something innocently green (forgive the unintended pun) about Jade that charmed audiences.

At least the celebrities who emerged from reality tv shows knew they had no talent. Like artless children who stumble on a stash of new Xboxes, they made the most of their good fortune. They usually busied themselves endorsing products, attending openings, making cds, appearing on talk shows; cashing in on their instant and, for most, transitory fame. In his *Understanding Celebrity*, Graeme Turner reflects on the types of response celebrities engender: "Audiences place individual celebrities somewhere along a continuum that ranges from seeing them as objects of desire or emulation to regarding them as spectacular freaks worthy of derision" (2004: 55).

He compares responses to Nicole Kidman and Anna Nicole Smith, the former attracting "more admiration" than the latter, even though Kidman's admirers may be mindful of the media apparatus and publicity machinery she has at her disposal. In other words, Turner suggests that audiences recognize something in Kidman that they do not in Smith and place her on a different part of the emulation/derision continuum.

Turner has a point, but his example is an awkward one. Kidman in the early twenty-first century was Hollywood royalty.

Emerging from the acclaimed low-budget Australian film *Dead Calm* in 1988, Hawaii-born, Australia-raised Kidman was offered a part opposite Tom Cruise in *Days of Thunder*. Late in 1990, she married Cruise, a deed that earned her more international recognition than any of her previous roles. Hollywood parts – like "Dr Meridian" in *Batman Forever* – followed, though her performances in independent films such as *To Die For* and *Portrait of a Lady* protected her from charges that her status owed more to her husband than to her own merit. Still, her marriage to Cruise, which ended in 2001, coincided with her becoming a featured actor and her elevation to celebrity status.

The other Nicole also married well: in her case to billionaire oil tycoon J. Howard Marshall, who died aged 90 in August 1995, thirteen months after the wedding. Smith was 26 when they married. The *Playboy* "Playmate of the Year" in 1992, Smith appeared in *Naked Gun 33 1/3: The final insult* and *The Hudsucker Proxy*, both in 1994. Yet it was her misalliance that aroused public interest, especially after it became known that she stood to inherit nearly $0.25 billion. Marshall's family contested the bestowal and a court battle ensued. Smith was awarded $88 million.

Just as she seemed destined to return to anonymity, albeit a plush anonymity, E! The Entertainment Channel capitalized on the rising popularity of the then-novel reality tv form by featuring Smith in a show that involved shooting her and her entourage as they navigated their way through shops, clubs, hotels, and anywhere else. *The Anna Nicole Show* débuted in 2002 and followed the earlier MTV show *The Osbournes* in straightforwardly recording the directionless activities of a bunch of people with lots of money and even more free time. Highlights included their having breakfast and playing video games. Somehow the inertia conjured the interest of viewers and Smith returned to the spotlight.

Maybe, as Turner suggests, Smith elicits a different response from consumers to Kidman. But are they more likely to look down on Smith and be in awe of Kidman? Cynics may spot parallels amid the divergent career paths. Others may suspect that, as we have noted before, celebrity culture rewards presence rather than anything as uncertain as talent or its correlates. Still others may regard both as products of an overpowering media that lends specious importance to anyone who can draw viewers to a screen and readers to a tabloid.

There is, as Turner reflects, a "paradoxical relationship between the celebrity and their public." Smith had no pretensions: she didn't say she could act (she had just one acting lesson) or sing; nor did she try to disguise her early lap-dancing job as a career interlude. She didn't even try very hard to contest the copious charges that she was a gold-digger. Yet clearly consumers took pleasure in watching her. This is what Turner regards as the "arbitrariness" of celebrity: "Sometimes no amount of publicity can generate public interest; at other times, the public reveals a mind of its own in its reactions to a specific individual" (2004: 55).

The best-selling computer game "The Sims" is another example of the pleasure we take from the commonplace. "What is significant about The Sims is that it is not about violence, killing competition; it is not fantasy or sci-fi," explains Myra Stark of *Brandweek* magazine. "The player creates a simulated person or family and helps them with the demands of daily life: getting and keeping a job, making friends, decorating houses, maintaining relationships in a family" (2003: 18).

Again, the democratizing tendency of celebrity culture is apparent. The reality tv form invited audiences to show their favor: they could advocate, ignore, tolerate, or support, even making representatives out of unlikely figures. Sometimes, celebrities were elected a little unsteadily above their stations and vanished without trace after their momentary fame. But other electives had more staying power.

: RU talentless?

There should be a name for the condition that afflicts pop stars when asked to reflect on contemporary culture. Selective amnesia doesn't quite capture it. Retrospective interpretation deficiency is nearer. Madonna's denunciation of television as "trash" and her refusal to let her children watch was rich indeed, coming from someone whose entire career was linked to television as response is linked to stimulus. Had she been starting out in show-business in the early twenty-first century, Madonna might easily have turned up in a talent quest tv show.

The likes of *PopStars* and *American Idol* exploited the possibilities offered by a generation which considered fame its only deliverance. "I want to be as famous as Persil Automatic," was the declaration of an early cohort member, Victoria Beckham, the former Posh Spice. Persil is Britain's best-known household detergent. So it seems fair to conclude that she did achieve her ambition. In fact, the Spice Girls were the perfect archetype of manufactured fame even if they didn't appear on reality tv. Responding to an ad in the March 1994 edition of the theater trade journal *Stage*, which ran: "RU 18–23 with ability to sing/dance?" Victoria Adams, as she then was, became one of five successful applicants for a job in a band. The five ingénues rehearsed for months, showcased for industry a&r workers and recorded a demo tape. After the first single "Wannabe" became a hit in 1995, the Spice Girls went on to become a global brand. *Forbes* ranked the band number six in its "Celebrity Power 100" in May 1999. These rating weren't based solely on numbers of cds sold or box office receipts, but on the value of the overall brand.

There had been manufactured bands before, of course; but the Spice Girls were made not from school friends, session musicians, or members of other bands. They had no track record to speak of and no obvious talent as individual performers. Their commercial success was proof that bands could be assembled like machines, people being the interchangeable parts. Those responsible for designing, developing, and marketing the end product were the ones who plotted the destiny. If they got it right, then there were Spice Girls. If they got it wrong, there was Hear'Say – the group put together on *PopStars* but which disbanded after only a year. Again, the democratizing tendency of reality tv offered a solution: let the audiences express their preferences interactively.

Consumers' powers of persuasion were evident in shows that exhibited untested entertainers, allowed music industry professionals to appraise them, then invited viewers to vote. In February 2002, 4.2 million Brits (7 percent of the total British population) voted Will Young the winner of *Pop Idol*. Within sixteen days, his first single "Anything is possible/Evergreen" was released and became the fastest-selling single ever in the UK. Four years later, Young's output was still selling, not only in Britain but internationally.

Young's US equivalent was Kelly Clarkson who won the first *American Idol* in September 2002. The ten-week series attracted 25 million viewers (compare this with the 52.5 million who watched the finale of *Friends*, as we saw in Chapter 9). Duplicating Young's success, Clarkson began recording immediately after the show and continues to sell cds globally.

The *Idol*-type shows were different to other reality shows: the production was more akin to conventional entertainment or teledrama, with eye-pleasing lighting and stage settings. There were also performances that were, in most cases, indistinguishable from those of other entertainment shows. To offset this, the shows included backstage histrionics, personality battles, and inconsolable anguish as well as the more conventional euphoria. The next generation of shows, such as *The X-Factor*, let audiences mock the ineptitude of those fame-hungry wannabes who were long on motivation but short on talent. The ritualistic excoriation by the likes of Simon Cowell became an attractive feature of the shows and disclosed a side to audiences that had been mined previously by confessionals, like *The Jerry Springer Show*.

The peeper's delight in watching others being denuded of their dignity in full view of millions might seem a world away from the callous pleasures taken by patrons of cock-fighting, bear-baiting, and other blood sports in previous centuries. Yet there was cruelty in both kinds of enjoyment. The confessionals showed how much malicious amusement there was to be had in listening to and watching ordinary people embarrass themselves by revealing intimate details of their mixed-up private lives. The unspoken *quid pro quo* was that, if any member of the audience were able to exchange positions, he or she would unhesitatingly disgorge their own innermost secrets in full view. The Springer show and its counterparts were perfectly consistent with the times. As the talent quest shows developed, they exploited consumers' malicious fondness for public shaming and the real attraction shifted from the victors to the heartlessly, hopelessly vanquished.

Any form of reality television carries this potential. Viewers patiently endure the endless formalistic routines in the hope that some spontaneously indiscreet behavior will erupt. Much like the way Andy Warhol fans might watch one of his early films, which consist of *longueurs* punctuated with occasional brief bursts of activity. So, as well as the blameless pleasure of witnessing painfully maladroit people humiliate themselves and be humiliated by a castigatory panel, there was the added thrill of a violent outburst from a defeated contestant or a moment of brazen intimacy or even the confession of a dark secret to whet the appetite. There was also, for those who wanted to look, an insight into what Hensher called the "shift in the nature of ambition." Young people, many with acumen and capabilities that, in a different era, would equip them for careers in industry or commerce, were mobilized for one thing: fame.

The quest shows had many antecedents including *Star Search* in the USA and Britain's *Opportunity Knocks*. Although shows that used viewers' votes to determine winners had only primitive technology, such as postcards and telephones, the spirit of interactivity was present. They also allowed consumers the rare pleasure of watching an incompetent or novelty act that had little chance of winning, but entertained nevertheless. But these shows effectively mimicked conventional entertainment rather than providing a counterpoint to it. Quest shows ostensibly strove for a glossy product, but provided audiences with much grubbier merchandise. There was also moral neutrality: before reality tv, programs would have fought shy of leaving viewers without some redeeming memorandum about why they should feel ashamed of laughing at the spectacle of others' mortification or at their indiscretions, or even at their manifest lack of talent.

Reality tv didn't just awaken interest in hitherto taboo areas: it absolved viewers from any culpability they might have felt as they woke up. One got the impression that contestants could have bled as they trooped off camera following a mauling from Cowell *et al.*, but viewers would have still felt in the clear morally. And, if they did feel a pang of guilt, they could always vote for that contestant.

: ordinary, not average

To say that there is more to reality tv than meets the eye is trite. But there is. My interest in this book is not in evaluating the genre in artistic terms, only in its relationship with celebrity culture. As I've pointed out, reality tv was brought into being by the dissipation of celebrity status and the widespread interest in celebrities *qua* people. Their pedestals dismantled, stars became human: we became fascinated with them, in viewing their capacities as mortal beings rather than otherworldly creatures. The fascination with ordinariness promoted reality tv and made it work. It also dissolved any spurious divisions between the deserving and the lucky. Celebrity status owed something to both, probably in equal measures. Once we understand this, we can see how reality tv is like the Van Gogh portrait beneath the dull wallpaper: it's worth peeling away the top layer to find something more interesting. What if we scrape some more? We might get lucky and find some Rembrandt doodles or, more likely, the bricks and mortar that hold the structure together.

Back in 1961, Daniel Boorstin offered an amusing tautology when he suggested there was a new class of people who were well known for their "well-knownness" (1992). At least it seemed a tautology – saying the same thing twice – when it was published. Now it seems a perfectly reasonable assertion. Well-knownness is an independent variable: it doesn't rely on anything else for its validity. Athletes, rock stars, models, actors, and a miscellany of celebrity lawyers, chefs, writers, and so on are not just known for their well-knownness. The source of their renown is their prowess. Once that has been noticed, they can garner recognition by their appearance, their partners, their presence at events, their endorsements, and practically anything that interests their audience, including porn videos, of course. We wouldn't have been interested in them in the first place if it hadn't been for their achievements.

It could be argued that reality tv has introduced a new generation of celebrities whose fame owes nothing to achievement and everything to appearance. Yet even this distinction is artificial by today's criteria. Appearing on a reality television show *is* an achievement; maintaining a presence in the show is an even bigger achievement. The genre has been successful because of changes in conceptions of achievement, but it has also promoted even further changes. There's no mystery about why we're attracted to the likes of Jade Goody: it's because of her achievements, not least of which was appearing in *Big Brother*.

Writing in 2001, the year after *BB*'s launch, Chris Rojek marked out three types of celebrity status: ascribed, which is gained by virtue of descent (aristocracy, for example), achieved, and attributed, when "ordinary" people "are vaulted into the public consciousness as noteworthy figures, primarily at the behest of mass-media executives pursuing circulation or ratings wars" (2001: 18). The triplex might have held together before the start of reality tv, but not now. Leaving aside the ascribed category, which applies to the small number of persons like kings and queens in whom celebrity status is seen as a transferable possession, there seems little to demarcate between achieved and attributed status. Celebrities that have come to the fore via reality shows would, on Rojek's account, have been attributed their status by the media rather than have achieved it.

Barry Smart's analysis of *Sport Stars* echoes this. "No matter how hard commentators, analysts and sponsors work . . . to subordinate the ethos of sport to the values of entertainment and commerce, sport retains a significant measure of authenticity" (2005: 93). In other words, Smart believes that there is something genuine or authentic about those athletes who have achieved excellence rather than just had celebrity status attributed to them. But do sports celebrities earn their status through swinging a baseball bat or forcing a ball across a white line? There is nothing intrinsic in their skills that make them worthy of celebrity status. The skill functions as an alert to the media and a diverse collection of other interested parties which, on the contrary, actually do subordinate the ethos of sport to market imperatives and, in the process, accredit the athlete with celebrity status. (I will return to Smart's argument when I look at sports in Chapter 12.)

It barely needs repeating – there is no divine right to fame: context is everything. As it changes, so do the conditions under which status is presented or taken away. There's no built-in reason why we should hail someone for propelling a football any more than we should praise another for entertaining us by giving birth in the Big Brother house, a feat accomplished by Tanja, a contestant in the Dutch version of the show. Whether in the house or on a South Pacific island, ordinary people without prior achievements have demonstrated a capacity for amusing audiences, however inadvertently. At other times in history, the owner of a prize-fighting cock, an explorer, or the originator of a bacteria-inhibiting serum might draw widespread acclaim. Not so much today.

Now, the distinction between ascribed, attributed, and achieved celebrity has been not so much blurred as erased. Not even a royal would become a celebrity without the attentions of the media. No one gets celebrity status attributed without doing something, however seemingly inconsequential that something might be – appearing in a reality tv show is *something*. And anyone who claims achievements, whether in sports or any other field of endeavor, will become widely known only with the assistance, collaboration, and support of the media and other branches of the culture industry.

This gives fuel to those critics who find reality tv "morally repugnant" and those, like Philip Hensher, who ask: "Isn't it worrying that so many people, inevitably failing in their fantastic dreams through lack of talent and lack of application, embark on a life they will always regard as second best?"

Fame-hunger is a malaise of our times. It's a hunger that's both promoted and satiated by perhaps the most maligned televisual genre ever. "It is damaging and sad that so many young people, aiming for celebrity at all costs, regard the kind of useful and, indeed, rewarding careers their parents would have regarded as appropriate ambition with contempt," Hensher concludes in the same *Independent* article quoted earlier.

In complete contrast, others see the democratizing impact of celebrity culture as modifying though not eliminating the impulse to succeed. "Fame typifies a particular idea of personal freedom and motivation to succeed that all should share," according to Jessica Evans (2005: 15). While Evans doesn't necessarily share this conception, it is one that has gained currency among a group she calls "populists" (by which I presume she means they claim to represent the whole of the people).

Reality tv strikes a blow for self-improvement and self-development: privilege and elite networks count for nothing. Hierarchies based on class, ethnicity, gender, or any other cultural contrivances have limited access to preferred areas of society. Anybody, literally anybody can fight their way into a reality tv show, become famous, even if only briefly, and grab their chance of success. It also urges us to rethink what it is to have talent. And perhaps: what is talent for? Is it a natural gift, or a capacity to enthrall us? If it's the latter, then the ordinary folk who seem to keep us rapt as effectively as a virtuoso violinist, a Shakespearean actor, a rock singer, or a sports star could lay claim to having it. Like it or not, reality tv featured people who *mattered* to audiences.

It was almost inevitable that reality tv would eventually succumb to temptation. Instead of using nondescript subjects, some shows featured people who had a public profile, no matter how low or eroded with age. While they didn't use scripts, cast members of both *Survivor* and *The Osbournes* accused producers of trying to influence their behavior. "The shows have denied doing so," wrote Dirk Smillie, in his article "So, this is reality?" before adding: "*Survivor* acknowledged restaging some scenes with body doubles" (2003: 23).

To some, this would have been tantamount to a corruption of the genre. To others, it would merely be an extension of a project that was never actually a window on reality. The purpose-built reality conveyed by reality tv was, to return to de Zengotita, part of the relentless move "from representation to representation."

As I stated earlier, my purpose in this chapter has not been to chart the rise of reality tv or to assess its merits, though readers may anticipate that I find much to commend in the genre (they can also find scholarly dissections in Holmes and Jermyn 2004; Murray and Ouellette 2004). In particular, the *Big Brother*-style formats might have qualified as pathbreaking social psychological experiments a few decades ago. The bewilderment offered by fragmented insights into several lives interacting can be as stimulating as it is mind-numbing. And the contrast with the linear narratives of conventional drama is often compelling. There is no room for stereotypes of any kind: viewers are continually reminded that they are watching real people. And here lies one source of their allure.

In agreeing with Dyer's early account, Matt Hills confirms: "Stars therefore represent society back to itself, functioning almost as cultural barometers" (2005: 151). Most of us check the tv, radio, or newspaper rather than a barometer for the weather forecast nowadays, but Hills' point is that celebrities are signs of the atmosphere, culturally speaking: they indicate to us what is going on in the rest of society. Mark Andrejevic expands this type of argument in his *Reality TV: The work of being watched*: we can inspect what might otherwise remain hidden aspects of culture by observing the interactions of people we don't know initially, but with whom we can identify (2004).

This may not – almost certainly does not – apply to all the celebrities of the constellation, but it surely rings true for those who came out of reality tv shows and maintained their attachments with us via the parasocial route we covered in earlier chapters. Those celebs may have terrified those who believed television's purpose was to uplift, enlighten, and enrich. For those who accepted that tv's primary purpose was to amuse, they were instructive: they showed that even though recognizably ordinary, normal, commonplace, run-of-the-mill people may be common, but they aren't average. Their appeal owed much to this lesson.

BLURRING/THE LINE

: soft news

Ask ten people "What's the biggest political event since the end of the cold war and the collapse of communism?" and there's a good chance at least six of them will answer "the Lewinsky affair." Monica Lewinsky was the White House aide whose affair with Bill Clinton became the subject of an investigation and indeed an international scandal. The affair was, without doubt, the biggest single news story of 1998. The media flexed their muscles and went into action at every new revelation. Consumers were absorbed by the affair that led to Clinton's nationally televised claim "I did not have sexual relations with that woman."

That same woman's admission that she had had oral sex with the President in the Oval Office transformed her from a nondescript intern into one of the most celebrated women in the world. And, while the US President is always a figure of great interest by virtue of his position (there's never been a female President), the several allegations of sexual peccadilloes that dogged Clinton marked him out as someone worthy of even greater interest. The relationship, or rather the coverage of its aftermath, dominated both the headlines and our attention. But was it a political event?

In a sense: Clinton was the US President for two terms of office and, for a while, under threat of impeachment. So the scandal could have had wider-reaching repercussions than it actually did. And the fact that Lewinsky actually worked in politics gave it added relevance. But, as the concupiscent details of the case unfurled – the semen-stained dress, the cigar, the secretly recorded phone conversations – interest tended to swing from the political to the prurient. For the final two years of the twentieth century, Lewinsky was one of the most famous women in the world. Her celebrity status manifested in several books about her, an assortment of well-paid endorsement deals, her own line of accessories, and a reality tv program in which she featured. She then faded from view.

Clinton remained as President till 2001, when he left office after serving his complete second term. He also acquired a status distinct from that of other politicians who leave legacies. Clinton could have been remembered for bringing together Israel's Yitzhak Rabin and Yasser Arafat of the Palestine Liberation Front on the White House lawn in 1993, or signing the 1994 Kremlin Accords that stopped the preprogrammed nuclear missiles, or organizing peace talks for Bosnia and Herzegovina in 1995, or ordering cruise missile strikes on Afghanistan in 1998. He could also be remembered for his consistently high approval rating among the "baby boomer" generation (those born in the immediate post-World War II period), for playing the saxophone, or for refining the soundbite as an effective mode of communication. Yet chances are he will be best remembered for the Lewinsky affair.

In the same year as the scandal, Kathy Koch wrote an article for *CQ Researcher* entitled "Can the media regain the public's trust?" (1998). As part of her research, she uncovered "the roots of newspapers' obsession with soft news" which, she argued, lay in two research projects of the late 1970s. One concluded that people read newspapers primarily for hard news, while the other, led by focus-group researcher Ruth Clark, found that readers favored lifestyle stories. This was the 1970s, remember.

Clark's conclusions were tempered by its subjects' realization that the media had responsibilities to inform and educate as well as to entertain, though this tended to be overlooked. "Predictably, perhaps, newspaper editors across the country embraced Clark's study," Koch reported. Politics started to give way to lifestyle. If any medium epitomized this move, it was *USA Today*, a national (and later international) newspaper launched in 1982, incorporating colorful graphics and relatively short (500-word) stories with lots of entertainment news and limited reporting on government or world politics. In a decade in which economic downturn affected most of the corporate sectors, including the media, the paper consistently turned a profit. It convinced its proprietors, Gannett Publishing, that it had hit on a successful formula.

As we noted in Chapter 2, the tabloids specializing in scandal were adversely affected around this time. Koch reckons that, during the 1980s, when independent and family-owned publications were taken over by large corporations, managers and proprietors started to take note of *USA Today*'s commercial success. Hard political news was either reduced or written in a personalized way. Politicians, their partners, or even their extramarital lovers, became the foci of political news; which was why, as Leo Braudy put it: "Everybody from the *New York Times* down starts a story – even one about ideas or policies – with an anecdote of some sorts" (quoted in Neimark 1995. I suspect Braudy might disapprove of this book too).

Lauren Langham believes image-led politics has a longer history than many suppose (2002). By the 1930s, both Hitler and Roosevelt had sensed the potential of radio and film to disseminate not only political information but images, especially images of great spectacles, such as rallies and marches. "With the growth of consumerism after WWII, aided and abetted by television, it would not be long until 'telepolitics' as a marketing strategy would join with consumerism as a means of 'selling' dreams, desires, and selfhood" (2002: 517).

Television's impact on the contemporary political process is scarcely news. Since the famous televised debates between John

F. Kennedy and Richard M. Nixon of 1960, there has been little doubt that image can overwhelm substance. Nixon may have held his own in the discussions, but his ghostly pallor and jowly cheeks made him appear a less attractive candidate than his fresh-faced opponent who emerged triumphant.

Since 1960, we have grown evermore reliant on television for our political information, as we have for all kinds of information. At the time of the Kennedy–Nixon debates, the printed medium was the most credible source of news. Despite its domestic growth over the previous decade, television was still something of a novelty and lacked the gravitas of newspapers and journals. By the time of the Lewinsky scandal, all remnants of solemnity and somberness had been obliterated as if by the touch of a remote control button. Television's mandate to entertain and divert, and its accent on the image over the word contrived to turn televised politics into a form of pleasure.

The title of Neil Postman's diatribe against television *Amusing Ourselves to Death* captures the self-destructive process he believes the medium, or rather our fixation with it, brought about (1985). Whereas once, populations would have flocked to meetings to watch, listen, and ask questions of politicians for anything up to four hours, they now grow impatient after a couple of minutes of watching tv. Even if we don't accept Postman's overall critique, we should acknowledge that television has pushed politics toward entertainment: and that the rest of the media has responded in kind. One implication of this is that the credibility once reserved for printed media has been dissipated widely among all media.

A parallel tendency has been for political systems to supply politicians who are ideologically indistinguishable and who are projected as much as entertainers as political leaders. How often have we heard politicians described as "boring" as if this was a heinous sin? The effort to produce aesthetically acceptable candidates whose ideas are subordinated to other, cosmetic considerations has brought what W. Russell Neuman calls "excessive sameness" in all politicians served up by television (2002). As we are only "partially attentive" when viewing and listening to them, eye-catching characteristics or memorable catchphrases linger in the mind of an audience that has become accustomed to passivity. Such characteristics and catchphrases come easily to some politicians, especially those versed in working the media.

: shining armor

The ascent of an actor whose filmography included *Cattle Queen of Montana* and *Hellcats of the Navy* to the Presidency of the United States was something of an object lesson in how to transfer values. Maybe Ronald Reagan wasn't a leading light of Hollywood in the 1950s, but he acquired enough expertise in the arts of presentation and communication to enable him to become a successful politician in the 1980s. Nowadays, the idea of a movie actor turning to politics isn't nearly so interesting or unexpected as it was when Reagan made the switch. Any number of movie and television actors have moved into politics, though without reaching the White House or 10 Downing Street. Sports stars too have made political challenges. Imran Khan capitalized on his international status as Pakistan's cricket captain when he entered politics. Soccer's George Weah failed narrowly in his attempt at the presidency of Sierra Leone.

The "white knight" phenomenon is how Darrell West and John Orman describe the success of celebrities who ride into politics (2003). Shining armor, a devotion to the service of the people, and chivalrous spirit of adventure are useful credentials in a world where politicians are typically regarded as self-serving hypocrites. Like knights, celebrities have rank or honor conferred on them as reward for personal merit or services outside politics. In this sense they haven't been smeared. Often, they have enough means to be above the corrupting influences that pervade politics. And, importantly, they have credibility: why would someone want to trade in a glamorous and lucrative lifestyle for something as prosaic as public duty if not out of a sense of service? But, perhaps even more important than this, they have recognizability: their image is known prior to their entry into politics. This saves a good deal of painstaking work and money in trying to establish a politician in the public consciousness.

In their book *Celebrity Politics*, West and Orman mark out five types of celebrities playing a role in politics: legacies, like those of the Kennedys and Bushes; newsworthies, such as Jesse Jackson; famed non-politicos of the Ronald Reagan or Sonny Bono type; famed non-politicos spokespersons, including Jane Fonda, Charlton Heston and the many others we will discuss in a later section; and event celebrities, like Monica Lewinsky (2003). The thrust of the book is that the line between news and entertainment has become blurred. Reagan probably did more than any contemporary politician to blur it.

By the time of his last movie appearance in 1964's *The Killers* Reagan had accumulated some political experience: he had served as president of the Screen Actor's Guild between 1947–52 and 1959–60, and openly supported the blacklisting of actors suspected of having communist sympathies. Paradoxically, he came from a family of Democrats and was a party member himself until switching in the 1960s, when he sensed the Republicans were better able to stem the suspected communist influences in Hollywood. After campaigning for the unsuccessful presidential candidate Barry Goldwater in 1964, he stood for Governor of California in 1966 and defeated the incumbent. He gained the presidential nomination at the third attempt, then ousted Jimmy Carter from the White House in 1980. Hints of what was to come emerged during the presidential election campaign. "A recession is when your neighbor loses his job. A depression is when you lose yours," Reagan contrived his maxim. "A recovery is when Jimmy Carter loses his." Short, crisp, witty, and endlessly quotable, it was trademark Reagan.

Reagan was re-elected in 1984 with a landslide win over Walter Mondale. Friends and enemies alike called him The Great Communicator: his expression of ideas in plain, easy-to-understand language was made for a culture in which the media was taking on greater importance. Simple, dismissive, often empty but memorable put-downs, like "there you go again" to rebut legitimate though sometimes complicated arguments were devoured by the media, as were his occasional gaffes, like joking "we begin the bombing [of Russia] in 15 minutes," or referring to Diana as "Princess David."

While it obviously wasn't planned, an attempt on Reagan's life in 1981 served to forge an improbable association with two entertainers: John Lennon, who was assassinated the year before and whose death was fresh in people's minds, and Jodie Foster. As we saw in Chapter 5, Reagan's would-be assassin, John Hinckley Jr, had had an erotomaniacal fixation on Foster.

Celebrity status has not always been as transferable as it was for Reagan: West and Orman remind us of the failure of astronaut John Glenn's presidential bid and athlete Bill Bradley's unsuccessful attempt to take the Democratic nomination. In contrast, the Philippines and India, among other nations, have traditions of politicians who first emerged as entertainers before switching to politics. After Reagan, there was a closer juxtaposition of spheres in the West: entertainment and politics moved side by side, occasionally overlapping. Celebrity culture forced politicians into making use of the same kinds of marketing and advertising techniques as popular entertainers and disposed popular entertainers to see politics as providing an open invitation to those with fame, money, and a yen for power.

Reagan was never what we would describe today as A-list. He was primarily a co-star: one of those faces you see in movies and recognize, but never expect to see in a starring role. While he might not have had much grasp of policy affairs or international trade agreements, he had a flair for image maintenance and quotable quotes, both essential in Hollywood. He also had experience in actors' union affairs and served an apprenticeship of sorts before becoming the US President.

Arnold Schwarzenegger, by contrast, built his reputation completely on image. While he had no know-how of politics prior to his election as Governor of California, Schwarzenegger was used to career transitions. A one-time body-builder, the Austrian featured in the 1976 film *Pumping Iron*, in which he played basically himself. Innovations on the same role followed in *Conan the Barbarian, Predator* and *The Terminator*, which reproduced itself in two blockbuster sequels. Reputed at one stage to be the highest paid actor in the world, Schwarzenegger made no firm indication that he sought political office before he launched his bid in 2004, but his campaign revealed that he had a canny grasp of the demands of politics. Far from being embarrassed by tabloid condensations, he encouraged them. FROM TERMINATOR TO GOVERNATOR-type headlines greeted his election. Schwarzenegger responded by promising to terminate taxes. His policies may have been opaque, but his slogans were communicable and memorable and, of course, his image was globally familiar. The same instantly recognizable image helped him raise money and attract the attention of the world's media. In these senses, Schwarzenegger made an extremely efficient political candidate.

His party warmly embraced Schwarzenegger. Shortly after his election, he addressed the Republican National Convention. "People pay $9 to go see Arnold Schwarzenegger in massive numbers," declared the Republican National Chairman Ed Gillespie. "So hopefully people will see him in massive numbers and support [presidential candidate George W. Bush] for re-election" (quoted in Raasch 2004). The logic was sound enough. Traditionalists would reply that being popular in one medium should not necessarily translate into popularity in another, especially when the latter carries with it obligations to help form and represent the opinions of rather than amuse the electorate.

While Schwarzenegger's foray into politics drew much attention, it could be argued that the principles underlying his election had been exploited earlier not just by Reagan but by Bill Clinton. "Clinton drew upon forms of self-presentation developed in the entertainment industries," maintains David Hesmondhalgh. "He studied the way in which television performers established a rapport with their audiences" (2005: 131).

Hesmondhalgh cites in particular the way in which music videos on cable and satellite tv channels had enabled performers to establish a new kind of rapport with viewing audiences. Perhaps more significantly, we should add the changes in presentational style occasioned by the 24-hour news stations with their fast-paced audio-visual economy that rarely tested the patience of viewers. "An intimacy at great distance," is how Hesmondhalgh describes the style essayed by Clinton. The President probably didn't realize just how intimate this relationship with his audience would become, as we saw at the start of this chapter.

Warren Beatty, who was initially a Clinton supporter, actually caricatured him in his 1998 movie *Bulworth*, in which a liberal politician is reduced to a corporate lackey. In fact, Clinton may have inadvertently politicized several Hollywood actors who were so dismayed by him that they became activists themselves. Susan Sarandon, Tim Robbins, Danny Glover, and Sean Penn found a new pole of political attraction on the streets of Seattle in 1999 when the anti-globalization protesters challenged the World Trade Organization.

This isn't necessarily a negative development. West and Orman acknowledge that many celebrities who ride into politics with their lances at the ready have limited political skills, particularly in conflict resolution. But they do bring with them a guile and persuasiveness with the media and are not often bound by restrictive party lines. So they can actually invigorate politics with new ideas. Schwarzenegger, despite being a Republican, supported affirmative action, environmental regulation, gay rights, and (conditionally) stem cell research. West and Orman are not alone in challenging the more orthodox view that celebrities have polluted politics. John Street, for example, argues that the celebrity politician is consistent with a liberal democratic ethos and that each celebrity needs to be evaluated on his or her own merits (2004). There remains, however, a suspicion that, for all the freshness and independence of thought celebrity politicians at first bring to the established arena, their absorption into the party process eventually limits their potential. They become, to return to Neuman's phrase, excessively the same as all the others. On the other hand, celebrities who pursue their political aims from outside the system avoid this assimilation.

: bards of the powerful?

In the 1970s, before Reagan had made it to the White House, Francesco Alberoni wrote of a "powerless elite," a class of entertainers "whose institutional power is very limited or non-existent, but whose doings and way of life arouse considerable and sometimes even a maximum degree of interest" (1972).

They were extremely famous, earned huge sums of money, and had considerable influence, but that influence was based on their image. As we've seen, images are manipulated in a way that makes celebrities persuasive endorsers of commercial products. Celebrities can also inspire people to wear certain types of clothes or jewelry, have their hair styled in a particular way, and even use new language. They may even change the way people think and feel about poverty, the environment, and other social issues, perhaps sparking debates. Still, they don't have the capacity to make decisions that actually change society in a significant and substantial way. That kind of capacity usually comes with political office.

Alberoni argued that stars who commanded strong and widely diffused followings operated in their own spheres and posed no effective challenge in a political sense. He was writing in the early 1970s, before the cultural shift that left celebrities of all kinds with a sense of self-importance that inclined them to try their hands at politics. Whereas rock stars, actors, or models once had influence without legitimate, governmental power, they assumed a kind of moral authority once associated with sages or charismatic leaders. And, after Reagan, several swapped spheres, opting to capitalize on their image in the sphere of institutional politics.

If the juxtaposition of politics and entertainment were any closer, then every pop or movie star would be potentially electable. This is not quite the case, though the situation has encouraged all manner of celebrities to offer themselves to politicians. Celebrities provide a valuable resource: attention. Celebrities popular with young people are particularly useful in conferring elusive credibility, though this hasn't always translated into votes. Jon Bon Jovi not only backed Al Gore in the 2000 election won by George W. Bush, but hosted fundraisers and, on one occasion, performed an acoustic set. Wesley Clark lost out to John Kerry in the 2003 Democratic nominations despite the support of Madonna.

It sounds trite to assert that today's celebrities are politically active. It suggests that yesterday's stars were not. Obviously, they were; it's just that consumers were not interested. So, why risk losing fans by disclosing political preferences when there was nothing to be gained and everything to lose? Celebrities are now open to inspection: fans can't be appeased with a few dismissive comments about being uninterested in politics or mistrusting all politicians. Those that honestly do mistrust all politicians often make their own personal views public and sometimes offer themselves as politicians-without-office.

Bob Geldof is something of an archetype in this respect. The former frontman for the 1970s band the Boomtown Rats, he was reincarnated as St Bob when he organized the global Live Aid concert of July 1985. It was an epic concert split across Britain and the USA, designed to raise money to alleviate a famine in which some 30 million people were starving as drought swept across sub-Saharan Africa. Cynics may point out that the concert provided many acts with invaluable global exposure and, certainly, several of the performers went on to epic careers. In particular, U2 had just released *The Unforgettable Fire*. Sting had recently left Police and was launching a solo career. Run DMC were poised to release their breakthrough single "Walk this Way." All prospered in the aftermath of the concert, but all, in their own ways, maintained their commitment both to the alleviation of poverty and other causes.

Obviously, there had been natural calamities and comparable human suffering, though the Live Aid concert used the medium of television to telling effect: viewers in the affluent West watched from the comfort of their homes as children died. Ninety-eight percent of all televisions in the world received the broadcast. In total, more than 1.5 billion tv viewers watched the event. The Live Aid concert raised $100 million, the most by far that had ever been collected for charity from a single event. So effective was the mass action that it announced the arrival of rock stars and other celebrities in global politics.

Geldof's reputation oscillated between that of a fading rock star trying to clamber back into the limelight and an earnest, socially aware campaigner for human rights and opponent of inequity. Over the next couple of decades, the latter won out. In fact, in 2005, he gathered another assembly of stars to stage another huge, multi-venue concert, this time under the rubric of Live8. The result was a dramatic increase in several nations' aid budgets.

Rock music lends itself to issue-based politics. The music itself was rebellious, at least when it emerged in the 1950s, and there has been a pulse of dissent beating ever since: Bob Dylan's scalding tirades of the 1960s, Billy Bragg's leftwing sermonizing in the 1970s, Bob Marley's sometimes mournful, sometimes blistering attacks on racism in the 1980s, REM's alignment with several liberal causes in the 1990s. Actors have been less conspicuous,

though Jane Fonda, Barbra Streisand, Susan Sarandon, and Woody
Harrelson are among several Hollywood celebs who have rallied
around particular issues, especially following September 11, 2001.
These and many others have kept the pulse going through the
decades. Geldof, though, disclosed a different kind of celebrity
politicking. He used his status to mobilize other musicians who,
in turn, mobilized millions from around the world.

The lesson wasn't lost on Paul Hewson aka Bono, Geldof's
confederate at both Live Aid and Live8. After 1985, he realized
what he once called "the currency of my celebrity." In 1987, the
value of that currency rose with the release of U2's *The Joshua
Tree*, an album that established them as one of the world's best-
selling bands. It afforded Bono himself a wider audience for his
campaigns for Third World debt relief and AIDS medication for
Africa. Clinton's successful presidential campaigns in the 1990s
had alerted politicians to the value of celebrity supporters (among
Clinton's fans was Fleetwood Mac, which supplied his 1993
campaign's theme song "Don't stop (thinking about tomorrow)").
It made sense for politicians to schmooze with celebrities, the
higher the celebrity currency, the greater the concession. At
least, Bono arrived at that conclusion. For example, in 2002,
he accompanied US Treasury Secretary Paul O'Neill on a tour
of Africa, using the opportunity to set up an organization called
DATA (Debt. AIDs. Trade in Africa). He spoke on behalf of
Canadian Prime Minister Paul Martin on the condition that
Canada increased its budget for foreign aid. He visited George
W. Bush at the White House when Bush unveiled a $5 million aid
package for the world's poorest countries with good human rights
records.

Trade-offs like these drew criticism from, among others,
George Monbiot, the environmentalist writer, who, in a *Guardian*
article, detected that, after Live8, Bono and Geldof had become,
as the title of his article indicates, "Bards of the powerful" (June
21, 2005). A bard is an honored poet. "I have yet to read a
statement by either rock star that suggests a critique of power,"

commented Monbiot, who censured Geldof and Bono for becoming so cozy with the world's political leaders that they had lost the capacity to express a thoroughgoing critique. Instead: "They are lending legitimacy to power."

The danger for any celebrity who secures concessions from politicians in exchange for collaboration if not backing is that they may be seen as ventriloquists' dummies, mouthing platitudes that serve the interests of politicians. This may be an unfair appraisal, but it is the import of Monbiot's appraisal. Contemporaries of Geldof and Bono, such as Sting, have maintained a distance from politicians, sniping from the margins, though, it could be argued, without actually achieving material gains. Sting appeared in both Live Aid and Live8 and remains a prominent advocate of human rights and the environment.

In some senses, there is a no-win situation awaiting any celeb who strikes up a political posture. In the twenty-first century, there is every chance that an opportunist politician's celebrity coordinator (and there are such agents) will snap them up, promise acknowledgments and a few dispensations, and make an ally out of them. If they remain silent, they risk appearing apolitical, unaware, and indifferent to world events. Even saying a few carefully chosen words on a single, poignant issue carries risks. When Kanye West observed in the wake of 2005's Hurricane Katrina that "George Bush don't care about black people," he could hardly have expected a response that would have been more appropriate to an act of treason. His critics ran from the far right to 50 Cent.

And, while anti-globalization campaigners greeted with approval Coldplay's Chris Martin's revelation "I don't really care about EMI [the company that releases his band's records] . . . I think shareholders are the greatest evil of this modern world," in 2005, the shareholders themselves must have been rubbing their hands at the dividends boosted by 9 million (and counting) sales of the band's third album *X&Y*. Observers would have spotted the comic irony.

Chances are that celebrities will not be silenced by a few embarrassments. One of the effects of celebrity culture has been to open up opportunities for celebrities to voice their political opinions in expectation that they will get an airing. Add to this the fact that every politician harboring thoughts of high office is constantly searching for the kudos that comes with celebrity support. Critics may complain that a cooptation is in progress and even the most severe celebrity critics can be accommodated within the political system. Apologists may point to writers like Frances Bonner, who argues that celebrities have become "a major way through which people apprehend how the world itself operates" (2005: 93). They may also contend that that seeing Coldplay support Oxfam's Make Trade Fair campaign or Robbie Williams applaud UNICEF motivates fans to recognize great causes. In this respect, "Celebrities may also be seen as 'navigational' aids," as Bonner puts it.

When, in her essay, "Celebrity, media, and history," Jessica Evans paraphrases Oxfam's reason for enthusiastically enlisting celebrities, she manages to capture this positive effect of celebrity culture on politics. The "function" of celebrities, she summarizes, is to convert "very complex economic and political arguments . . . into digestible and easily understandable chunks of information that will fit into the contexts of media viewing" (2005: 42).

Some will find this laudable: celebrities have helped keep concerns about, for example, global warming, toxic waste, and animal rights at the forefront of public consciousness. Others are convinced that it is symptomatic of a culture where the media's unparalleled power has perverted the entire character of politics, turning it into just another diverting amusement.

: defining the events themselves

When Lauren Langham describes an "amusement society" in which image-makers have "blurred the differences between leaders and stars . . . electoral politics has become a moment of entertainment" and politicians are marketed like "soap, cars or toothpaste," the allusion is to a dramatic carnival-like spectacle in which the stage and props are owned by media corporations (2002: 516).

Like all great entertainments, politics has continually changed to suit new contexts. From the moment television viewers warmed to the unsullied complexion of Kennedy and cooled on Nixon, politics as an institution started to adapt to what Postman calls the age of television. As we have seen, research in the following decade revealed a growing keenness for lifestyle news, and the media overlooked consumers' abiding interest in hard news of government and current affairs in their efforts to maintain market share. By the early 1980s, a fledgling *USA Today* had thrown down a gauntlet, challenging other media to replicate its commercial success.

In the background, mergers and takeovers served to concentrate ownership of the world's media into the hands of a few powerful global corporations. While fearmongers' claims that the media can make or break politicians and possibly entire political systems have seemed exaggerations, they can't be dismissed totally. The trend toward consolidation in the newspaper industry was paralleled in other media, with national corporations becoming global conglomerates. This gave rise to fears that cozy relationships between political leaders and media tycoons could militate against critical coverage. As the title of Robert McChesney's book *Corporate Media and the Threat to Democracy* suggests, the profit-maximizing mentality of the global media industry worked to the detriment of democracy, a system in which members are supposed to have a right to participate in decision-making. One episode in particular highlighted how commercial considerations could subordinate political matters.

As Clinton's imbroglio over Lewinsky began, the publisher HarperCollins, which is part of News International, Rupert Murdoch's group of companies, pulled a memoir by former

Governor of Hong Kong Chris Patten from publication. Patten's text contained less than kind statements about China. Murdoch had – indeed, still has – extensive network outlets throughout China, a country with a one-party rule political system, a record of abusing human rights, and a habit of stamping down on protest, as evidenced in Tiananmen Square in 1989. It also has the world's fastest growing economy and a population of over 1.3 billion. As such, it represents a fertile market.

The episode sent up two flares. One signaled the immense power of media conglomerates to shape the information that eventually gets into books, newspapers, and the other media on which we depend. The 1997 Bond movie *Tomorrow Never Dies* envisioned a megalomaniac media mogul with designs on creating as well as reporting the news. The plot seemed less fantastic than those of many other Bond films. The second flare was about the ability of global corporations to censor political news. To an extent, fears about this were offset by the expansion of the internet, which made anyone with access to a computer a potential publisher. Perhaps more importantly, it turned consumers into active interpreters rather than passive receivers of news and other kinds of data. Readers of computer screens had to stay mindful of the source of news, the motivation of its originators, and its reliability. It could be argued that tv viewers and newspaper readers should do the same, though they probably don't: they may disagree with the opinions or the slant, but they rarely challenge the source.

To some extent the softening tendencies of journalism were arrested by the rise of CNN and the various other television channels dedicated to exposition, comment, and analysis as well as straightforward reportage. And, while the internet may not have galvanized consumers as it had seemed to promise, its value lay in prompting television's response. At the time of the Lewinsky affair, the internet was getting into its stride as a news source and this made the race for fresh information between media more competitive.

The 24-hour news channels were effectively television's response to the challenge of the online sites that were like a rolling tableau of events, constantly updated and never-ending. CNN was founded in 1980 by Ted Turner and later acquired by Warner Bros, itself absorbed into Time-Warner, which later became AOL Time-Warner. Unique in its day, CNN was later joined by, among others, Murdoch's Fox News Channel and MSNBC (Microsoft-NBC), as well as Britain's BBC News 24 and SkyNews (another Murdoch enterprise). "The prophecies about the Internet soon emerging as the prime medium for news are crumbling to dust," declared Rueven Frank in 2001. After considering the rivalry between television's 24-hour news channels and their internet rivals, Frank was in no doubt about which emerged not only victorious, but also more influential: "The media coverage of major events has often come to define the events themselves and has exerted profound influence on the public's perception." CNN, in particular, "influences the decisions of leaders and shapes public opinion" (2001: 38).

Even allowing for a degree of overstatement and a failure to anticipate how other tv news channels would catch up with CNN, at least in terms of audience, if not influence, Frank had a strong point: television commands great authority in affecting the decisions that contribute to political events and in shaping the consumers' understanding of those same events. People now talk in terms of the "CNN effect" when considering how the transmission of images of suffering from around the world can influence both viewers' understanding and Western governments' policies.

As we've seen in previous chapters, we can no more understand celebrity culture without the media than make omelets without eggs. Politics is, by definition, a public sphere. Yet perhaps never quite as public as it is today. As well as being able to relay news instantly from every part of the world to every part of the world, the news media enable viewers to scrutinize their political leaders to an extent unheard of as recently as the 1990s.

The surveillance carried out by news media is more invasive and perhaps more meddling than ever.

Celebrity culture itself is, in some senses, an accommodation of this, celebrities surrendering any trace of a private life in exchange for publicity. Politicians too have had to strike the bargain. They play by the same rules of engagement, as we called them in Chapter 3. As Clinton discovered, this is not necessarily a bad thing for a politician's credibility. As well as being depicted as a philanderer, he was, at various intervals, accused of being a dope-taker, a draft-dodger, and an embezzler. Yet his popularity rating remained high, especially among women. Reagan might have been the first politician to exploit the media's weakness for pictures and platitudes, but Clinton, as Langham puts it, "clearly understood the new realities, or hyperrealities, of simulated images in a media age."

Langham means that media have created an environment in which politics itself has become a form of amusement. The space it has reserved for politicians is one in which they can prosper or perish, depending on their response to the visibility. One tactic employed – indeed, pioneered – by Clinton and adopted by just about every other politician is to hobnob with celebrities from outside politics: even if they don't publicly endorse the candidature, the association alone has its rewards. As we've seen, many celebrities have responded to this, some even swapping careers, others supplementing showbusiness with political credentials. Still others snipe from the edges.

CREATING/LEGENDS

: first of the breed

Picture this. It's the middle of the 1960s, the decade of release when young people, stirred into protesting against war in Vietnam and excited by the prospect of great cultural change, are asserting their difference. Their membership of a new generation is evident in their clothes, their music, and even the way they talk. Concerned citizens worry about their long hair, their drugs, and their open rebelliousness against anything that smells of "establishment."

Some parts of the establishment are inviolable, of course. Sports, for example. If there was any doubt that, despite the changes swirling about it, sport remains a conservative institution, it comes in 1968, when Olympic athletes Tommie Smith and John Carlos thrust their gloved fists into the air in a defiant Black Power salute. African Americans and young whites everywhere are making the same gesture. The big difference is that Smith and Carlos do it on the victory rostrum in full view of television viewers around the world. They are thrown out, never to return to competitive sports.

This couldn't happen in football, one of the most conservative of pursuits, encrusted in traditional, some might say archaic values. Suddenly, someone pops up to remind everyone that even this sport is in flux. This player looks like he might have been in the Who or the Byrds, or a member of the cast of *A Hard Day's Night*. He wears clothes that were probably bought from a fashionably expensive boutique (as the upscale clothes stores are called), grows his hair voguishly long, and sports facial hair every so often.

He also has the kind of dark handsome features that invite a rock star following among young women. And he exploits this fully. The media chronicle his *affaires de cœur* keenly, affording him the kind of coverage typically reserved for showbusiness libertines like Warren Beatty and Mick Jagger. In fact, he rubs shoulders with movie and rock stars, often to the embarrassment of his football club. The club is further compromised when he opens his own late-night club, where he is often seen drinking with "beautiful people," as they are known.

Endorsements are also distractions: advertisers are lining up to offer him well-paid assignments and, for a while, his image seems unavoidable. If he's not on tv playing, he's in the commercial breaks advertising men's grooming products or in the papers, promoting clothes, food, and practically anything else he can help sell. Yet, it's easy to forgive him: when he's on the football field, his play is sublime. He is inspirational in his club's most prestigious and historic victory and is acknowledged as one of the most gifted players of his time.

Then, unexpectedly, he quits, disappears, returns, though without ever recapturing his best form. The advertisers lose interest and the media's emphasis turns to his habitual drinking. Gradually, he fades from public view, surfacing every so often to do media work, though without showing much aptitude for this. Occasional stories about his drinking suggest he has a problem and he undergoes rehab. It is a sorry end to a glittering career, though mention of his name continues to awaken the echoes. Readers will have guessed that name.

British readers: he is, of course, George Best.

American readers: he is, of course, Joe Namath.

There is a remarkable parallelism about the careers of Best and Namath. Apart from the above description of their lives – which can be applied to either without modification – they were both misfits, square pegs in round holes, fishes out of water, odd men out. In an era when athletes were athletes, Best and Namath were celebrity athletes. Today, there is any number of sports stars who fit comfortably into that role. In fact, virtually any athlete who has public visibility is handed endorsement contracts, requests for talk show appearances, and possibly a media retinue of their own. In the 1960s, there were a few standouts, Muhammad Ali being the most obvious, but he rose to global fame on account of his boxing, his refusal to take the Vietnam draft, and his affiliation to the segregationist Nation of Islam rather than his sybaritism. Fascination with lifestyles is something we associate with today's celebrities. As Best's biographer Joe Lovejoy writes, in a phrase that could equally apply to Namath: "As the first of the breed, he had no precedents" (1999: 201).

It's possible to cite Joe DiMaggio, who created enormous interest beyond sports, especially after marrying Marilyn Monroe. Before him, Babe Ruth and Jack Dempsey had been international figures, famed almost as much for their lifestyles as their competitive prowess. But none of them attracted a public besotted with images. Best and Namath were able to do this: a media that had been changed by the arrival of television powered their ascent. After their demise in the 1970s, it was at least a decade before the emergence of other athletes with comparable capacities to enchant.

Now, skip to the early twenty-first century. Two other athletes hold sway. Neither Best nor Namath was especially popular outside their own countries. By contrast, Tiger Woods and David Beckham are globally recognized as celebrity athletes. They enjoy followings practically everywhere football and golf are played and in many places where they are not. There were other celebrities from sport, of course: Serena and Venus Williams, Allen Iverson, Kobe Bryant, and Michael Schumacher, for instance. All acquired followings that went beyond the confines of their sports. The first four became emblematic of a new type of black person, or, to use Wiley Hall's phrase from Chapter 7, "a different kind of White person." But Woods and Beckham seemed hypnotically, almost incomprehensibly, captivating. They were genuinely charismatic; and, by this, I mean they held the capacity to inspire followers with devotion and passion – not that they had any special gift or talent. Some may argue that both *did* have special talents that separated them from other athletes. Maybe so. But surely this isn't sufficient to explain their inspirational power. There have been plenty of great golfers and footballers, though none that has moved what at times seemed like entire populations.

In their day, Best and Namath were unruly, insubordinate, and openly defiant. They talked, behaved, and looked like they had respect for nothing and no one: they followed their own impulses rather than others' rules. Clashes with authority were frequent, with both athletes, at intervals, threatening to or actually quitting their sports rather than succumb to the official imperatives. Far from being virtuous characters, they acquired well-earned reputations for philandering and the high life. They were flawed, irredeemably in the case of Best, who died in 2005 after an illness occasioned by alcohol abuse.

In no sense did either represent, symbolize, or exemplify mainstream cultural values. And yet they were priceless cultural figures. This was the 1960s, remember: before society had developed an apparatus for producing and refining characters who would amuse and enliven though without necessarily inciting us to iniquitous behavior. It was a time when "the emergence of celebrity figures was a haphazard and arbitrary voyage of discovery," as David Andrews and Steven Jackson put it in their *Sport Stars: The cultural politics of sporting celebrity* (2001: 4). They add: "Today the process is considerably more proactive in its focus on the cultivation of potential celebrities." Even from the world of sport.

: harmonious blends

In their essay "Stories of sport and moral order: unraveling the cultural construction of Tiger Woods," Judy Polumbaum and Stephen Wietling argue that Woods' fame has sources in his golfing talent but is "augmented" by stylized media coverage (1999). Drawing on Nick Trujillo and Leah Vande Berg's 1994 analysis of the baseball player Nolan Ryan, Polumbaum and Wietling notice how, in the 1980s and 1990s, the pitcher performed great sporting feats in the diamond, but was also depicted by the media as a "manifestation of mainstream cultural values," including the work ethic, honesty and fairness, wholesomeness, and a "humble lifestyle." He played till he was 46 and, though composed, could react aggressively when provoked.

When they were writing in the late 1990s, Polumbaum and Wietling could only suggest that Woods' connection to such values was "tenuous." His ethnicity combined with insinuations of "irreverence" made the perfect Ryan-type match improbable. But, of course, mainstream values are neither constant nor undisputed: they are challenged and changed.

By the time Woods became the world's highest-paid sports endorser with an annual income of $54 million/£32 million, in 2002, his image was congruent with the values of the times (by the mid-2000s, he was up to $87 million pa). His work ethic was beyond dispute, as was his sense of fairness and his wholesomeness. And, while humility had probably lost some of its approval rating since the days of Ryan, Woods was hardly P. Diddy when it came to flamboyant consumption. More importantly, Woods was a black man, who consciously promoted his multicultural heritage, which included both Asian and African ancestry. He embodied, as Polumbaum and Wietling put it, "the harmonious blend of American diversity."

C. L. Cole and David Andrews are in broad agreement with this assessment. They describe Woods as an "American supericon: a commercial emblem who makes visible and concrete modern

America's narrative of itself as a post-historical nation of immigrants" (2001: 72). They go on: "Woods is coded [by the media] as a multicultural sign of color-blindness" (2001: 81).

Woods introduced a new kind thread in the narrative of race and ethnicity. He was a black man for all to see; yet his speech, demeanor, views, and all-round "cultural literacy" made it possible for him to reassure the United States – and, we should add, the world – that America's history of racial violence and segregation were a thing of the past (hence, the phrase "post-historical").

This "hybrid" image, as Polumbaum and Wietling call it, became even more apposite after September 11, 2001, when national unity became a paramount concern for the USA. Presumably, these writers would find the argument presented in Chapter 7 consistent with their approach. Like Beyoncé, Woods sells a kind of amnesia, helping erase the morally disfigured past as he projects a benign and flawless "face of America's future citizenry," the kind of presence that "reinvigorates, rather than contests, white cultural prestige" (2001: 85).

Beckham was also a decent, clean-living family man, his seeming devotion to his children securing his wholesome image. The values he was portrayed as personifying were in keeping with early twentieth-century mores. Although he was white, it was often said that his tastes, particularly in ostentatious jewelry, r&b music, and inventive hairstyles made him "black" in a cultural sense. While his marriage to former Spice Girl, Victoria Adams, herself a bona fide member of the fashionistas, put his sexual proclivities beyond doubt, he enjoyed a considerable gay following and, at times, deliberately wooed this with photoshoots in gay magazines. He confirmed on national British television that he wasn't embarrassed by his gay fandom – an admission that would have guaranteed purgatory for any other soccer player.

In every other respect, the mild-mannered Beckham was utterly bland. He held no known opinions on issues other than sport and his family. In the early phases of his emergence, he gave interviews sparingly and offered photo opportunities only under strict conditions. He almost gave the impression of being inscrutable. At one point, he retreated Garbo-like and surfaced only to train or play. Teasing or just plainly annoying the media like this can have its rewards. Beckham presented a *tabula rasa*, that is a blank slate onto which anything could be written, and audiences inscribed whatever they wanted. Beckham, or rather "Beckham" (the mediated image) took on an existence independent of time and space: he became the possession of countless fans, who each constructed their own version of how they wanted him to be.

Already Britain's premier celebrity athlete, Beckham was made the captain of the England football team, a position that obliged him to engage more with the media. "Engage" is hardly an apt verb: he dispensed inanities about soccer and chatted smilingly about his burgeoning family. There was a freshly plucked innocence about Beckham the family man, doting father and talismanic leader of English soccer. He was, to invoke the cliché, a good role model. Even neater, Beckham reverberated with inclusiveness. White, but with black tastes; straight, but adored by gay men; male, but with a penchant for nail varnish, body-waxing, and androgynous attire.

Skillfully steered by a wife who was, as we saw in Chapter 10, well-versed in the art and science of celebrity production, Beckham moved from Manchester United to Real Madrid, launched a new line of sportswear with adidas, carved open Asian markets, endorsed Gillette, Pepsi, and many other products and still found time to play football. In 2004, news of an affair spoiled the image of the blissfully contented family man. But, by this stage, the piety was probably becoming burdensome and a streak of devilishness may have actually enhanced his image.

Unlike Woods, Beckham had no hesitation about switching between the juxtaposed spheres of sport and entertainment. He could hardly avoid it: his ascent had been calibrated with a perfection typically associated with a rock star. The influence of his wife was apparent in almost every move, right down to, for example, requesting digital press cameras so that stills could be viewed and approved there and then prior to publication.

Woods and Beckham were alpha males, but with New Man sensibilities and few, if any of the deviant tendencies that made both Best and Namath appealing mavericks. But, while the latter two were incongruous characters in the 1960s, the former pair was in complete harmony with the 2000s. They epitomized valued properties, like excellence, merit, and propriety. It's doubtful whether a hard-drinking womanizer with spotless macho credentials and a habit of showing the finger to authority would fit into the contemporary celebrity suite. Control is one of the most important requirements: celebrities must be manageable, if not dirigible – willing to be guided in any direction. And while, in the past, the odd individualist could be accommodated, an unpredictable, wayward spirit could not. The most recent of these is probably subversively cross-dressing Dennis Rodman, "an unmistakable embodiment of 'bad' blackness," as Mélisse Lafrance and Geneviève Rail describe him (2001: 40). Or Paul Gascoigne, who inherited both Best's fortune as a "football genius" and his bane as an alcoholic.

Why did the more anodyne and inoffensive defenders of the status quo displace the eccentric, nonconformist champions? This actually isn't a fair question: they were not displaced. There are still plenty of maverick types about; they just don't attract the kinds of contracts that became indispensable to a celebrity career. There was no need for arbitrary and haphazard voyages, to repeat Andrews and Jackson, when there were precise map coordinates available.

: putting the sex into sport

"Here's the exchange," an advertising executive once said to a sports agent. "I'll pay your man double what he earns from his sport in a year and plaster his face all over the hoardings, tv screens and newspaper pages. In return, your man just stays out of trouble." These may not have been the exact words, but they carry the essence of the kind of deals that were reached during the late 1980s. Before long: "Sports had arguably surpassed popular music as the captivating medium most essential to being perceived as 'young and alive,'" according to Donald Katz, author of *Just Do It: The Nike spirit in the corporate world*. "Sports, as never before, had so completely permeated the logic of the marketplace that by 1992 the psychological content of selling was often more sports-oriented than it was sexual" (1994: 25–6).

Sport came of age. Its innocence had been lost many years before, perhaps as far back as 1858 when baseball players divided up the money collected from admissions, or 1864 when professionalism was allowed into English soccer. But it had never laid its virtue on the line in the pursuit of pure manna. Once sport climbed into bed with market forces, the new liaison was irrepressible.

Of all the deals of the 1980s or 1990s, Nike's arrangement with Michael Jordan was the most unusual, yet most influential. Jordan left university without graduating to join the NBA club, Chicago Bulls. While most players do deals with sports goods manufacturers, Jordan was granted a guaranteed minimum plus royalties from Nike. In other words, he received a percentage of every piece of apparel or footwear bearing his name. Jordan made about $130 million from Nike over the course of his playing career, according to David Halberstam (1999: 412). As we pointed out in Chapter 9, Nike sold $5.2 billion-worth of Air Jordan over the same period, according to the estimates of Roy Johnson and Ann Harrington (1998).

The Nike/Jordan relationship was something of a harbinger. Athletes had always regarded endorsement contracts as sidelines, while advertisers had sought out only elite sports stars whose profiles worked for their products, such as razors and breakfast cereals. Nike used Jordan to construct a brand, something that worked as a product in its own right. Its jaw-dropping success alerted others to the limitations of exploiting existing markets. Nike's program was to create new markets. Jordan became its universal delivery service: he carried the Nike banner to every part of the world. There was reciprocity, as Naomi Klein points out in her *No Logo*: "It was Nike's commercials that made Jordan a global superstar" (2001: 52).

The idea of affixing the name of an athlete to a product seems ridiculously obvious nowadays. It's hardly possible to get through a newspaper without seeing some football or baseball player citing the benefits something or other (Pelé's approval for Viagra was noteworthy). Yet, prior to the 1980s, sports stars were recruited only sporadically to lend their support to products: they had almost oddity value. Why did athletes suddenly become ubiquitous?

Unlikely as it seems, I'll begin my answer in South Korea. Here, two of the best-known figures in recent years are Taiji Seo, a rock musician, and Chanho Park, the pitcher who migrated to Major League Baseball in the US. Heejon Chung describes both as "cultural icons," though "if they could be placed on an ideological continuum, they would be located at right and left extremes." In his scholarly analysis of the two celebrities, "Sport star vs. rock star in globalizing popular culture," Chung reveals: "Seo is the symbol of progressiveness, resistance and deviation, Park is that of conservatism, adaptation and normality" (2003: 104).

Recall the characters we have highlighted so far. Like Park, Beckham and Woods are conservative, well-adapted ciphers of "normal" family life, as, of course, was Jordan. In the 1960s, Best and Namath were acclaimed because of their devil-may-care rebelliousness. They attracted a few endorsement contracts, but, as I pointed out earlier, were too exceptional, too "unsafe" for most advertisers. In any case, athletes, though often lauded and praised, were parts of a sphere that was by definition unpredictable.

Entertainers, being under the control of agents, managers, and pr people were typically safer bets. But not scandal-proof, as the incidents covered in Chapter 8 indicated. In the late 1980s, athletes began to appear more secure. Figures like Ben Johnson, who was demonized by the media after failing a drugs test and being ejected from the 1988 Olympics, were a rarity. Sports competitors more typically embodied an uprightness, respectability, and all-round honesty that advertisers craved.

In answering the question "Why has sport moved from the periphery to the centre of popular culture?" John Horne writes in his *Sport and Consumer Culture*: "The media, sponsors and marketing agencies are merely exploiting a growing interest in sport, which has been created by increasing media coverage of sport" (2006: 80). Yet surely they weren't "merely exploiting": they were actively propelling sport to its central position. Advertisers made the athletes featured in campaigns more visible, recognizable, and, in a self-fulfilling way, more attractive to other advertisers.

Horne believes that there were other factors at work, the interest in health, fitness, and the overall well-being of the body being another. In Chapter 4 we saw how the culture of narcissism nourished an awareness of the body. Sport provided an arena in which hale and hearty bodies were displayed.

A more decisive change was, as we saw in Chapter 3, the proliferation of television channels and their obvious requirement: programs. Sports provided relatively cheap content: production costs were low compared to drama and, for commercial tv companies, the advertising income more than offset them. ESPN's venture in 1980 was every bit as audacious as that of MTV (launched in 1981). While the latter filled its airtime with music, ESPN showed nothing but sports. By 1998, the channel was received by 70 percent of all US households and broadcast 23 percent of all televised sports. The network's reach extended to 160 different countries and it provided services in 19 languages.

Surely, you can have too much of a good thing: but not when it comes to sport, it seems. Emboldened by ESPN's growth, mainstream television networks filled their channels with football, golf, tennis, and other sports. In 1984, David Stern became commissioner of the ailing National Basketball Association (NBA) and remodeled basketball in a way that made it more attractive to advertisers and hence television. Already shown on ESPN (which was bought by Disney in the same year), the NBA sought mainstream airtime. By 1991, with Jordan in his ascendancy, Stern was able to land a $600 million four-year deal with NBC. Basketball was watched by young people of all ethnic backgrounds, the kind of people who also had their remotes' favorite channels programmed to MTV – a perfect demographic for advertisers.

The NBA, like other major sports, provided, as Horne puts it, " 'killer content' to attract audiences to advertisers, new channels and new technologies, which in turn provided new means of consuming the spectacle" (2006: 89). Television viewers acquired access to visual angles, virtual reconstructions, and amplifications undreamt of as recently as the 1990s. Sport was presented in much the same way as other forms of entertainment, whether music, drama, or news. And, as it was also consumed in the same way, it seems reasonable to argue that sport actually became entertainment. This may not sound defamatory today, but it would once have been a slight against the competitive endeavors that separated heroes from other mortals and provided events that were regarded by many with spiritual reverence.

At the same time, the rogue elements of sport were domesticated. There was no place for rebels or political protestors. Resistance was turned into stylistic affectation, making people like Andre Agassi, Eric Cantona, and Dennis Rodman seem like insurgent forces instead of the housetrained poseurs they really were. Nike, more than any other advertiser, expertly honed their images to represent youthful insolence. More likely they were agents of containment working on behalf of an organization that "positioned itself as a rebellious, maverick, and anti-authoritarian company," as Jim McKay describes Nike (1999: 418).

One wonders how Nike would have managed Muhammad Ali, Diego Maradona, or the previously mentioned Smith and Carlos. Or even Billie Jean King, whose sexuality became the source of scandal in 1981 when her secretary took legal action against her and outed her as a lesbian.

In their own ways, these and many other athletes resisted conformity, whether protesting against war, consorting with communist leaders, or transgressing sexual norms. As such, they were internationally known, admired more than abhorred. But they were not celebrities. Their private lives weren't pored over, they weren't hunted by paparazzi, and their reputations were built from deeds, not advertisements. Even after the scandal surrounding her, King was able to resume her tennis career without perpetual intrusion.

As sport morphed into popular entertainment, its main characters were subject to the same treatment as other celebrities. The rewards were great: $20 million is no longer such an extraordinary yearly income for many elite performers. For such earnings the surrender of any residual private life, a promise not to misbehave, and an outward commitment to "conservatism, adaptation, and normality" must seem a fair exchange.

: global designs

As we've documented in the previous chapters, there's a kind of worldwide exchange system in which celebrity is a common currency. Globalization may well have been prompted by worldwide migrations of labor, the international sourcing of materials, the distribution of production, the detachment of politics from nations, and the time-space compression initiated by technology, among other things. But underlying these is the development of a common culture predicated on consumption. As we saw in Chapter 9, the development has brought with it the nexus between what we buy and how we think about ourselves. As Derek Layder writes: "The pervasive effects of consumerism link identity and social status to the market for commodities" (2006: 53). The *global* market for commodities.

One medium, perhaps above all others, has made this development possible. "Advertising, in particular, seeks to sell products by depicting idealized Western lifestyles, often under the universalizing themes of sex, status and the siblinghood of humanity," reasons Malcolm Waters in his *Globalization* (2001: 203).

It's often assumed that sport itself has contributed substantially to this idealization of Western lifestyles. There is sense in this: as the various translations suggest, *Fußball*, *fútbol* or *voetbal* is the most global of global games, originating in England and migrating almost everywhere in the world. Its most glamorous players, like Beckham, are international celebrities, personifying the glamour and wealth of the West. Basketball has circumnavigated the world in the successful pursuit of new markets in far-flung places where the average weekly wage would be like tip money to an NBA player. Other sports, such as cricket, rugby, and baseball are played in both hemispheres of the globe.

Yet there is also sense in Waters' claim that advertising should be credited, or perhaps held responsible – depending on one's perspective – for hastening globalization. There's no contradiction, of course: the use of athletes to promote commodities in advertising campaigns is not confined to one territory (unless the contract stipulates so). In the 1990s, Jordan's image could be seen in Nike ads virtually anywhere in the world. Today, the world traveler will collide with representations of any number of sports celebrities. Wherever sports are played or watched, there are ads depicting celebrity athletes.

Sports stars have become so effective as marketing instruments that corporations with markets across the world have consciously sought out athletes regardless of their actual competitive achievements. When she turned professional in 2005, aged 16, Michelle Wie had tied up promotional contracts with both Nike and Sony, which guaranteed her $10 million independently of her golfing achievements. The Korean-American's package paled alongside the reported $90 million Nike paid LeBron James when he short-circuited college basketball and went straight from high school to the Cleveland Cavaliers in 2003. Exceptional as they were, deals like these were becoming increasingly commonplace in the twenty-first century, producing an interesting crossover phenomenon: the global celebrity athlete whose status is based on marketing rather than sporting accomplishments.

Wie and James are examples of "a new kind of citizenry, of people who work and live borderless and bordered lives." That's the term used by Lloyd Wong and Ricardo Trumper to describe Wayne Gretzky and the Chilean soccer star Iván Zamorano. In their article "Global celebrity athletes and nationalism," Wong and Trumper analyze the "transnationalism" and "deterritorialism" now apparent in sport (2002). Celebrities have become metaphors for globalization in the sense that they actually "belong" to no particular territory: their physical presence is unimportant as long as their representations are carried "via telecommunications technology such as cable and satellite television" (2002: 182). And, we should add, the internet.

So, the fact that Yao Ming was born in China and drafted to Houston Rockets in 2002 was no hindrance to his marketability. Quite the opposite, in fact: he was "an exemplary vehicle for the NBA's global designs," according to Thomas Oates and Judy Polumbaum, "a well-behaved alternative to the bad-boy stereotype of the African American athlete" (2004: 187). Troubled by the scandal surrounding Kobe Bryant and the associations between black players and gangsta culture, the NBA found in Yao Ming a marketing dream. As did several other global corporations, including Apple, Gatorade, Nike, Toyota, Visa, and several Chinese companies, such as China Unicom and Yanjing Beer. All closed endorsement deals with him.

At the time of Yao Ming's move, NBA games were televised in 205 countries, with commentary in 42 languages, reaching more than 650 million households. Merchandise sales outside the USA were worth about $300 million (£180 million) per year. The league's marketing ambitions were similar to those of other US-based organizations with more obvious commercial remits (sports, while driven by commercial imperatives, are not supposed to be solely motivated by profit, of course).

In 2004, Oates and Polumbaum reported on Yao Ming's "marketable persona": "As a transnational figure, Yao has already proven extraordinarily adaptable commercially as well as athletically and culturally, which suits the demands of his multiple constituencies in the global marketplace." The fact that he came from the nation with the world's fastest growing economy and a 1.3 billion population did not harm his marketing potential.

If Yao Ming were tea, he would have been decanted into an American Coca-Cola bottle before being sold back to the Chinese. While he and many of the other celebrity athletes that have risen to international prominence were born outside the USA, they, or, more pertinently, their representations were created, fashioned, refined, and distributed – that is, packaged – by multinational businesses which had their primary markets in the US. Merrill Melnick and Steven Jackson call this "globalization American-style" and use it as the basis of an investigation into what they describe as the "psychosocial consequences of the intersection of global forces and local cultures" (2002: 430).

In their study of 510 young people in New Zealand, they examined the effects of "identifying with American popular cultural icons such as Tiger Woods [and] Venus Williams." Their results backed up an argument advanced in Chapter 3: that traditional forms of leadership have given way to new varieties. Sir Edmund Hillary, himself from New Zealand, was the first man to climb Everest and, as such, was described by the study's authors as "a living legend." In the 1950s (his ascent was in 1953), 1960s, 1970s, and possibly beyond, he would surely have commanded supreme admiration, respect, and even iconolatry, especially in his native land. In the study, he was totally eclipsed by Jordan as the most popular hero (highlighting the point made previously about the decline of confidence in traditional leaders). Jordan, remember, is American and played a sport far removed from the rugby and cricket at which Kiwis excel. NBA games were televised in New Zealand and, of course, the ubiquitous Nike had a presence there.

While Melnick and Jackson were keen to point out that identifying with American athletes or other types of celebrities didn't necessarily impact the lives of New Zealand youth "in significant ways," their research underlined the influence of global on local culture, or, put another way, "the extent to which worldwide commodified images impact on national identity" (2002: 445).

Studies such as this suggest caution before we assert the overwhelming globalizing power of media-borne celebrities. Oates and Polumbaum contend "patterns of cultural production and consumption which already have transformed North America are enveloping much of the rest of the world." But we are still only guessing at the extent of the transformation. Melnick and Jackson accept that there is a wholesale adoption of American – and presumably American-styled – celebrities, especially from sport. Yet, they're not convinced that admiring or even identifying with them translates into buying Nike, drinking Gatorade, or any of the other products endorsed by the celebs. "How are American/foreign products resisted and/or transformed and made sense of by local youth?" they ask.

Certainly there has been a worldwide anti-Nike backlash and Naomi Klein, among others, has revealed and contributed to the tendency to reject American-originated global corporations that she believes have usurped indigenous cultures (2001). There have also been vacillating fortunes for many of those corporations, including Nike, The Gap, McDonald's and Starbucks, all of which have had to endure consumer recoil of one kind of another. But they're all still standing. Nike and Gap, in particular, have used celebrity endorsers effectively to bolster their market share (Sarah Jessica Parker is widely credited with restoring Gap to financial stability), once more highlighting the point made in Chapter 9: credible celebrity endorsers can be deadly efficient in cutting into the toughest markets and combating the fiercest consumer resistance.

: genuine articles

Do we imagine today's celebrity athletes are like yesterday's sports stars in any respect other than playing ability? Where there were once "colorful characters" or superstars, there are now icons – images created by corporate interests for the purpose of selling in a market that respects no national boundaries. In this vital respect, they are closer to showbusiness entertainers than athletes. Corporations like Nike waste no time in co-opting teenagers into their grand projects, determining their value separately from their competitive accomplishments. Celebrity athletes are given the same kind of treatment as any other kind of celebrity: they're turned into commodities and made to function as marketing vehicles.

Some writers prefer to see them differently. Barry Smart, in his *The Sport Star*, insists that it is impossible to "subordinate the ethos of sport to values of entertainment and commerce." Unlike other celebrities, especially those whose transitory fame comes via reality tv, sports stars have "authenticity." This is a term Smart uses throughout his text to stake out the difference between athletes and all other celebrities. He means that, in order, to become known, they must first demonstrate competence, if not excellence in their sport. There are occasionally, lamentably inept athletes at major tournaments who are widely publicized for their gameness. But their time in the sun is usually short and, for the most part, athletes who rise to global fame "confirm the authenticity of their exceptional status, their significant difference, if not their uniqueness" (2005: 195).

Smart isn't so dazzled by this that he doesn't recognize that: "Since the 1960s a series of economic and cultural processes have transformed the world of sport" (2005: 18). The "threat" posed to authenticity – "a vulnerable quality," he reckons – by commercial interests is apparent everywhere. And yet: "The authenticity of sporting figures like Michael Jordan, Tiger Woods and David Beckham ultimately derives from the quality of their playing performance, from their records of success in competition" (2005: 195).

Authenticity is one of those words that create an illusion: it looks like a simile for genuineness or legitimacy, whereas it hides a transaction, as we revealed in Chapter 9. "Authenticity is a tricky concept," concluded Deborah Root in a different context. "The term can be manipulated and used to convince people they are getting something profound when they are just getting merchandise" (1996: 78).

Root wasn't writing about sport, though her argument travels well. When she refers to a "commodification of authenticity," she could be referring to the way in which various areas of the culture industry work to turn playing skills into "pure artistry," "natural talent," or even "genius." These are terms to which sports fans have become accustomed. Undeniably, there are athletes who have convinced everyone they possess them: Wayne Gretzky, Lance Armstrong, Michael Schumacher, and Roger Federer are among an elite group of sportsmen who utterly dominated their particular sports for unfeasibly long periods. Their achievements are a matter of record and defy contrary arguments.

There are also athletes who have dominated sports who register little recognition beyond those sports. David Bryant was supreme in lawn bowls, as was Geet Sethi in billiards and Phil Taylor in darts. Netball's Vicki Wilson and squash's Heather McKay were leaders of their respective sports. They and many other peerless athletes resist categorization as "cultural products," at least in the way Chung means it in his reference to Seo and Park. Much garlanded as Bryant and the others were, they were never afforded the kind of celebrity status enjoyed by the athletes mentioned earlier in this chapter. Being in the right sport – one that receives media attention – at the end of the twentieth or start of the twenty-first century is what mattered. Context, as ever, is vital to understanding why some athletes have been and still are acknowledged as authentically great and others remain largely unknown. We don't have to deny Smart's claim that some athletes are better than others: we simply have to point out that this may, in some contexts, have a bearing on their status, while, in others, it may not.

In other words, we need to treat celebrity athletes like other celebrities and, for purposes of analysis, distinguish between what the *Economist* magazine calls "a celebrity's craft and their celebrity rating, which has a trajectory of its own" (September 3, 2005, p. 29). In celebrity culture, the latter outweighs the former. The point I made in Chapter 10 about the "craft" of reality tv stars bears repeating: there's nothing intrinsically valuable, worthy, or precious about talent, or whatever other term we use to describe the faculty we appear to be rewarding with our attention and money. We're really paying for the pleasure we derive from watching, reading, or talking about someone; and that pleasure is affected by the manner in which that someone is made available to us, usually on screens or in publications.

ANSWERING/
THE BIG QUESTION

: why?

April, 2005: Reese Witherspoon says she's been chased across town from her gym by paparazzi who encircled her in the Hollywood Hills and only retreated after she appealed to a private security guard at the entrance to a gated community. A photographer is later charged with child endangerment and battery after allegedly hitting a five-year-old child with his camera and pushing away another to take pictures of Witherspoon and her children.

June, 2005: Driving her Mercedes-Benz, Lindsay Lohan is in collision with a pursuant minivan driven by a photographer who is subsequently charged with assault with a deadly weapon – the vehicle. The photographer is later cleared, though the case encourages Governor Arnold Schwarzenegger to sign legislation allowing celebrities to collect large damage awards from paparazzi who harass them.

August, 2005: Several cars follow Scarlett Johansson as she leaves her Hollywood home for Disneyland in her Mercedes. In her attempt to escape them, she bumps a Daihatsu carrying a mother and daughter to whom she apologizes. Johansson's agent tells the *Los Angeles Times*: "At least two or three of them [paparazzi] had been camping outside of her house for five days . . . she's left Los Angeles. You can't deal with it any more."

September, 2005: The *Daily Mirror* newspaper carries a story based on a 45-minute video that purports to show Kate Moss preparing and snorting five lines of cocaine in a London recording studio, where her boyfriend Pete Doherty – who has a well-documented history of drug dependency – was working with his band. Earlier, the *Daily Mirror*'s sister paper, the *Sunday Mirror*, had paid out "substantial damages" after publishing a story claiming that Moss had collapsed after taking coke in Barcelona in 2001.

October, 2005: After disappearing in 1993, Kate Bush re-emerges from her self-imposed exile to release a new album. She became a recluse to escape the media and to raise a family away from the glare of the kind of publicity to which she had become accustomed since her first single "Wuthering Heights" became an international hit in 1978.

When Kate Bush receded from the public view, we let her. When I say "we" I mean everybody, not just the paparazzi, the television crews, and the other members of the media, but everybody who licensed them, however unwittingly. Despite avoiding scandals, she must have sensed that it was going to be hard to slide between professional and personal lives. The membrane separating them was getting evermore permeable. She opted for the personal. By the time she decided to return to her recording career, things had changed appreciably. It's likely that had she started her recording career today, she would be pursued as vigilantly – and in Moss's case, the pursuit was downright vengeful – as any of the other female celebrities in the vignettes that opened this chapter.

It could be argued that it's a small price to pay. After all, celebrities earn serious money and, much as some deny it, they wallow in the admiration if not outright adoration. Having your home staked out and having a perpetual tail of media personnel, as they say, goes with the territory. My purpose in this book is not to put the case for or against the celebrities. Rather, it's to understand the changes that have led to the collective preoccupation with them. The vignettes are not untypical. On the contrary, they are representative illustrations of the lengths to which the media will go just to satisfy our appetites for pictures and news of, or just gossip about, people whom we don't know but feel we do know. When all's said and done, celebrities should make no lasting impact on most of our lives, apart from prompting the occasional emotion: like the joy we take in listening to their music; or the contentment in watching their acting; or the thrill of just seeing them; or maybe the ecstasy in fantasizing about them. But there's more. We spend an inordinate amount of time and money reading about them, staring at pictures of them, discussing them, and, in some cases, obsessing over them. All of which leads us to our final question. Why?

Why? is a loaded question, of course. On what grounds? Under what conditions? In what circumstances? For what reason? With what purpose? If you've read this book chapter-by-chapter rather than dipping in and out, you'll have one answer ready. But there are others, many of which I've alluded to throughout the text. In concluding, I will formalize them.

Celebrity culture has been with us just about long enough to generate a body of literature. A glance at the bibliography of this book indicates the scale of work already available. Like any other subject-based literature, there is a branch devoted to theorizing. This is where the Why? question gets answered, though, as we will see, in a number of different, sometimes contrasting ways. We shouldn't expect anything less: celebrity culture, like any other aspect of study, defies any once-and-for-all answers. Instead, there are perspectives, models, accounts, and conceptual approaches, all of which offer a way of answering questions and asking a few more.

Most of the theorists of celebrity culture have appeared earlier in the book, their one- or two-line wisdoms helping advance the overall argument. In this, the final chapter, I will consider their work again, this time with the intention of disclosing their overall designs. The perspectives are those of the twenty-first century: the influences of earlier writers such as Leo Braudy and Richard Dyer are clear enough, though my interest is in how these influences have been distilled into contemporary analysis.

: the new Ecclesiastes

Religion. It enchants us. I mean this literally. We are caught in a spell we either can't break or don't want to break because we have faith. Faith replaces the need for evidence. Our belief in whatever particular complex of beliefs we call our religion dictates that we believe *in* it rather than believing it conditionally. Adherents of religions don't, for example, say: "I'm prepared to accept that there is a superhuman, controlling power such as god and that god should be worshipped, but only on the condition that, at some stage, I'll be supplied with proof of this." More typically, we devote ourselves and organize our mental outlook and conduct accordingly without ever needing even a sign. Those who do search for signs usually find them in the quotidian, that is, the common everyday things that most people take for granted.

Religion has been under threat since before the eighteenth-century Enlightenment, which used reason and individualism to challenge traditions of prejudice and superstition. Science and technology addressed many of the questions asked and answered by religion and poured them into a different mould. It reshaped them in a way that invited answers, without any recourse to faith. Science offered proof.

This occasioned a gradual decline not so much in religious belief but in the significance religion had in society, especially Western European societies. Secularization spread, though perhaps not as universally as enthusiasts of science would like. Religion has held fast and still dominates the politics and culture in some parts of the world. In others, it's retreated temporarily, only to return with renewed influence. But science meant that religion's power to bewitch had been weakened. The overall project started by the Enlightenment brought with it disenchant-ment. This has led some writers to conclude that celebrities have served to re-enchant a world in which deities have either been abandoned or emptied of their power, leaving a "post-God world."

"Celebrities are our myth bearers; carriers of the divine forces of good, evil, lust and redemption," declared Jill Neimark, marshaling the historical work of Leo Braudy to bolster her claim (1995: 56). Braudy's *The Frenzy of Renown: Fame and its history*, was, as its subtitle indicates, a historian's perspective on fame (1997). First published in 1986, just before the changes that animated our intense interest in celebrities, it examined the triumphs of famous figures long before the age of celebrity. In fact, Braudy identifies Alexander the Great as the first truly famous person. As long ago as the third century BCE Alexander regarded himself as no other human: more a deity or a hero of Homeric legend. With no media in the sense we understand it today, Alexander made use of an alternative apparatus for spreading news of himself and his achievements. He commissioned authors to chronicle his battles, artists to depict his likeness, and engravers to design shields, coins, and other artifacts bearing his profile. Alexander actively encouraged worship and exaltation by fashioning himself after the gods and demigods of ancient Greece.

Alexander may be a prototype of the godlike human, but he certainly wasn't a celebrity (at least, only when played by Colin Farrell, in the movie *Alexander*). All of his efforts at immortality and indeed those of the many Roman emperors, who vain-gloriously followed his example, were aimed at separating themselves from their subjects. They deliberately flouted legal and moral rules as a way of confirming their extraordinary status: rules applied to humans, not gods. In a similar way, the Pharaohs of ancient Egypt, such as Akhenaten and his wife Nefertiti, ordered the building of edifices to commemorate their existences and the European aristocracy of the Middle Ages commissioned portraits of themselves to ensure their posterity. They cultivated the popular conception that their world was not that of ordinary mortals; they were untouchable.

There are remnants of this type of behavior in today's celebrity temple. For example, Mariah Carey's famous refusal "to do stairs" assisted her elevation above both her audience and the rest of her entourage. Outlandish demands worked for the likes of Cleopatra, so presumably today's celebs think they will work for them. But, no one seriously thinks the celebrities are deities. Or do they?

"Post-God celebrity is now one of the mainstays of organizing recognition and belonging in secular society," writes Chris Rojek (2001: 58). Celebrities appear as gods in human form or simulacra of departed deities. Celebrity culture, in this view, becomes a functional equivalent of religion, with beliefs and practices associated with religion "converging" with those of celebrity culture.

As we have seen in previous chapters, what was once a vast gulf between Them and Us has been narrowed to the point where celebrities have become touchable. The likes of Lohan, Johannson, and indeed Carey appear on celluloid, but hawkish photographers make sure that most of the widely circulated images show them tracksuited on their way to the shopping mall, often bedraggled, and sometimes annoyed enough to greet their watchful media with all-too-human gestures (Cameron Diaz was famously photographed giving the finger to paparazzi). So it appears to make little sense to regard them as godlike beings rather than ordinary people who have bad hair days like everyone else. Rojek suggests that the "glut of mass-media information" which personalizes the celebrity has turned them from being distant figures, not just into ordinary people but "significant others." "They are also symbols of belonging and recognition that distract us in positive ways from the terrifying meaninglessness of life in a post-God world" (2001: 95).

This might strike some readers as decaf phenomenology, with the "terrifying meaninglessness" in fact being a resignation to the mundane monotony of everyday life, and with the "positive ways" in which celebrities distract us being retail therapy. But there is more complexity to the argument. "Celebrities offer peculiarly powerful affirmations of belonging, recognition, and meaning in the midst of the lives of their audiences (2001: 53).

Secularization may have been overstated, but religion has certainly had to adapt in order to survive in many parts of the world. In some important respects, it has reconfigured so that it can respond to the "uprooting effect of globalization." In striving to meet the needs of the rootless flock, religion has borrowed the style of celebrity culture. Its leaders are charismatic tv personalities, its sermons arrive in people's homes via television or the internet, and it elevates its showbusiness devotees into standard bearers. This is part of a convergence. The other part is celebrity culture's ability to supply experiences that, for fans, are every bit as meaningful as religious experiences. This is why fans spend more time reading tabloids than they do the Good Book. As Rabbi Shmuley Boteach put it: "MTV and Access Hollywood has supplanted Ecclesiastes and Proverbs" (2002: 1).

While Rojek describes this as a "hypothesis," other writers have put it to the test. Lynn McCutcheon and John Maltby are part of a team of psychological researchers who have explored the manner in which consumers engage with celebrities. In Chapter 5, we covered several of their research projects, many of which explore what the researchers call "celebrity worship." The term makes clear allusions to religion, though we should remain mindful that the word worship derives from the Old English *weorthescipe*, meaning, basically, worthy. To worship someone or something means to show respect or acknowledge merit. Paying reverence to deities is but one meaning of the term. Celebrity worship sounds less profound once this is borne in mind, though the research of McCutcheon *et al.* delivers a somewhat surprising conclusion: many of those who follow celebrities do so with a zeal that actually does resemble religious fervor (2002, 2003; Maltby *et al.* 2004).

Celebrity worship is measurable on a Celebrity Worship Scale, low worship describing what many of us do: watch and read about celebrities. At the other extreme, there is the level at which worshipful followers show "a mixture of empathy with the celebrity's successes and failures, over-identification with the celebrity, compulsive behaviours, as well as obsession with details of the celebrity's life" (McCutcheon *et al.* 2002: 67). This is the kind of uncompromising and extreme disposition we might regard in a different context as religious zealotry or fanaticism (remember: some trace the origins of the word fan to fanatic, which has religious connotations, as we saw in Chapter 5).

Adoring or even obsessing over celebrities as idols or role models is a "normal part of identity development in childhood and adolescence," according to McCutcheon *et al.* (2003: 309). It's a form of parasocial interaction. We may identify with cartoon characters or the fictional characters played by actors, rather than the actors themselves. But we may also idolize rock stars, movie stars, and any other kind of celeb that attracts us. It becomes a psychologically abnormal state when it continues into adulthood, perhaps leading to the worshipper's neglect of everyday duties. It may lead to the believer's having deluded conceptions about the nature of his or her relationship with one or more celebrities. Or even what the researchers call "addiction to a celebrity."

McCutcheon and her colleagues are specifically interested in the psychological origins and effects of celebrity worship on the individual, rather than its cultural sources or its wider ramifications. As such, they don't address the question of whether celebrity worship has converged with or even replaced religious worship, as Rojek suggests. Their evidence is, however, persuasive: the intensity of emotional involvement, the impact on the life of the believer, the pattern of engagement with the rest of the world (from sociability to withdrawal) are all features of celebrity worship that have religious counterparts. As I pointed out in Chapter 5, the scholars question the usual separation of stalkers from other devotees: "The distinction between pathological and nonpathological worship is somewhat tenuous" (2002: 69).

The team's findings are complemented by those of Susan Boon and Christine Lomore, also psychologists, who discovered that fans were not simply influenced by the way celebrities dressed, made up, wore their hair, or by their overall demeanor: "they took note of their attitudes and values, especially on issues of morality" (2001). Such a finding invites comparisons not only with prophets, preachers, or sages, but with priests, pastors, and ordained ministers responsible for the spiritual leadership of a church or other religious organization.

: the world through a lens

In the 1960s, when Daniel Boorstin was completing the first edition of his *The Image: A guide to pseudo-events in America,* he wondered about the effects of living in an "illusory" world of created characters. Mediated, two-dimensional images were becoming as important to us as real people: we only needed to flick a switch or open a magazine and we were in the alternative world. Compared to this, our own world must have seemed color-less and uninteresting. In Boorstin's world, people exchanged ideas and gossiped about stars and tv characters rather than learning about each other and, by implication, about themselves.

The early 1960s: the Beatles, Martin Luther King, Motown, George Best, *Cleopatra*. The names seem to be from a different age. They are. Yet we know them all. And they're all compre-hensible and not just as historical entities. The media supports a vivid imagination. We may be detached observers, but we feel we know, perhaps do actually know, all about the Beatles and the story of Motown without having to delve into the history books. The media is just *there* like a Greek chorus, different voices singing different things simultaneously and continuously.

This is where our story of celebrity began, of course. The early 1960s witnessed the beginning of our new enchantment. Our senses were massaged or manipulated by a newly tenacious media that fed on the real people behind the image. Of course, what they were doing was delivering new images to replace the old.

There were potent images that lingered in the mind long after the early 1960s: the first live transatlantic television broadcast via the Telstar satellite in 1962; the assassination of John F. Kennedy in 1963; the first spacewalk in 1964; England's World Cup win in 1966 (watched by about 400 million tv viewers). These were delivered by television. The "illusory" world grew both bigger and smaller to viewers watching "live" transmissions of events 250,000 miles away.

Essentially the same media that delivered the first moon landing delivered celebrities. To be precise, images of celebrities. David Giles provides an illustration, inviting his readers to put themselves in the shoes of a famous female recording artist. After a harrowing experience with the paparazzi, she is summoned to the studios by her record company to make a second album, a single from which is going to be released ahead of the album. When the single becomes available (downloads are typically around before the cd), the press office arranges over 100 interviews and the singer is whisked around the country to make tv and radio appearances. "You are replicated furiously," Giles assures the hypothetical singer/reader. "Dozens of newspapers and glossy, full-colour magazines carry photographs of you . . . The video, for a start, receives heavy 'rotation' on specialist TV channels and several plays on terrestrial TV" (2000: 52).

The single sells well, prompting another few weeks of "saturation media coverage" and every time the song is played whether on radio, tv, iPod, or whatever, "you stroll into their living room . . . you are *there*" (2000: 52).

The singer obviously isn't physically there: Giles means that her presence is summoned by a visual or audile representation that registers in the imagination. Jessica Evans tenders a phrase to capture this: "Mediated persona is a useful term in that it reminds us how celebrity as a category *is absolutely dependent on the media* to create and disseminate a persona to an audience" (2005: 19).

Evans's emphasis reveals the colossal importance she places on the role of the media in the creation and perpetuation of celebrity. Giles is equally convinced of the media's efficacy in bringing celebrity culture into being, though his inflection is on the way in which technology has taken matters to a new level.

Braudy's history of fame alerts readers to the manner in which primitive media were used not only to circulate news but to glorify and lionize rulers, whether kings, generals, priests, or saints. "So it can be argued that there is much continuity between the representations of the famous in the past and the present," writes Evans (2005: 20).

Citing examples from history, Evans argues that even the "pseudo-events" Boorstin believed were stage-managed episodes specific to the twentieth century have much older precedents. Louis XIV (the seventeenth-century French king, not the San Diego band) was adept at making carefully designed public rejoicings appear spontaneous. The point is: public relations is not as new as we think and the media, even before the age of print, were used as promotional vehicles. Fame then has always involved some mediating agency that represents and disseminates news and images. Edited collections, such as James Monaco's 1978 *Celebrity: The media as image makers* and Lisa Lewis's 1992 *The Adoring Audience: Fan culture and popular media*, as their titles suggest, concentrated on the power of the media in both in governing the depiction of celebrities and influencing the experience of consumers through the twentieth century.

While her approach accentuates historical continuity, Evans identifies the period 1890–1930 as "crucial" when "the mass media invented a particular kind of 'star' persona" (2005: 23). This is slightly later than the take-off phase identified in Chapter 4, though Evans's argument is in broad agreement: in making the private lives of entertainers a part of their overall public persona, the emerging media in concert with the film industry nurtured a new kind of relationship between the famous and their audiences. Between them, there were texts, defined by Evans's collaborator Frances Bonner as "socially constructed assemblages of items such as spoken or written words, or pictures (2005: 59). (An "assemblage" is something made of unrelated things joined together, so the text is basically anything that's intelligible to the consumer, or the person doing the "reading.")

In Evans's model then, there are three conceptual elements: the production, text, and reception. While each contributes to making celebrity a meaningful social entity, the relationship between them is variable. Culture industries may produce a particular set of images or personae of celebrities, but there is no guarantee that audiences will interpret them in the way intended: the texts may be quite different. "Reception" is perhaps a poor choice of words in that it implies passivity, whereas consumers are seen as discriminately selecting and decoding media messages in a way that resists manipulation.

Although the media and the elaborate organizations that augment them drive celebrity production and, as such, remain the engine of the model, the texts that circulate in a way have a life of their own once in the public discourse (actually "in" the public discourse isn't quite appropriate as the discourse is actually constituted or made by the public).

Giles sees less historical continuity. New media technologies rupture developments, opening up unanticipated opportunities for aspiring celebrities. They did so in the fourteenth century when the modern theater became popular, providing a "vehicle . . . for creating fame." Then again in the fifteenth century with the invention of the printing press; engravings were a popular way of portraying the human face before photography. "Celebrity is essentially a media production, rather than the worthy recognition of greatness," says Giles, echoing Evans and naming hype as its "purest form."

Hype has no object of any value: it just implies "that a phenomenon can be made to appear valuable, even when its value is non-existent" (2000: 20). While he doesn't go into the etymology of the term, note that its root is *huperbole*, Greek for excess, from which we get hyperbole, an exaggerated statement. Giles cites P. T. Barnum as the pioneer of hyping: the techniques he used for publicizing the exhibits of his shows were much the same as those used today. The Hollywood film industry's publicity machine refined and perfected what was an art for Barnum into something resembling a science. After the 1950s, domestic television became a new medium for creating celebrities *par excellence*. There had been nothing to compare with tv: it served to shrink the distance between viewers and events and the people who featured in the events; but it also began to create events of its own – shows, performances, competitions, and even news items specifically made by and for television. The video recorder pushed things further, allowing viewers to play events over and over again. As with Evans, Giles's stress is on the media as the engine that drives celebrity culture. The actual celebrities are almost incidental to the theory.

Giles believes that there is a long-standing and even desperate desire for fame among human populations. Changing forms of media have effectively made it possible for more and more people to gain the kind of mass exposure that brings fame. Myriad media around the globe rapidly and exponentially reproduce images of people. "The proliferation of media for publicizing the individual has been reflected in a proliferation of celebrated individuals," writes Giles. "As the mass media has expanded, so individuals have had to do less in order to be celebrated" (2000: 32).

The process copies itself like a replicating DNA. Technological developments in the media have enabled humans to reproduce images of themselves "on a phenomenal scale, thus providing an evolutionary rationale for the obsessive pursuit of fame" (2000: 53).

While both Evans and Giles acknowledge that other writers (and I need to include myself in this group) see something qualitatively distinctive and exceptional about contemporary celebrity culture, they highlight the continuity in the role of the media. Admittedly, Giles pinpoints the bewilderingly fast reproductive properties of today's media as crucial to the fleeting celebrities that flit across our screens today and disappear next week. But celebrity culture is continuance masquerading as uniqueness. The media were always pivotal: their forms have changed; their effects haven't.

: in the service of capital

The Roman poet Juvenal might have been reflecting on the way his countryman in the first century of the common era assigned celebrity status to gladiators when he coined the phrase *panem et circenses*. Translated as "bread and circuses" it describes the way in which ancient Roman leaders would provide food and entertainment to the underprivileged plebeians, allowing them access to the spectacular gladiatorial contests and chariot races at the Colosseum and other vast stadiums. Without the agreeable distractions and a full stomach, the masses might have grown discontented and started to wonder why they had little money, lived in inadequate accommodation, and, unlike their rulers, could never afford life's luxuries. Immersing themselves in the excitement of the contests and cheering on their champions diverted their attention away from more mundane matters.

Juvenal was alluding to power, specifically the uneven distribution of it and how this imbalance was maintained. The sections of the populations that had little power and no real chance of gaining the advantages that go with it had to be placated somehow. If not, they might have grown restless and begun to ask searching questions that could destabilize power arrangements. Keeping them satisfied maximized the chances

ANSWERING/THE BIG QUESTION 261

that they wouldn't notice. The entertainment may have been good wholesome fun – well, as wholesome as pitching humans against lions can be – but it also served an ideological purpose. It fostered a style of popular thinking that was compatible with a particular type of political and economic system.

Critics of sports such as Paul Hoch (1972) and Jean-Marie Brohm (1978) wrote challenging polemics in the 1970s, identifying athletics events as key amusements that kept the working class preoccupied. Too preoccupied, it turned out, to oppose capitalist systems that were designed to exploit them. Drawing on Marx's opiate thesis, in which he likened religion to a drug that dulls the senses and provides a temporary sensation of well-being, critics saw sports as a kind of functional equivalent of religion, commanding the attention of millions of fans without delivering any tangible improvements to their lives. Sports and, by implication, other types of popular entertainment have ideological utility: they reinforce the status quo.

This invites the kind of images I mentioned in Chapter 1, with heads of mega-corporations gathered around a table to hatch plots designed to keep the working classes from noticing how the system works against them. Neither Hoch, Brohm, nor any of the other theorists who followed their leads pictured the scene so melodramatically. Sports and entertainment today may be overpraised and soak up too much of our time and money, but they haven't been designed to assist society's ruling power-holders. They are best viewed as convenience rather than connivance.

Celebrities do ideological work too. This is hardly profound: more a statement of the obvious. They massage our senses in a way not totally dissimilar to the gladiators. Like the citizens of ancient Rome, we are captivated, enthused, and thrilled by people we don't know and who probably don't care about us. Maybe we don't have the same deprivations from which we have to be distracted, but there are serious issues that impact on everybody: climate change, globalization, war, for instance.

These and other issues already provoke widespread dissent and, often, outright protest. The prospects for even more forceful protests might be great were it not for the diverting power of celebrities. At least, that's what theorists of the bread and circuses school would argue. They'd find an ally in the comic Chris Rock who offered his own take on celebrity culture in 2004: "It's a trick to get your mind off the [Iraq] war. I think [George] Bush sent that girl to Kobe's room. Bush sent that little boy to Michael Jackson's house. Bush killed Laci Peterson [whose mysterious disappearance stirred up widespread curiosity] . . . all to get your mind off the war!" (quoted in *Maclean's*, June 21, 2004).

Even those who are not persuaded by the basic version have converted its premise into a more sophisticated model, the engine of which is still ideology. The title of P. David Marshall's book *Celebrity and Power: Fame in contemporary culture* is a clue to his approach (1997). He sees the concept of individuality as vital to both contemporary capitalist democracy and consumerism. Celebrities are not just people; they are influential representatives. The represent "subject positions that audiences can adopt or adapt in the formation of social identities" (1997: 65). There is a "celebrity-function" which is to "organize the legitimate and illegitimate domains of the personal and the individual within the social" (ibid.: 57).

Matt Hills interprets this: "The celebrity or star appears to give rise to, and anchor their very own authenticity and individuality. But what appears as a natural property of the charismatic celebrity is actually produced by discourses of celebrity" (2005: 151). Giles pares this down to basics: "The capitalist system uses celebrities to promote individualism and illusions of democracy (the 'anyone can do it' myth) [. . .] capitalism retains its hold on society, by reducing all human activity to private 'personalities' and the inner life of the individual" (2000: 19 and 72).

Multiplying numbers of celebrity escapees of the *Big Brother* house and other reality television shows have appeared since the publication of Marshall's book, though he would surely use the "ordinary" celebrities as further proof of his thesis. And, despite the attempts of the previously mentioned Mariah Carey and the others who strive to keep the purdah that separates Them from Us intact, consumers have seen through the veil.

Graeme Turner has adopted Marshall's framework in his book *Understanding Celebrity*. In particular, he points to Marshall's potentially useful "spin": "His proposition [is] that the celebrity-commodity provides a very powerful form of legitimation for capitalism's models of exchange and value by demonstrating that the individual has a commercial as well as a cultural value" (2004: 25).

Celebrities then have social functions. Like the proto-celebrity gladiators, they serve political ends as well as providing pleasure for the masses. They participate, however unwittingly, in a process that entices – some might say inveigles – Us into thinking about ourselves and Them in a particular way: as freestanding individuals living in a merit-rewarding society; and one, we might add, in which the good life advertised by celebrities is open to anyone with enough money. This is, for Turner, the primary function: "Celebrities are developed to make money" (2004: 34). In the kind of competitive market system fostered by capitalism, only ever-increasing consumption can keep the system running.

Vertical integration features in Turner's analysis. This describes the tendency of large corporations, especially media corporations, to incorporate a range of industrial processes in its portfolio. News Corp., for example, can produce the content of tv, film, and other media, market it through its agencies and distribute it to consumers through its multimedia networks. It can also promote its own films or programs through its print media and cross-promote other products. Straightforward product placement is commonplace in all media, though the movie *Tomorrow Never Dies* took it to a new level. 007 used an Ericsson JB988 phone, which was advertised using the movie as a frame, while the movie was promoted in a complementary process of brand integration – an arrangement we covered in Chapter 9.

While Turner doesn't mention this movie, nor its star Pierce Brosnan, whose own value was elevated by the cross-promotion, he seems to have something like them in mind when he writes: "The celebrity's usefulness to the cross-media expansion of the major media and entertainment industry conglomerates has translated into an enhanced value for the celebrity as a commodity" (2004: 34).

Turner would find evidence for this in the way celebrities are used to transfer brand "values." Mercedes-Benz, for example, linked up with TAGHeuer, a global brand in its own right endorsed by, among others, Brad Pitt and Tiger Woods. Figures like these may not represent Mercedes directly, but their associations with the watch company that produced the Mercedes watch were useful in establishing credibility. Turner would surely find this kind of cross-brand development complementary to the cross-media expansion he cites.

So, when we learn about the kind of situations presented at the start of this chapter and either sympathize with, abhor, or just laugh at the celebs' displeasure, we should remain mindful of how: "The expression of interest, in turn, provides them with the power to elicit an adulatory photo feature in *Hello!* or to demand approval of the writer assigned to prepare a profile on them for *Vanity Fair*" (2004: 36). (Within two months of her coke exposé, Kate Moss appeared on the cover and across eleven pages of this very publication.)

Celebrities perform important functions in a mature capitalist economy in which consumer demand is paramount. A competitive market needs ever-increasing consumption to keep the system moving. The "accelerator of consumer demand," to use the phrase we took from Zygmunt Bauman in Chapter 1, has to be kept hard down at all times. Turner himself uses a similar analogy when he writes of the constant, urgent need for new celebrities to whet the appetites of consumers: "The industrial cycle of use and disposal ... does seem to have radically accelerated in response to the demand created by new media forms" (2004: 85).

Celebrities and the culture they epitomize are products themselves. They can be bought and sold, much like the merchandise they advertise. As such, they are parts of an industrial process that maintains our spending levels while keeping us pleasantly occupied. Turner doesn't dismiss other purposes the celebrities may have in, for instance, the fan's sense of self and individuality. He even quotes Rojek who believes that celebrities offer "peculiarly powerful affirmations of belonging, recognition, and meaning" (2001: 94).

Yet, with Marshall, Turner insists that any account of celebrities must be predicated on the recognition that "the interests served are first of all those of capital." Capitalism's growing dependence on what some call hyper-consumerism has led to an ethic of hedonism and health, excess and extravagance. Prudence, self-denial, deferred gratification, and all manner of frugality have been rendered old-fashioned by a culture that continually tries to develop discontents that can be salved only by buying commodities. Celebrities have to be understood in this context: they operate with the advertising industry – almost *as* an advertising industry – to persuade, cajole, and convince consumers that dependence is nothing to be ashamed of. If we depend on commodities, so what? As long as we have money enough to assuage the urge to consume, there is no problem.

None of the contemporary theorists on celebrity culture subscribes to the crude bread and circuses explanation. If that were so, celebrities would be no more that eye-catching diversions that prevent us noticing more pressing issues. Yet, there is a sense in which both Marshall and Turner understand the utility of celebrities to the capitalist enterprise and believe that this is their *raison d'être* – the purpose that accounts for their very existence.

So, we return to a question asked by all the writers covered in this chapter: what are celebrities for? Are they new replacement gods, media-born creations, or commodity representatives of a capitalist system that thrives on consumption? This is not an either/or question, of course. The media, as we've seen in previous chapters, have become increasingly obsessed with the young and prosperous, with glamour, money, and the kind of power that they confer. We, the consumers, have become fascinated, often to the point of prurience, with their well-chronicled lives. Celebrities have become godlike objects to us and we seem to delight in their sense of self-importance, their scandalous behavior, and their eagerness to deplore the media's intrusions, while inciting their interest with any device available.

The sometimes fanatical devotion we show has tempted several writers into seeing celebrity culture as a secular religion; impulse seems to dictate the behavior of some consumers more certainly than calculation. As we've seen, there is empirical support for this perspective: as there is for the other perspectives that attribute the rise of celebrities to the media and to capitalist consumerism. Neither secularization, the media, nor capitalism can be absolved; but nor can they be burdened with the whole shebang.

Celebrity culture is guided by the logic of consumerism and the celebrities are guided by this basic message: enjoy novelty, change, excitement, and every possible stimulant that can be bought over a shop counter or an internet website. The message falls on receptive ears. Consumers thrill to the sight and sound of celebrities, not because they're dupes, suckers, airheads, or simpletons, but because they have become willing accomplices in the enterprise. They too are guided by the logic of consumerism.

Appetites that were once damned as the cause of unhappiness and instability are extolled. An expansion of demand for commodities and a continuous redefining cycle of what's luxury and what's necessity has led to the elevation of new groups into the sphere of consumption we know as celebrity culture.

: supremely cultivated

As the first wave of theories of celebrity culture arrived, much of the critical impulse concerned its democratizing effect. The pronouncement of death for the old-style stars and egalitarian promises of fame for all seemed to herald a new continuous communion in which celebrity status was available to everyone, regardless of talent, if only for short periods. Reality television, as we saw in Chapter 10 seemed to confirm the promise.

Accompanying this and integral to it was what we could call a democratization of taste. Consumer items that may once have been associated with the rich and famous became widely available. Everyone could participate in a version of the good life. The once-unbreachable wall between Them and Us was replaced by gossamer-thin gauze that was thin enough to be seen through and occasionally torn. Consumers defined themselves by the commodities they bought. As we noted before, Derek Layder alludes to this in his *Understanding Social Theory* when he observes: "The pervasive effects of consumerism link identity and social status to the market for commodities" (2006: 53). "The compulsive buying of new fashions and new products" is one manifestation of this.

In 1991, Christopher Lasch wrote of the kind of society he dreaded, one in which abundance would appear to be available to everyone, while in reality being restricted to the wealthy: "The progressive conception of history implied a society of supremely cultivated consumers" (1991: 531). We now have them. In this sense, celebrity culture has been successful: the seamless unity occasioned by the end of the traditional Them and Us has brought delirious pleasure to billions the world over. Consumers devour magazines, movies, downloads, and practically everything else bearing the image, signature, or just aura of celebrities. And celebrity culture has been even more successful than Lasch could have imagined. It thrives in painlessly easing money away from people who, in a genuine sense, feel themselves part of the communion, which is less about spiritual unity, more about market harmony.

Celebrity culture does not, of course, come with a free pullout panacea for all the problems that afflict us in the early twenty-first century. For all the well-intentioned efforts of the campaigning celebrities we discussed in Chapter 11, we have to conclude that they have prompted big questions, though without answering them. But there may still be opportunities: after all, there has probably never been a comparable time in history when so many people have held the ability to influence, inspire, and perhaps incite others to action. We've seen glimpses of this when celebrities confront particular issues, such as global warming, globalization, or debt relief. But, so far, no wide-ranging vision shapes the way in which people view the world.

This is probably asking too much: what celebrity is prepared to risk rearranging the thoughts of his or her fans in a way that will undermine their devotion? "Stop buying my cds, don't rent dvds, or go to the movies. And don't buy clothes or the jewelry just 'cause you see celebs wearing something similar. But, above all, become interested in people who say things that enlighten or do things that matter!" This would be like trying to stop a car with no brakes while driving it.

Celebrity culture has offered us a distinctive vision, a beguiling one too: one in which there are few limits, an expanding range of opportunities, and inexhaustible hope. Celebrities themselves are, as I've stressed throughout, the living proof of this. Ideas like restraint, prudence, and modesty have either been discredited or just forgotten. Celebrity culture has replaced them with impetuosity, frivolity, prodigality. Human impulses like these were once seen as vices; now they are almost virtuous.

Universal consumption, the promise of luxury for all, and an endless cycle of insatiable desire have been introduced not through political discourse but through the creation of a new cultural group. Celebrities have energized our material expectations, helping shape a culture in which demand is now a basic human experience. What were once luxuries are now regarded as necessities. What was once improvement is now replaced by upgrading. For all the fantasy and escapist tendencies it radiates, celebrity culture's most basic imperative is material: it encourages consumption at every level of society.

Celebrity culture's paradoxical feat is not in advancing a worldview in which social discontents have their causes in the scarcity of material commodities, so much as promoting an idea that we shouldn't think about this long enough to distract ourselves from what we do best – consume even more of those very commodities.

TIMELINE

18th Century

- The Age of Reason advances scientific discoveries that undermine religious ideas and hastens secularization. Energized by the Enlightenment, the Industrial Revolution, which begins late in the century, creates new wealth and eventually gives the West political and economic hegemony. Education and political power are diffused through the class structure. The revolution is given impetus by the inventions of the steam engine and the spinning wheel, their respective creators, Watt and Arkwright earning international acclaim in the 1760s. Military leaders such as Nelson and Napoleon are held in reverence. Kant and Rousseau are renowned intellectuals, the latter being an influence behind the French Revolution of 1789. Goya, Voltaire, and Beethoven are prominent literary and artistic figures. Newspapers have been in evidence since 1665 when the *London Gazette* began publishing; the *Boston News-Letter*, which began publishing in 1704, is America's first recorded newspaper; only the educated minority read newspapers.

19th Century

1829
- George Stevenson builds his steam train "The Rocket," which becomes crucial to the industrial process.

1831
- Michael Faraday's experiments with electromagnetism stimulate work on broadcasting, leading to radio.
- The term "fancy" — a possible forerunner of "fan" — is in popular use to describe aficionados of prize-fighting.

1832
- A rotary device called a phenakistoscope demonstrates motion pictures; the zoetrope is a similar experimental machine.

1837
- Samuel Morse pioneers telegraph signaling; news and information can be transmitted almost instantaneously.

1842
- Charles Dickens crosses the Atlantic to tour America and further his renown.
- The rotary press is introduced; this becomes crucial to publishing.

1852
- William Fox Talbot's experiments suggest that tones can be reproduced by means of photographic screens.

1859
- Blondin (aka Jean-François Gravelet) first crosses Niagara Falls on a tightrope, a feat that adds to his growing international renown.

- Darwin's *The Origin of Species* is published, introducing a theory of natural selection that adds to secularization; Darwin becomes, according to Janet Browne (writing in 2003), "a nineteenth-century scientific celebrity."

1861

- Blondin appears in London's Crystal Palace, turning somersaults on stilts on a rope stretched across the central transept, 170 feet (52 meters) off the ground.

1871

- P.T. Barnum launches what becomes known as "The Greatest Show on Earth," using contrived stories to publicize his show in a manner that foreshadows what is later known as hyping.

1876

- Alexander Graham Bell exhibits his telephone at the World's Fair in Philadelphia.

1879

- A primitive form of radio is introduced.

1880

- The multiple reproduction of photographs and illustrations in halftone — that is, composed of minute dots — by newspapers and journals heralds the beginning of a "graphic revolution" in which the ability to reproduce images mechanically improves and images become central to popular culture, at first through photography and, later, television **CONDITION**

1882

- Already a major literary and theatrical figure, Oscar Wilde tours America.

1883

- Buffalo Bill Cody's Wild West Show starts touring; it becomes one of the most popular forms of entertainment in the Western world.

1887

- German sociologist Ferdinand Tönnies writes about the replacement of *Gemeinschaft*, or community, with *Gesellschaft*, which describes modern society.

1894

- Thomas Edison's kinetoscope, a device that makes the exhibition of motion pictures possible, is demonstrated in New York; this is one of the precursors to cinema, another being the Lumière brothers' *cinématographe*, which is unveiled the following year.
- The term "fan" is in popular use to describe baseball enthusiasts.

1895

- Marconi perfects the radio, or wireless.

1896

- Blondin gives his final performance in Belfast

1899

- "Conspicuous consumption" is a phrase used by economic theorist Thorstein Veblen to describe the emerging pattern of signifying membership of a social group through consumable items. **CAUSE**

20th Century

1900

- Prominent figures are renowned for their achievements and include discoverers (for example, Stanley and, later, Peary), inventors (Edison, Marconi), military leaders (Lee, Kitchener), political leaders (Theodore Roosevelt, Disraeli), scientists (Pasteur, Lister), literary figures (Dickens, Melville) and financial and industrial leaders (Rockefeller, Ford, who starts his motor company in 1903). Florence Nightingale, the nurse, is famous for her heroic work caring for soldiers in the Crimean War. Prominent artistic and literary figures, such as Tchaikovsky (who died in 1893) and Renoir are noted for the body of work they produce. Incumbents of senior religious positions, such as Popes and Archbishops are revered. Entertainers and athletes are regarded as less worthy of attention.

1901
- Queen Victoria, a monarch of international prominence, dies, ending her 64-year reign as Queen of England and closing a period characterized by temperance and prudishness.

1904
- Sir J. A. Fleming invents the radio valve, which is designed to detect radio waves in the air, and improves the quality of wireless transmission.

1905
- Neon signs are introduced; these are used for advertising and become literally a sign of fame (" … your name in lights").

1907
- *Scientific American* is the first journal to use the word "television."

1910
- The faked death of Florence Lawrence to create publicity for "The Biograph Girl" presages the start of the "star system."
- Film magazines such as *American Magazine* go into print, reflecting the growing interest in film gossip.

1913
- Harry Houdini performs his most famous feat, escaping from a straitjacket suspended upside down in a glass and steel tank filled with water.
- Between now and 1928, the average amount of fabric needed to dress a woman declines 36 percent from 19.25 yards (17.6 meters) to 7 yards (6.4m), suggesting a sharp move away from Victorian traditions.

1921
- Roscoe "Fatty" Arbuckle is arrested for the sexual assault and manslaughter of a female actor at a party in San Francisco; although he is cleared, his films are withdrawn and his film contract canceled; he dies destitute in 1933.

1922
- RCA begin selling "radio music boxes," effectively heralding popular broadcasting; by the mid-1930s, about 60 percent of homes in the USA and Britain have radios, even though the broadcasts they receive are limited.

1925
- Greta Garbo, of Sweden, signs a contract with MGM, becoming Hollywood's leading female actor, first in silent films, then in talkies; her taciturn, often cold, attitude and refusal to talk to journalists creates a mysterious aura that reinforces her iconic status.
- The telephotographic ("telephoto") lens is invented by C. Francis Jenkins; this makes it possible for photographers to gain images of distant objects.

1927
- Five radio listeners die supposedly from heart attacks during the Gene Tunney–Jack Dempsey world heavyweight title fight.
- Charles Lindbergh earns international recognition for the first transatlantic flight; his renown is enlarged later by tragedy when his son is kidnapped and murdered.
- Warner Brothers release *The Jazz Singer*, the first motion picture to include dialogue; the first all-talking film *Lights of New York* is released the following year.

1929
- There are 23 million cars in the USA; a steep rise from 8 million ten years before; greater mobility assists both physical and social liberation.

1931
- *The Public Enemy* is the first of a series of films in which James Cagney adopts the tough, gangster image that will become emblematic of his Hollywood career.

1932
- The film of Ernest Hemingway's *A Farewell to Arms* is released; by this time, a public "Hemingway" image has emerged.

1935
- In *Captain Blood*, Errol Flynn introduces the swashbuckling hero-adventurer screen persona that Flynn emulates in his private life.
- Howard Hughes, the industrialist and film producer, is acknowledged as a hero for breaking the air speed record, though he achieves even greater renown from the mid-1950s when he mysteriously refuses to be seen in public. He dies a recluse in 1976.

1938
- Sociologist Robert Merton's study "Social structure and anomie" is published, highlighting the influence of consumer aspirations and the power of the market economy on individuals. **CAUSE**

1939
- John Wayne's role in *Stagecoach* creates an enduring persona that Wayne lives through during his career: strong, heroic, patriotic, and traditionally masculine.

1945
- World War II ends and its military heroes such as Eisenhower and Montgomery are held in reverence, as are statesmen like F. D. Roosevelt and Churchill. Throughout the immediate postwar period, they, together with scientists and discoverers, such as Baird, Curie, Einstein, Goodyear, and Whittle, and explorers, such as Amundsen, Fuchs, and Hillary, are exemplary figures with the quality of moral leadership. The authority of such heroic figures slowly erodes over subsequent decades, confidence discharging more rapidly in the 1980s. **CONDITION**

1946
- Television is exhibited at the World's Fair in New York; sets for domestic use become available. **CONDITION**

1948
- Lucille Ball is cast as "Liz Cugat" in *My Favorite Husband*, a CBS radio show that develops into *I Love Lucy*.
- *TV Guide* begins publication; by the 1970s it is one of the best-selling magazines in the USA.
- Community Access Television begins in Pennsylvania; this later develops into cable tv.
- Gandhi is assassinated; his efforts in the Indian struggle for independence from British rule distinguished him as a charismatic leader.

1949
- Baseball player Eddie Waitkus is shot by a fan in Chicago, becoming the first victim of what later become known as stalkers.

1950
- *The Lonely Crowd: A study of the changing American character* by David Riesman and his colleagues is published; it documents the fragmentation of social life anticipated by Tonnies 63 years earlier.
- James Stewart negotiates a contract allowing him a share of the profits for the movie *Winchester '73*, which is released this year. (The eponymous lever-action rifle was itself a popular icon, being used by a variety of western entertainment figures, including Buffalo Bill and John Wayne.)

1951
- *I Love Lucy* begins; it becomes the most commercially successful television show of the 1950s, turning Lucille Ball into one of the best-known women in the world.

1954
- The Senator Joseph McCarthy hearings are televised.

1955
- Solomon Asch's psychological studies disclose the importance of peer groups in influencing judgment and opinions.
- Commercial television starts in Britain, ending the BBC's monopoly; the development opens new opportunities for advertisers, including American advertisers.

1956
- Psychologists D. Horton and R. R. Wohl publish their article "Mass communication and parasocial interaction" in the journal *Psychiatry*; it suggests how tv viewers can form one-sided relationships with figures they have never met.

1957
- The Soviet Union sends the first satellite *Sputnik 1* into orbit.
- Vance Packard's *The Hidden Persuaders*, a book that reveals the extensive influence of advertising, is published; it is complemented in 1959, with the author's *The Status Seekers*, an analysis of how people crave consumer goods not for their use but for the prestige they confer on the owner. **CAUSE**

1958
- In his *The Affluent Society*, economist J. K. Galbraith argues that basic material needs have been satisfied by mass affluence and that advertising has become crucial in creating excessive consumption and a corresponding consumer debt. **CAUSE**
- Tazio Secchiaroli, a freelance newspaper photographer, sparks pandemonium in Rome when taking shots of King Farouk, Ava Gardner, Anita Ekberg, and others without their permission. Pictures of the events appear in various publications.
- Telephoto lenses for use on 35 mm cameras are now in regular production.

1960
- Federico Fellini's film *La Dolce Vita* features a Secchiaroli-like "Signor Paparazzo" (described by his mistress as a "vulture") and introduces a new generic noun to the popular vocabulary.
- The televised John F. Kennedy–Richard M. Nixon presidential election debates highlight the power of television in shaping perception.
- About 90 percent of homes have a television set.

1961
- In his book *The Image* Daniel Boorstin offers what seems at the time an amusing tautology suggesting there is an emergent class of people who are well known for their "well-knownness."

1962
- Marcello Geppetti takes his influential photograph of Elizabeth Taylor and Richard Burton. **TRIGGER**
- *Telstar 1* provides an eight-minute transmission; *Telstar 1* is the first of several communications satellites capable of sending signals to earth that go into orbit over the next several years; they provide the stimulus for the development of a global media. **CONDITION**

1964
- Taylor marries Burton in Montreal; Burton is Taylor's fifth husband; after ten years, the world's most renowned couple divorce, only to have a secret wedding ceremony in Africa in 1975, followed by a second honeymoon 16 months after splitting up.
- The summer Olympics in Tokyo are broadcast internationally "live."

1966
- Former Hollywood actor Ronald Reagan is elected governor of California; he is re-elected in 1970.

1967
- George Best's fame broadens as he features in Manchester United's win over Benfica in the European Cup Final.

1968
- The *National Enquirer* moves headquarters and changes policy; circulation increases.
- Athletes Tommie Smith and John Carlos expose the power of global television to highlight social and political issues when they make Black Power gestures on the Olympic victory rostrum in Mexico City.

1969
- *Apollo 11* beams images from the moon's surface back to earth.
- Britain's *Affluent Worker* study discloses a materialistic working class with bourgeois aspirations. **CAUSE**
- Joe Namath leads the New York Jets to an upset victory in the Super Bowl.
- Andy Warhol launches his magazine *Inter/View*, in which he famously predicts: "In the future, everyone will be world-famous for fifteen minutes."

1971

- Philip Zimbardo's prison simulation experiments disclose interest in human interaction, which later manifests in reality television.

1972

- Photographer Ron Galella receives a federal court order barring him from approaching within 50 yards of Jacqueline Kennedy Onassis or her children.
- The *Star* magazine launches, prefiguring an increase in publications specializing in gossip.
- Computer scientists show an early version of what is later to become the internet.

1973

- *An American Family*, a fly-on-the-wall documentary is shown; it anticipates the format of reality tv; a similar British show *The Family* features the same approach.

1974

- Cher and Sonny Bono divorce; the *National Enquirer* builds popularity by carrying full details of the breakup.
- Psychologist Stanley Milgram's study *Obedience to Authority* shows how effectively human behavior can be manipulated given the appropriate circumstances.
- *People* magazine launches.

1976

- HBO begins full transmission, showing the Muhammad Ali Joe Frazier fight from Manila; it uses a transponder on a commercial satellite, which relays signals to cable systems; the technology allows the global exchange of television (or telephone) signals by means of microwaves directly to the home, without the need for relay stations; within two years, HBO, which specializes in movies and sports, is the most popular cable channel with 1.5 million subscribers. **CONDITION**

1977

- The *National Enquirer* sells 7 million copies of the issue featuring pictures of Elvis Presley in his coffin.

1979

- *The Culture of Narcissism* by Christopher Lasch is published; it describes a culture increasingly reliant on the media to define its "needs." **CONDITION**

1980

- Reagan is elected President of the USA; he is re-elected in 1984.
- ESPN starts transmission; by 1998, it broadcasts to 160 countries.
- CNN starts operations; within 20 years, it reaches 212 countries, with a combined audience of 1 billion

1981

- Diana marries Prince Charles.
- MTV starts transmission; in 1987, the first of several analogous stations around the world is launched.
- Assassination attempt on Reagan by a fan fixated on Jodie Foster
- Revamped *Us Weekly* adds to the growing number of celebrity magazines

1982

- *USA Today* is launched by Gannett Publishing.

1983

- Madonna releases her first self-titled album.
- Michael Jackson's "Billie Jean" is entered onto MTV's playlist after a dispute with CBS.
- The Reagan administration announces a program of deregulating (decreasing government control of) business and broadcasting and facilitates more competition among American media companies.
- 50 major media corporations dominate the global industry.

1984

- Burton dies of a cerebral hemorrhage; Taylor's apprehension about the media deters her from attending the funeral.
- *The Cosby Show* begins airing; by the early 1990s, the African American consumer market is estimated to be worth $200 billion.

- Michael Jordan leads the US national team to Olympic gold medal; he later turns professional and signs a landmark deal with Nike; the Olympic games are broadcast in stereo.

1985
- Live Aid concerts in aid of a famine in sub-Saharan Africa signify the power of popular entertainers to raise awareness of social issues through the media.

1986
- Oprah Winfrey's Chicago talk show goes on national television.

1987
- There are now only 29 corporations that dominate the global media.

1989
- Madonna's *Like a Prayer* album is released; Pepsi pulls out of a $5 million endorsement deal with her.
  TRIGGER
- Sky satellite tv channel is launched.
- Explicit tapes featuring Rob Lowe circulate; ten years later, he reappears triumphantly in the tv show *The West Wing*.

1990
- Warner Communications and Time Inc. merge in a $14.1 billion deal to create the world's largest media corporation; together with other media corporation takeovers and realignments, it combines to reduce the number of dominant media corporations to 23.
- Madonna's "Justify my love" is excluded from MTV's playlists.

1991
- CNN reports on the Persian Gulf War "live."
- The film *Truth or Dare*, or *In Bed With Madonna*, as it is entitled in Britain, goes on general release.
- *The Jerry Springer Show* begins broadcasting.
- William Kennedy Smith is acquitted of rape after a highly publicized trial.

1992
- Mike Tyson's rape trial is a global *cause célèbre*; Tyson is sentenced to three years' imprisonment
- Diana and Charles announce their separation.
- Madonna's book *Sex* goes on sale at $50 (£30).
- MTV starts *The Real World*, a precursor of reality television.
- Two serious books on fans, Henry Jenkins' *Textual Poachers* and *The Adoring Audience* edited by Lisa A. Lewis, challenge popular conceptions by viewing fandom as a form of empowerment.
- Bill Clinton accentuates the importance of image management during his successful US presidential election campaign.

1993
- Critics berate *Body of Evidence*, featuring Madonna.

1994
- The O. J. Simpson trial commands the attention of the world's media.
- A fan of tennis player Steffi Graf stabs her rival Monica Seles during a game in Germany.
- Michael Jackson marries Lisa Marie Presley, daughter of Elvis, in a secret ceremony in the Dominican Republic that evades the purview of the paparazzi; the couple deny they are married for two months; 18 months later, Presley files for divorce.

1995
- The Spice Girls' "Wannabe" is released and launches a band that is later listed by *Forbes* as one of the top global "brands"; the band portends the rise of other "manufactured" performers.
- Hugh Grant is fined and put on two years' probation after pleading no contest to charges of lewd behavior with prostitute Divine Brown on Hollywood's Sunset Strip; in the following years, he makes several successful films, including *Bridget Jones's Diary*.

1996

- Tiger Woods makes his professional début and signs a five-year deal with Nike valued at $40 million.
- Disney takes over Capital Cities/ABC for $19 billion, creating a movie, tv and publishing giant with capacity for vertical integration; it is the biggest media deal to date and reduces the number of dominant media corporations to twelve.
- Madonna earns plaudits for her lead role in the film *Evita*.
- The US Telecommunications Act deregulates the media industry, giving corporate Hollywood a near-monopoly of cinema ownership and cable tv (permitting more vertical integration); President Bill Clinton negotiates first rights for US companies in Latin American broadcasting and gives himself "fast track" approval on trade deals for media companies.

1997

- The *Daily Mirror* pays a reported £265,000 ($450,000) for British rights to publish shots of Diana and Dodi Al-Fayed on their vacation off Sardinia. The photographer Mario Brenna earns an estimated $7 million from global sales of the pictures.
- Diana dies in a car accident in Paris; the photographers who chase her prior to the crash are later cleared of wrongdoing. **TRIGGER**

1998

- Clinton's affair with Monica Lewinsky dominates the media and sparks impeachment proceedings; Clinton remains in office until 2001.
- George Michael is fined and ordered to do community service after being found guilty of lewd behavior in a public lavatory in Los Angeles.
- Madonna is subpoenaed to give evidence against a stalker.
- 66 percent of US homes have cable tv.

1999

- Viacom purchases CBS for $34.5 billion. the biggest media acquisition at this point; there are now only eleven dominant media corporations.
- Hollywood actors join anti-globalization protesters challenging the World Trade Organization conference in Seattle.
- *Heat* launches in Britain as a general entertainment magazine; after a year of disappointing sales, it adopts a celebrity-centric approach and its sales soar.
- John de Mol launches a new show he has designed on Dutch television; within six years, 70 versions of *Big Brother* are shown in countries around the world.
- *PopStars*, a documentary series following the creation of an all-girl group, True Bliss, from 500 contestants is shown on New Zealand television; it is a seminal program with many variations being produced globally over the following years.

21st Century

2000

- British and American versions of *Big Brother* start; in the USA *Survivor* begins.
- AOL acquires Time-Warner in a deal valued at $166 billion (£100 billion) to create the biggest of the ten dominant media corporations in the world.
- French tennis player Natalie Tauziat criticizes the priority the media afford "aesthetics and charisma" in sport; it is a veiled reference to Anna Kournikova, 12th-ranked women's tennis player, but the world's highest-paid female athlete with income over $10 million, only 6.4 percent of which is prize money, the rest from endorsements and photoshoots for, among others, *Esquire*, *GQ*, and *Maxim*.
- *OK!* magazine secures the exclusive contract with Michael Douglas and Catherine Zeta-Jones to cover their New York wedding; arch-rival *Hello!* publishes unauthorized photographs.
- A British version of *PopStars* begins, its eventual winners emerging the following year.

2001

- Hear'Say, the band formed from the British *PopStars* becomes the first group to top the British single and album charts simultaneously with début releases; the band begins to break up within a year; Liberty X, a band formed out of losing contestants, has more commercial success than the winners.
- *Pop Idol* starts in Britain.

- Wynona Ryder is arrested for shoplifting in Beverly Hills.

2002

- *American Idol*, the US counterpart to Britain's *Pop Idol*, starts; by 2006, it averages 27 million viewers and becomes the US's most expensive program for advertising after the Super Bowl, with 30-second spots costing $700,000 (£420,000).
- There are just nine dominant media corporations: AOL Time-Warner, Disney, Bertelsmann, Viacom, TCI, General Electric, Rupert Murdoch's News Corp., Sony, and Seagram, all with vertical integration capacities.
- A team of British and US psychologists introduces the "celebrity worship scale" to measure individuals' intensity of interest.
- Venus Williams signs a $45 million promotional deal with Reebok; this is thought to be the most lucrative endorsement contract held by a female.
- Beyoncé features in her first film *Austin Powers in Goldmember*.

2003

- Michael Jackson is interviewed on television and indicates that he has shared his bed with children.
- Arnold Schwarzenegger is elected Governor of California.
- Excerpts of a tape featuring Paris Hilton are uploaded; 13 million viewers watch the tv show *The Simple Life* in which she features; over the next three years, she is contracted to appear in eight films.
- Jennifer Aniston appears on the cover of *Vogue*'s best-selling issue of the year (and again in 2004). *InStyle* also features her in its best-selling edition.
- Madonna kisses both Britney Spears and Christina Aguilera at MTV Music Awards.
- Beyoncé's first solo album *Dangerously in Love* sells 6 million copies.
- Douglas and Zeta-Jones are awarded £14,500 damages from *Hello!* magazine for breach of privacy and rights "of confidence"; Zeta-Jones famously says in her evidence that £1 million is not very much money to her and to spend three times that amount [in legal costs] to recover less than £15,000 defies all logic.
- Oprah Winfrey is valued at over $1 billion by *Forbes*.
- Kobe Bryant is tried for sexual assault; he is subsequently cleared.
- LeBron James turns professional and signs a reported $90 million contract with Nike.
- David Beckham moves from Manchester United to Real Madrid after globally reported transfer negotiations.

2004

- Beckham is involved in an internationally publicized scandal after reports of an extramarital affair.
- Martha Stewart begins a five-month prison sentence; she is released in 2005 to find her companies prospering.
- Princess Caroline of Monaco wins a key ruling from the European Court of Human Rights, which confirms that the publishing of paparazzi photographs of the princess in a public place was a violation of her right to privacy.
- Cosmetic surgeries increase at a yearly rate of 17 percent in the USA (now 214,200 procedures; or 1 person in every 1,168) and 35 percent in Britain (16,350; or 1 in 3,670). When nonsurgical cosmetic procedures, such as Botox, laser hair removal, and chemical peels, are added, the totals are: USA: 8 million; UK: 500,000.
- The US publication the *Star* is revamped as a glossy magazine; it started as a tabloid in 1972.

2005

- Michael Jackson is cleared of child molestation charges after one of the most publicized trials in history; over 1,000 journalists are sent to Santa Maria, California to cover the event.
- A Los Angeles court jails for three years a stalker who threatened to cut Catherine Zeta-Jones into pieces.
- *Hello!* magazine wins a legal battle to overturn a ruling which would have forced it to pay £2 million ($3.5 million) to *OK!* for publishing unauthorized shots of the Douglas/Zeta-Jones wedding; the previous ruling on damages (from 2003) stood.
- *OK!* launches an American edition.
- *Vanity Fair* has its all-time best-selling issue, featuring a tell-all cover story on Jennifer Aniston whose breakup with Brad Pitt was given extensive global media coverage, including a record five successive weeks on the cover of *Us Weekly*.
- Kanye West is reproached for his criticism of George Bush following the devastation of New Orleans by Hurricane Katrina.

- There are 22,000 cosmetic surgery operations in Britain (1 person in 2,727); this is a third more than in 2004.
- Michelle Wie turns professional, aged 16, with $10 million-worth of endorsement contracts.
- Kate Moss loses several modeling contracts, worth an estimated £6 million ($10 million) after being pictured by a British newspaper using cocaine.

2006

- Kate Moss attracts several new modeling contracts, worth an estimated £12 million ($20 million) months after being exposed by a British newspaper for using cocaine.
- Governor Arnold Schwarzenegger signs a California law that increases penalties against overly aggressive paparazzi.
- *People* magazine records sales of 3.6 million copies.
- Madonna provokes condemnation from Christian groups by performing in a crucifixion pose on a 20ft-high cross during her Confessions tour, which is the most lucrative tour ever undertaken by a female artist, grossing $200m.

BIBLIOGRAPHY

Adorno, Theodor and Horkheimer, Max (1972) *The Culture Industry: Enlightenment as mass deception*, New York: Herder & Herder.

Alberoni, Francesco (1972) "The powerless: elite theory and sociological research on the phenomenon of the stars," pp. 23–51 in McQuail, Dennis (ed.) *Sociology of Mass Communications*, Harmondsworth: Penguin.

Alperstein, Neil M. (1991) "Imaginary social relationships with celebrities appearing in television commercials," *Journal of Broadcasting and Electronic Media*, vol. 35, no. 1 (Winter), unnumbered.

Altman, Howard (2005) "Celebrity culture," *CQ Researcher*, vol. 15, no. 11 (March 18), pp. 1–32.

Andersen, Robin (1995) *Consumer Culture and TV Programming*, Boulder, CO: Westview.

Andrejevic, Mark (2004) *Reality TV: The art of being watched*, Lanham, MD: Rowman & Littlefield.

Andrews, David L. and Jackson, Steven J. (2001) "Introduction: sport celebrities, public culture, and private experience," pp. 1–19 in Andrews, David L. and Jackson, Steven J. (eds) (2001) *Sport Stars: The cultural politics of sporting celebrity*, London: Routledge.

Anonymous (2004) "Face value: star power," *The Economist*, vol. 372, no. 8387 (July 8).

Anonymous (2005) "Britain: the fame machine – making and marketing celebrities," *The Economist*, vol. 376, no. 8442 (September 3), p. 29.

Asch, Solomon (1955) "Opinions and social pressures," *Scientific American*, vol. 193, pp. 31–5.

Basil, Michael D. (1967) "Identification as a mediator of celebrity effects," *Journal of Broadcasting and Electronic Media*, vol. 40, no. 4 (Fall), pp. 478–96.

Bauman, Zygmunt (2001) "Consuming life," *Journal of Consumer Culture* vol. 1, no. 1, pp. 5–29.

Bechtel, Andy, Daniels, LeAnne, and Sylvester, Judith (1999) "When celebrities, race and news collide," *Quill*, vol. 87, no. 8 (November), n.p.

Biography Resource Center (2004) "Errol Flynn" *Biography Resource Center* http://galenet.galegroup.com/servlet/BioRC. Farmington Hills, MI: Thomson Gale.

Blum, Virginia L. (2003) *Flesh Wounds: The culture of cosmetic surgery*, Berkeley, CA: University of California Press.

Bogle, Donald (1998) *Toms, Coons, Mulattoes, Mammies, and Bucks: An interpretive history of blacks in American films*, 3rd edition, New York: Continuum.

Bonner, Frances (2005) "The celebrity in the text," pp. 57–95 in Evans, Jessica and Hesmondhalgh, David (eds) *Understanding Media: Inside celebrity*, Maidenhead: Open University Press.

Boon, Susan D, and Lomore, Christine D. (2001) "Admirer–celebrity relationships among young adults: explaining perceptions of celebrity influence on identity," *Human Communication Research*, vol. 3, pp. 432–65.

Boorstin, Daniel (1961/1992) *The Image: A guide to pseudo-events in America*, New York: Random House.

Boteach, Shmuley (2002) "Idol worship: the dark side of celebrity," *Forward*, vol. 106, no. 31,395, p. 1.

Braudy, Leo (1997) *The Frenzy of Renown: Fame and its history*, 2nd edition, New York: Vintage.

Briggs, Asa and Burke, Peter (2005) *A Social History of the Media: From Gutenberg to the Internet*, 2nd edition, Cambridge: Polity.

Brohm, Jean-Marie (1978) *Sport: A prison of measured time*, London: Ink Links.

Bronfen, Elisabeth (2002) "Celebrating catastrophe," *Angelaki: Journal of the Theoretical Humanities* vol. 7, no. 2 (August), pp. 175–86.

Brooks, Carol (2004) "What celebrity worship says about us: gossip can serve a purpose," *USA Today*, News section (September 14), p. 21a.

Browne, Janet (2003) "Charles Darwin as a celebrity," *Science in Context*, vol. 16, pp. 175–94.

Campbell, James T. (2000) "'Print the legend': John Wayne and postwar American culture," *Reviews in American History*, vol. 28, no. 3, pp. 465–77.

Carlson, Margaret (1997) "Blood on their hands?" *Time*, vol. 150 (September 8), p. 46.

Chung, Heejoon (2003) "Sport star vs. rock star in globalizing popular culture: similarities, difference and paradox in discussion of celebrities," *International Review for the Sociology of Sport*, vol. 38, no. 1, pp. 99–108.

Cole, C. L. and David L. Andrews (2001) "America's new son: Tiger Woods and America's multiculturalism," pp. 70–86 in Andrews, David L. and Jackson, Steven J. (eds) (2001) *Sport Stars: The cultural politics of sporting celebrity*, London: Routledge.

Cotts, Cynthia (2003) "Fame by numbers," *Village Voice*, vol. 48, no. 49 (December 3–9), p. 32.

Cox, Donna (1999) "*Diana: Her true story*: post-modern transgressions in identity," *Journal of Gender Studies*, vol. 8, no. 3, pp. 323–38.

Cushman, Philip (1995) *Constructing the Self, Constructing America: A cultural history of psychotherapy*, Reading, MA: Addison-Wesley.

Cushman, Philip (1999) "Why the self is empty: toward a historically situated psychology," *The American Psychologist*, vol. 45, no. 5, pp. 599–611.

Dalton, Stephen (2005) "Heroes of their degeneration," *The Times*, times2 section (September 30), p. 22.

De Tocqueville, Alexis (2003) *Democracy in America* (translated by Gerald Bevan, edited by Isaac Kramnick), London: Penguin.

de Zengotita, Thomas (2002) "The numbing of the American mind," *Harper's Magazine*, vol. 304, no. 1823 (April), pp. 33–41.

deCordova, Richard (1990) *Picture Personalities: The emergence of the star system in America*, Urbana, IL: University of Illinois Press.

Deutsch, Helene (1986) "Some forms of emotional disturbance and their relationship to schizophrenia," pp. 74–91 in Stone, Michael H. (ed.) *Essential Papers on Borderline Disorders: One hundred years at the border*, New York: New York University Press.

Duerden, Nick (2005) "Beyond doubt," *Independent Magazine*, August 28, pp. 12–14.

Dyer, Richard (1979) *Stars*, London: British Film Institute.

Ellroy, James (1990) *LA Confidential*, New York: Warner Books.

Evans, Jessica (2005) "Celebrity, media and history," pp. 11–56 in Evans, Jessica and Hesmondhalgh, David (eds) *Understanding Media: Inside celebrity*, Maidenhead: Open University Press.

Evans, Jessica and Hesmondhalgh, David (eds) (2005) *Understanding Media: Inside celebrity*, Maidenhead: Open University Press.

Flick, Larry (2003) "The second coming of Robbie Williams," *The Advocate*, no. 889 (May 13), pp. 34–42.

Foucault, Michel (1979) *The History of Sexuality*, vol. 1, London: Allen Lane.

Fowles, Jib (1992) *Why Viewers Watch: A reappraisal of television's effects*, Newbury Park, CA: Sage.

Fowles, Jib (1996) *Advertising and Popular Culture*, Newbury Park, CA: Sage.

Frank, Rueven (2001) "The shifting shapes of TV news," *The New Leader*, vol. 84, no. 2 (March/April), pp. 38–40.

Fraser, Benson P. and Brown, William J. (2002) "Media, celebrities, and social influence: identification with Elvis Presley," *Mass Communication and Society*, vol. 1, no. 2 (May), pp. 183–207.

Galbraith, John Kenneth (1958) *The Affluent Society*, New York: Houghton Mifflin.

Gamson, Joshua (1992) "The assembly line of greatness: celebrity in twentieth-century America," *Critical Studies in Mass Communication*, vol. 9 (March), pp. 1–24.

Gamson, Joshua (1994) *Claims to Fame: Celebrity in contemporary America*, Berkeley, CA: University of California Press.

George, Nelson (1988) *The Death of Rhythm and Blues*, New York: Pantheon.

Giles, David (2000) *Illusions of Immortality: A psychology of fame and celebrity*, London: Macmillan.

Goldthorpe, John, Lockwood, David, Bechhofer, Frank, and Platt, Jennifer (1968) *The Affluent Worker: Industrial attitudes and behaviour*, Cambridge: Cambridge University Press.

Gomery, Douglas (2005) *The Hollywood Studio System: A history*, London: British Film Institute.

Gray, Herman (1995) *Watching Race: Television and the struggle for "blackness"* Minneapolis, MN: University of Minnesota Press.

Green, Michelle (2002) "Those lips, that face . . ." *People*, vol. 61, no. 15 (April 19), pp. 127–8.

Halberstam, David (1999) *Playing for Keeps: Michael Jordan and the world he made*, New York: Random House.

Hall, Wiley A. (2002) "Urban rhythms: hooray! Halle Berry is a 'Bond girl' now," *Afro-American Red Star*, vol. 111, no. 16, p. A2.

Haney, C., Banks, W. C., and Zimbardo, P. G. (1973) "Interpersonal dynamics in a simulated prison," *International Journal of Criminology and Penology*, vol. 1, pp. 69–97.

Harris, Cheryl (1998) "A sociology of television fandom," pp. 41–54 in Harris, Cheryl and Alexander, Alison (eds) *Theorizing Fandom: Fans, subculture and identity*, Cresskill, NJ: Hampton Press.

Harris, Cheryl and Alexander, Alison (1998) (eds) *Theorizing Fandom: Fans, subculture and identity*, Cresskill, NJ: Hampton Press.

Henderson, Amy (1992) "Media and the rise of celebrity culture," *Organization of American Historians Magazine of History*, vol. 6 (Spring), pp. 1–6.

Hesmondhalgh, David (2005) "Producing celebrity," pp. 97–134 in Evans, Jessica and Hesmondhalgh, David (eds) *Understanding Media: Inside celebrity*, Maidenhead: Open University Press.

Higham, Charles (1980) *Errol Flynn: The untold story*, New York: Doubleday.

Hills, Matt (2005) *How To Do Things With Cultural Theory*, London: Hodder Arnold.

Hilton, Paris and Ginsberg, Merle (2005) *Confessions of an Heiress: A tongue-in-cheek peek behind the pose*, New York: Simon & Schuster.

Hoch, Paul (1972) *Rip Off the Big Game: The exploitation of sports by the power elite*, New York: Anchor Doubleday.

Holmes, Su and Jermyn, Deborah (eds) (2004) *Understanding Reality Television*, London: Routledge.

Home Office (2003) *Statistics on Women and the Criminal Justice System: A Home Office publication under Section 95 of the Criminal Justice Act 1991*, London: HMSO.

Hooper, Nancy (1995) "Celebrities at risk," *Risk Management*, vol. 42, no. 5 (May), pp. 18–34.

Horne, John (2006) *Sport in Consumer Culture*, Houndmills: Palgrave Macmillan.

Horton, D. and Wohl, R. R, (1956) "Mass communication and parasocial interaction," *Psychiatry* vol. 19, pp. 215–29.

Hoskyns, Barney (1996) *Waiting for the Sun: The story of the Los Angeles music scene*, London: Viking.

Illouz, Eva (2003) *Oprah Winfrey and the Glamour of Misery: An essay on popular culture*, New York: Columbia University Press.

Ingram, Billy (nd) "A short history of the *National Enquirer*" (two parts), www.tvparty.com/tabloids.html.

Insight Media (1990) *Quiet Rage: The Stanford prison experiment*, DVD/ VHS, New York: Insight Media.

Jenkins, Henry (1992) *Textual Poachers: Television fans and participatory culture*, New York: Routledge.

Jhally, Sut and Lewis, Justin (1992) *Enlightened Racism:* The Cosby Show, *Audiences, and the Myth of the American Dream*, Boulder, CO: Westview.

Johnson, Brian D. (2001) "We like to watch: 'reality TV' is the new pornography, mainstream voyeurism," *Maclean's*, vol. 114, no. 5 (January 29), p. 56.

Johnson, Roy and Harrington, Ann (1998) "The Jordan effect," *Fortune*, vol. 137, no. 12 (June 22).

Kates, Steven M. (2002) "The protean quality of subcultural consumption: an ethnographic account of gay consumers," *Journal of Consumer Research*, vol. 29, no. 3 (December), pp. 383–400.

Katz, Donald (1994) *Just Do It: The Nike spirit in the corporate world*, Holbrook, MA; Adams Media.

King, Natalie, Touyz, Stephen, and Charles, Margaret (2000) "The effect of body dissatisfaction on women's perception of female celebrities," *Journal of Eating Disorders*, vol. 27, pp. 341–7.

Kirby, David (2001) "Will the real out celebrities please stand up?" *The Advocate*, nos. 828/9 (January 16), pp. 56–8.

Klein, Naomi (2001) *No Logo*, London: Flamingo.

Knight, Jennifer L., Giuliano, Traci A., and Sanchez-Ross, Monica G. (2001) "Famous or infamous? The influence of celebrity status and race on perceptions of responsibility for rape," *Basic and Applied Social Psychology*, vol. 23, no. 3, pp. 183–90.

Koch, Kathy (1998) "Can the media regain the public's trust?" *The CQ Researcher*, vol. 8, no. 48 (December 25), pp. 1–25.

Kushnick, Louis (1981) "Racism and class consciousness in modern capitalism," in Bowser, B. and Hunt, R. (eds) *Impact of Racism on White America*, Beverly Hills, CA: Sage.

Lafrance, Mélisse and Rail, Geneviève (2001) "Excursions into otherness: understanding Dennis Rodman and the limits of subversive agency," pp. 36–50 in Andrews, David L. and Jackson, Steven J. (eds) (2001) *Sport Stars: The cultural politics of sporting celebrity*, London: Routledge.

Lange, Rense and Houran, James (1999) "The role of fear in delusions of the paranormal," *Journal of Nervous and Mental Disease*, vol. 187, no. 3, pp. 159–66.

Langham, Lauren (2002) "Suppose they gave a culture war and no one came: Zippergate and the carnivalization of politics," *The American Behavioral Scientist*, vol. 46, no. 4 (December), pp. 501–37.

Lapham, Lewis H. (1997) "Fatted calf," *Harper's*, vol. 295 (November), pp. 11–14.

Lasch, Christopher (1980) *The Culture of Narcissism: American life in an age of diminishing expectations*, London: Abacus.

Lasch, Christopher (1991) *The True and Only Heaven: Progress and its critics*, New York: W. W. Norton.

Layder, Derek (2006) *Understanding Social Theory*, 2nd edition, London: Sage.

Leff, Leonard (1997) *Hemingway and his Conspirators: Hollywood, Scribners and the making of American celebrity culture*, Lanham, MD: Rowman & Littlefield.

Lewis, David and Bridger, Darren (2001) *The Soul of the New Consumer*, London: Nicholas Brealey.

Lewis, Lisa A. (ed.) (1992) *The Adoring Audience: Fan culture and popular media*, London: Routledge.

Lovejoy, Joe (1999) *Bestie: A portrait of a legend*, London: Pan.

Luna, David and Forquer Gupta, Susan (2001) "An integrative framework for cross-cultural consumer behavior," *International Marketing Review*, vol. 18, no. 1, p. 45.

McChesney, Robert (1997) *Corporate Media and the Threat to Democracy*, New York: Seven Stories.

McCutcheon, Lynn E., Lange, Rense, and Houran, James (2002) "Conceptualization and measurement of celebrity worship," *British Journal of Psychology*, vol. 93, no. 1, pp. 67–87.

McCutcheon, Lynn E., Ashe, Diane D., Houran, James, and Maltby, John (2003) "A cognitive profile of individuals who tend to worship celebrities," *Journal of Psychology*, vol. 137, no. 4 (July), pp. 309–14.

MacDonald, J. Fred (1992) *Blacks and White TV: African Americans in television since 1948*, 2nd edition, Chicago, IL: Nelson-Hall.

McKay, Jim (1999) "Book review: Robert Goldman and Stephen Papson,

Nike Culture: The sign of the swoosh," *International Journal of Cultural Studies*, vol. 2, no. 3, pp. 418–21.

Maddox, Alton H. (2003) "Oh no! Kobe joins Tawana as racial victim," *New York Amsterdam News*, vol. 94, no. 30 (July 24), p. 12.

Madonna, Meisel, Steve (photographer) and O'Brien, Glenn (ed.) (1992) *Sex*, New York: Vintage/Ebury.

Maltby, John, Day, Liza, McCutcheon, Lynn E., Gillett, Raphael, Houran, James, and Ashe, Diane D. (2004) "Personality and coping: a context for examining celebrity worship and mental health," *British Journal of Psychology*, vol. 95, pp. 411–28.

Marshall, P. David (1997) *Celebrity and Power: Fame in contemporary culture*, Minneapolis, MN: University of Minnesota Press.

Melnick, Merrill J. and Jackson, Steven J. (2002) "Globalization American-style and reference idol selection: the importance of athlete celebrity others among New Zealand youth," *International Review for the Sociology of Sport*, vol. 37, nos. 3–4, pp. 429–48.

Meloy, J. Reid (1997) "The clinical management of stalking: 'someone is watching over me . . .'," *American Journal of Psychotherapy*, vol. 51 (Spring), pp. 174–84.

Merschman, Joseph C. (2001) "The dark side of the web: cyberstalking and the need for contemporary legislation," *Harvard Women's Law Journal*, vol. 24 (Spring), pp. 255–92.

Merton, Robert K. (1969) "Social structure and anomie," pp. 254–84 in Cressey, D. R. and Ward, D. A. (eds) *Delinquency, Crime and Social Process*, New York: Harper & Row.

Milgram, Stanley (1974) *Obedience to Authority: An experimental view*, New York: Harper & Row.

Monaco, James (ed.) (1978) *Celebrity: The media as image makers*, New York: Delta.

Murray, Susan and Ouellette, Laurie (eds) (2004) *Reality TV: Remaking television culture*, New York: New York University Press.

Nataraajan, Rajan and Chawla, Sudhir K. (1997) "'Fitness' marketing: celebrity or non-celebrity endorsement?" *Journal of Professional Services Marketing*, vol. 15, no. 2, pp. 119–30.

Nederveen Pieterse, Jan (1992) *White on Black: Images of Africa and blacks in Western popular culture*, London: Yale University Press.

Neimark, Jill (1995) "The culture of celebrity," *Psychology Today*, May/June, pp. 54–7, 87–90.

Neuman, W. Russell (2002) *The Future of the Mass Audience*, Cambridge: Cambridge University Press.

Newbury, Michael (2000) "Celebrity watching," *American Literary History*, vol. 12, nos. 1 and 2, pp. 272–83.

Oates, Thomas and Polumbaum, Judy (2004) "Agile big man: the flexible marketing of Yao Ming," *Pacific Affairs*, vol. 77, no. 2 (Summer), pp. 187–211.

Packard, Vance (1957) *The Hidden Persuaders*, New York: Random House.

Packard, Vance (1959) *The Status Seekers*, Chapel Hill, NC: University of North Carolina Press.

Packard, Vance (1960) *The Waste Makers*, New York: McKay & Co.

Polumbaum, Judy and Wietling, Stephen G. (1999) "Stories of sport and moral order: unraveling the cultural construction of Tiger Woods," *Journalism and Communication Monographs*, vol. 1, no. 2 (Summer), pp. 67–118.

Ponce de Leon, Charles (2002) *Self-Exposure: Human-interest journalism and the emergence of celebrity in America, 1890–1940*, Chapel Hill, NC: University of North Carolina Press.

Postman, Neil (1985) *Amusing Ourselves to Death*, New York: Penguin.

Raasch, Chuck (2004) "Entertainers blur line between celebrity, politics," www.usatoday.com/news/politicselections/nation/president/2004–08-30-celebrity-politics_x.htm.

Reinstein, Mara (2003) "Britney and Madonna – new best friends," *Us Weekly*, no. 448 (September 15), p. 52.

Rich, Joshua (2002) "Leave it do diva," *Entertainment Weekly*, no. 654 (May), p. 84.

Richards, David (1997) "Paparazzi's flashes of fame: in NY, a photohistory of the celebrity-chasers," *Washington Post*, September 9, p. E01.

Riesman, David, with Glazer, Nathan and Denney, Reuel (1950) *The Lonely Crowd: A study of the changing American character*, New Haven, CN: Yale University Press.

Rodriguez, Rene (2002) "J.Lo: Success makes the best revenge," *Hispanic*, vol. 15, no. 6, pp. 36–40.

Roediger, David R. (2003) *Colored White: Transcending the racial past*, Berkeley, CA: University of California Press.

Rojek, Chris (2001) *Celebrity*, London: Reaktion.

Root, Deborah (1996) *Cannibal Culture: Art, appropriation, and the commodification of difference*, Boulder, CO: Westview Press.

Sacks, Danielle (2003) "Who's that girl?" *Fast Company*, no. 76 (November), p. 32.

Sandvoss, Cornel (2005) *Fans: The mirror of consumption*, Cambridge: Polity.

Schor, Juliet B. (2004) *Born to Buy: The commercialized child and the new consumer culture*, New York: Scribner.

Schudson, Michael (1993) *Advertising, the Uneasy Persuasion: Its dubious impact on American society*, New York: Routledge.

Sharkey, Jacqueline (1997) "The Diana aftermath," *American Journalism Review*, vol. 19, no. 9, pp. 18–25.

Sherif, Muzafir (1936) *The Psychology of Social Norms*, New York: Harper & Row.

Sherman, Len (1992) *Big League, Big Time: The birth of the Arizona Diamondbacks, the billion-dollar business of sports, and the power of the media in America*, New York: Pocket Books.

Smart, Barry (2005) *The Sport Star: Modern sport and the cultural economy of the sporting celebrity*, London: Sage.

Smillie, Dirk (2003) "So, this is reality?" *New York Times Upfront*, vol. 135, no. 9 (February 7), pp. 22–3.

Smith, Robert and Seltzer, Richard (2000) *Contemporary Controversies and the American Divide: The O. J. Simpson case and other controversies*, Lanham, MD: Rowman & Littlefield.

Snyder, Robert W. (2003) "American journalism and the culture of celebrity," *Reviews in American History*, vol. 31, no. 3, pp. 440–8.

Sorlin, Pierre (1994) *Mass Media*, London: Routledge.

Spears, Britney (2004) "Madonna," *Rolling Stone*, no. 946, pp. 124–5.

Spencer, Nancy E. (2004) "Sister Act VI: Venus and Serena Williams: 'sincere fictions' and white racism," *Journal of Sport & Social Issues*, vol. 28, no. 2 (May), pp. 115–35.

Stark, Myra (2003) "You, me, celebrity: insights into what consumers are thinking, how they're acting and why," *Brandweek*, vol. 44, no. 21 (May 26), pp. 17–19.

Steele, Shelby (1990) *The Content of Our Character: A new vision of race in America*, New York: HarperCollins.

Street, John (2004) "Celebrity politicians: popular culture and political representation," *British Journal of Politics and International Relations*, vol. 6, no. 4 (November), pp. 435–52.

Strozier, Charles B. (2002) "Youth violence and the apocalyptic," *American Journal of Psychoanalysis*, vol. 62, no. 3 (September), pp. 285–99.

Susman, Warren I. (1984) *Culture as History: The transformation of American society in the twentieth century*, New York: Pantheon.

Sweet, Matthew (2005) *Shepperton Babylon*, London: Faber & Faber.

Taraborrelli, J. Randy (1991) *Michael Jackson: The magic and the madness*, New York: Birch Lane Press.

Tönnies, Ferdinand (1957) *Gemeinschaft und Gesellschaft* (translated by Charles Loomis) Ann Arbor, MI: Michigan State University Press.

Trujillo, Nick and Vande Berg, Leah R. (1994) "From wild western prodigy to the ageless wonder: the mediated evolution of Nolan Ryan," pp. 221–40 in Drucker, Susan J. and Cathcart, Robert S. (eds), *American Heroes in a Media Age*, Cresskill, NJ: Hampton.

Turner, Graeme (2004) *Understanding Celebrity*, London: Sage.

Underwood, Nora (2000) "Body envy," *Maclean's*, vol. 113, no. 33 (August 14), pp. 36–40.

Unorthodox Styles (2005) *Sneakers: The complete collector's guide*, London: Thames & Hudson.

Walters, Ron (1994) "Celebrity and racial neutrality," *Washington Informer*, vol. 30, no. 51, p. 17.

Waters, Malcolm (2001) *Globalization*, 2nd edition, London: Routledge.

West, Darrell M. and Orman, John M. (2003) *Celebrity Politics*, Englewood Cliffs, NJ: Prentice Hall.

Wilson, Clint C. III and Gutiérrez, Félix (1985) *Minorities and Media: Diversity and the end of mass communication*, Newbury Park, CA: Sage.

Wilson, John Morgan (2006) "There won't be trumpets," *The Advocate*, no. 954 (January 17).

Wong, Lloyd L. and Trumper, Ricardo (2002) "Global celebrity athletes and nationalism: *fútbol*, hockey, and the representation of nation," *Journal of Sport and Social Issues*, vol. 26, no. 2 (May), pp. 168–94.

Wood, Nona L. and Wood, Robert A. (2002) "Stalking the stalker: a profile of offenders," *FBI Law Enforcement Bulletin*, vol. 71, no. 12 (December) pp. 1–7.

FILMS

About a Boy, Chris and Paul Weitz, 2002.
About Last Night, directed by Edward Zwick, 1986.
Adventures of Don Juan, The, Vincent Sherman, 1948.
Adventures of Robin Hood, The, Michael Curtiz/William Keighley, 1938.
Alamo, The, John Wayne, 1960.
Alexander, Oliver Stone, 2004.
Arthur, Steve Gordon, 1981.
Austin Powers in Goldmember, Jay Roach, 2002.
Aviator, The, Martin Scorsese, 2004.
Babe, The, Arthur Hiller, 1992.
Bad Influence, Curtis Hanson, 1990.
Batman Forever, Joel Schumacher, 1995.
Bend it like Beckham, Gurinder Chadha, 2002.
Blood and Wine, Bob Rafaelson, 1996.
Body of Evidence, Uli Edel, 1992.
Boogie Nights, Paul Thomas Anderson, 1997.
Bottom's Up, Erik MacArthur, 2006.
Bridget Jones's Diary, Sharon Maguire, 2001.
Buffalo Bill, William Wellman, 1944.
Bulworth, Warren Beatty, 1998.
Caligula, Tinto Brass, 1979.
Captain Blood, Michael Curtiz, 1935.
Cattle Queen of Montana, Allan Dwan, 1954.
Charlie's Angels, McG, 2000.
Cleopatra, Joseph L. Mankiewicz, 1963.
Color Purple, The, Steven Spielberg,1985.

Conan the Barbarian, John Milius, 1981.
Days of Thunder, Tony Scott, 1990.
Dead Calm, Phillip Noyce, 1988.
Deliverance, John Boorman, 1972.
Dempsey, Gus Trikonis, 1983.
Dirty Harry, Don Siegel, 1971.
Dolce Vita, La, Federico Fellini, 1960.
Dreamgirls, Bill Condon, 2006.
ET: The extra-terrestrial, Steven Spielberg, 1982.
Evita, Alan Parker, 1996.
Fan, The, Tony Scott, 1996.
Farewell to Arms, A, Frank Borzage, 1932.
Fellini's Casanova, Federico Fellini, 1976.
Fighting Temptations, The, Jonathan Lynn, 2005.
Fistful of Dollars, A, Sergio Leone, 1964.
For Whom the Bell Tolls, Sam Wood, 1943.
From Here to Eternity, Fred Zinneman, 1953.
Funny Girl, William Wyler, 1968.
Funny Lady, Herbert Ross, 1975.
Glenn Miller Story, The, Anthony Mann, 1953.
Great Expectations, David Lean, 1946.
Green Berets, The, John Wayne/Ray Kellogg, 1968.
Hard Day's Night, A, Richard Lester, 1964.
Hellcats of the Navy, Nathan Juran, 1957.
Home Alone, Chris Columbus, 1990.
Houdini, George Marshall, 1953.
House of Wax, Paige Edwards, 2005.
Hudsucker Proxy, The, Joel Coen, 1994.
Hustler, The, Robert Rossen, 1961.
Ipcress File, The, Sidney J. Furie, 1965.
Jazz Singer, The, Alan Crosland, 1927.
Julius Caesar, Joseph L. Mankiewicz, 1953.
Killers, The, Don Siegel, 1964.
King of Comedy, The, Martin Scorsese, 1982.
LA Confidential, Curtis Hanson, 1997.
Lethal Weapon, Richard Donner, 1987.
Lights of New York, Bryan Foy, 1928.
Lindbergh, Stephen Ives, 1990.

Long Hot Summer, Martin Ritt, 1958.
Love Actually, Richard Curtis, 2003.
MacArthur: The rebel general, Joseph Sargent, 1977.
Maltese Falcon, The, John Huston, 1941.
Manchurian Candidate, The, John Frankenheimer, 1962.
Money Train, Joseph Ruhin, 1995.
Moulin Rouge, Baz Luhrmann, 2004.
Mr and Mrs Smith, Doug Liman, 2005.
Mulholland Falls, Lee Tamahori, 1996.
My Cousin Rachel, Henry Koster, 1952.
Naked Gun 331/3: The final insult, Peter Segal, 1994.
Natural, The, Barry Levinson, 1984.
Nell Gwyn, Herbert Wilcox, 1934.
*Network, Sidney Lumet, 1976.
Ocean's Twelve, Steven Soderbergh, 2004.
Pink Panther,The, Shawn Levy, 2006.
Pledge This!, William Heins, 2005.
Portrait of a Lady, Jane Campion, 1996.
Predator, John McTiernan, 1986.
Pretty Baby, Louis Malle, 1977.
Prime Minister, The, Thorold Dickinson, 1941.
Private Life of Henry VIII, The, Alexander Korda, 1954.
Prizzi's Honor, John Huston, 1986.
Public Enemy, The, William Wellman, 1931.
Pumping Iron, George Butler/Robert Fiore, 1976.
Richard III, Laurence Olivier, 1955.
Sands of Iwo Jima, Allan Dwan, 1949.
Saturday Night Fever, John Badham, 1977.
Scenes from the Class Struggle in Beverly Hills, Paul Bartel, 1989.
Selena, Gregory Nava, 1998.
sex, lies and videotape, Steven Soderbergh, 1989.
Shallow Hal, Peter and Bobby Farrelly, 2001.
Smokey and the Bandit, Hal Needham, 1977.
Somebody Up There Likes Me, Robert Wise, 1956.
St Elmo's Fire, Joel Schumacher, 1985.
Stagecoach, John Ford, 1939.
Star Wars, George Lucas, 1977.
Terminator, The, James Cameron, 1974.

To Die For, Gus Van Sant, 1995.
To Have and Have Not, Howard Hawkes, 1945.
Tomorrow Never Dies, Roger Spottiswoode, 1997.
Truman Show, The, Peter Weir, 1998.
Truth or Dare/In Bed with Madonna, Alek Keshishian, 1991.
Wayne's World, Penelope Spheeris, 1992.
Weird Science, John Hughes, 1985.
White Heat, Raoul Walsh, 1949.
Winchester '73, Anthony Mann, 1950.
Wiz, The, Sidney Lumet, 1978.

INDEX

DATE DUE

	MAY 0 2 2007		
	OCT - 3 2007		
DEC 1 8 2007			
MAR 8 2011			
JUN 2 2 2011			

Demco, Inc. 38-293